RED WATER
BLUE WATER
SALT WATER

A Novel
About Sailing Away…
As A Family

RED WATER
BLUE WATER
SALT WATER

A Novel
About Sailing Away…
As A Family

by
Todd Scantlebury

Carribbean Passage Routes — 1988 & 1998

Table of Contents

<u>Proviso</u>: While all of the events in this book are drawn from our actual experiences as a family sailing through the Caribbean, I have fictionalized names and some facts in order to protect the innocent and the guilty. The following story should not be construed as an actual representation of people, places, events or entities. Let us not get technical, and let us not be litigious. Let us simply have a good time.

maggie and millie and molly and may
went down to the beach to play one day
maggie discovered a shell that sang
so sweetly she couldn't remember her troubles
millie befriended a stranded star
whose rays five languid fingers were
and molly was chased by a horrible thing which
raced sideways while blowing bubbles
may came home with a smooth round stone
as small as the world and as large as alone
for whatever we've lost like a you or a me
it's always ourselves we find at the sea

— e.e.cummings

Dedication

To my parents: You taught me I could do anything I put my mind to, and even though you must have squirmed a bit when you saw where I put it, you never flinched. To my family: Diane, you are the best reader and editor I will ever know, and I am not just talking about the written word. Sawyer and Riley, without you, there would have been no story. Thank you for bringing such adventure to my life.

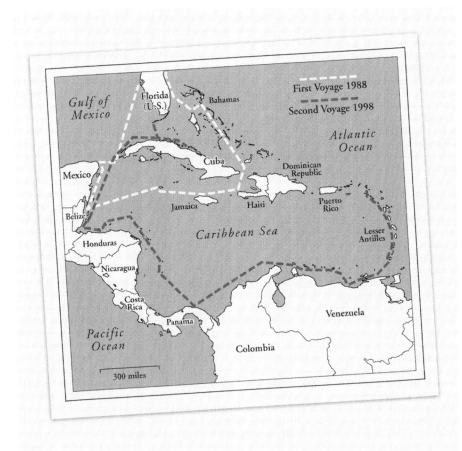

Carribbean Passage Routes - 1988 & 1998

Introduction

I rarely read introductions, prefaces or acknowledgments. I am too eager to get on to the story. Introductions tend toward sermons, and acknowledgments are about as lively as acceptance speeches. Though there are a few appetizers here, you have my permission to move on to the main course. The heart of the meal is there. And my only hope is that, when you push away from the table, you will be satisfied.

This is a story about being a family in the twenty-first century. It is written from the only perspective I have, that of a father - a role as ill defined and wanting today as it has ever been. My wife and all mothers, I believe, have a more profound perspective on family – a perspective we fathers will never entirely understand. It is a product of their mothering impulse, a connection that grows during months of child bearing and blossoms at birth. As Robin Williams has pointed out, even if we fathers stand bedside, sweating and hopeful, we cannot actually *share* in the birthing experience. To truly share in the experience, we would have to open an umbrella up our backsides.

Still, fathers do have their own particular *fatherly* feeling for their families, and they can help shape the course their family life will take. And so, just before the second millennium, I quit my corporate job and took my family of four, my wife Diane and my two daughters Sawyer and Riley, aged four and seven, on a voyage. We lived and traveled on the Caribbean Sea aboard a catamaran, a sailboat that looks a bit like two boats tied together with a UFO-shaped pod squeezed between them and a trampoline stretched out front.

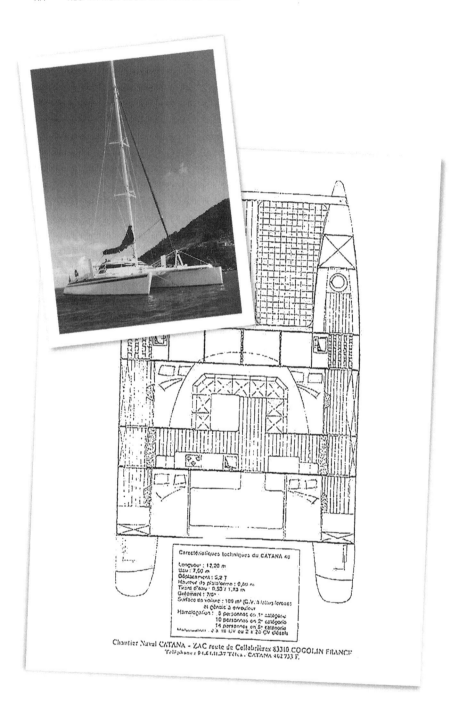

Catana 40 Catamaran Profile and Layout

We sailed over 7,000 ocean miles in two and a half years. And one afternoon, after we had returned to the United States, we sat together on *terra firma* in a Chinese restaurant. I told my two daughters, grown to seven and ten years, that I hoped to write a story about our adventure and I hoped that they would help. I had formed a mental list of ideas for the story - rewarding and life affirming experiences we could tell - but as a reality check and in a bow to authenticity (for by then I had learned to value my daughters' surprising insights), I asked them to tell me what they would want to tell other kids about life on the ocean.

Sawyer, my eldest daughter and a tactful lady, sensed my enthusiasm, and she bent her head and stirred her vegetable fried rice for a moment before answering: "Well," she said, "you read a lot."

Riley, an outspoken girl with a deadly aim at the Truth and, in those days, little tact in telling it, was inspired by her big sister's honesty. "Yeah," she said, "and you try not to barf."

I was flummoxed. After traveling throughout the Caribbean and peopling our world with Cubans and Cuna Indians, after walking the trackless beaches of uninhabited islands, after stroking sea turtles, wrestling with octopus tentacles and staring into the metallic eyes of six foot sharks, my daughters' most vivid memories of living on a boat were how they whiled away the slow times and got seasick? But before I protested, I caught myself. After all, patience had been one of the big lessons of our voyage, and the girls, I knew, were telling the Truth. I suddenly realized that if I were to ask kids from Manhattan or Montana about living in penthouses or on ranches, they would most likely shrug their shoulders and tell me that their lives were nothing special really, sometimes boring, and fraught with crowded streets or saddle sores.

But now, years after the Chinese restaurant, my girls are beginning to understand their adventure. They can look out from the shore, as it were, and across the sea with some perspective. They understand that what they did was special, and you will find their thoughts in the last chapter entitled "In Their Own Words." Perhaps youth is not wasted on the young after all.

As I finish this book, over six years since we left to go sailing and three years since I began staring at a blank computer and searching for the right words, the voyage seems distant - another world far away from the landlocked Arizona farm where we now live. The girls are fourteen and eleven. Their world is filled with farm animals, friends and school. Though they were little girls when we left to go sailing, they are young women now. The World Trade Center and the war in Iraq color our world. We have returned to the workaday world and a busy population trying to deal with the 21st century. But every once in a while, the sailing comes back to us – in a song, in the satisfactory tug of a rope secured with a tidy bowline knot, in the appreciation of a hot shower, a cold drink or, as a storm rages against the secure windows of our home set on concrete footings, a safe and immobile bed.

On land or at sea we remain a family; but the basics, the special connections we made on our voyage are unique gifts. I suppose these connections could have happened in other ways and in other places; but for us, they occurred as we sailed across the water far away from the United States. Today if we climb onto the roof of our home, hold hands and stare up at the infinite stars under our Arizona sky, the memories come back to us. We are huddled together in our life vests, safety harnesses attached to jack lines and eyebolts. We sail on a night passage in the middle of a great, empty sea, black waves rising and falling about us like hills in motion. In metaphor we still voyage beneath the same, brain piercing stars, but our experiences as a family on the water, good and bad, and the connections they helped us make are why we sailed. They are the connections that made me write this book. They are the gifts I think all families should share.

And They're Off

It was spitting snow as we drove away from our home. It was May of 1998, and my wife Diane and my daughters Sawyer and Riley were riding with me in our van. We towed a fourteen foot trailer packed to the ceiling with scuba gear, mattresses, spare seawater pumps, cases of toothpaste and shampoo, medical supplies, courtesy (country) flags, outboard engine parts, dolls, school books... everything we thought we might need to live on a sailboat for two years in the Caribbean. We even carried a forty-pound anchor, which the chuckling UPS man had lugged up to our porch and called the oddest thing he had ever delivered to Flagstaff, Arizona - a mountain town seven thousand feet above and three hundred miles from the nearest ocean.

After two years of planning and preparation, we were finally leaving. We had quit our jobs, rented out our home, loaded up our belongings and said tearful goodbyes to friends and extended family. The dripping rain mixed with snow should have been just the right sendoff - a reminder that we would not miss everything about Flagstaff.

But at the moment, the cold sky felt only sad and grey. Flagstaff had been our home for twenty years. As young college graduates, Diane and I had met and married there. We had camped in Arizona's red rock canyons, hiked through the mountain lupine and watched the mountain peaks turn scarlet in summer thunderstorms. We had held hands as the girls were born at the hospital up the hill. We had rebuilt an historic home, gotten a dog and pushed the kids on swings in the back yard. We knew everyone in town and Flagstaff was our home.

And so it had become easy to live in Flagstaff, and it had become impossible. As we drove through the slushy furrows in the road, my wife and I were so tied up with conflicting emotions - our minds still amuck with endless to-do lists, things to bring, people to call, bank accounts to close, insurances and taxes to pre-pay (we even had a master list that listed all of our other "to-do" lists) - that we could only glance at each other, force nervous smiles and try not to notice the strain of panic in our eyes.

As my mind raced back through our departure checklist, I realized we had done one thing right: we had remembered to bring our daughters. I reminded myself that no matter what else we had forgotten, remembering that the girls were our only critical cargo was a good start. Seven-year-old Sawyer was scribbling in her diary. She wrote, "We are going today. I am sad but I am also excited...," then she looked up at her mother and asked why she was crying. Riley, age four, was strapped in her car seat. She was trying to get Sawyer's attention. She wanted Sawyer to admire the rings on her fingers, but she had grown frustrated, so instead she was mashing Play-do into the crevices of the upholstery. For now, this was just another car trip.

As we pulled away from our home, I tried to push the doubts out of my mind and focus on the positives: Let's see...we were leaving a safe home, lifetime friends, familiar schools, good teachers and a high paying job; and we were heading toward an old and questionable sailboat, a French island where we knew no one, our first attempt at home schooling and no income whatsoever. Hmm.... I decided to try again. It would certainly be warmer. Leaving snow boots and parkas behind would be nice. I was also leaving behind a job, which though it had once been a passion that had pulled me from my bed each morning, had become a routine I resented. In fact, the more I resented my job, the more I felt I should be paid. (Can you imagine such idiocy?) There would be no more sad farewells at the airport, as I left for yet another interminable business trip. And there was more madness we were leaving in our rear view mirror: morning dashes to beat the school bell, angry town meetings about the growing traffic snarl, junk mail, phone solicitations...

Yes, on the positive side, we were leaving behind many headaches and heading toward one of our greatest passions: travel. There would be new people, different ideas, exotic foods and strange plants and animals in new lands. In fact, with only brief intermissions for births and diaper changes, Diane and I had been traveling ever since we had first met. Our first major trip had been a backpacking adventure using Eastern Airline's "Three-Weeks-Fly-Anywhere-to-as-Many-Places-as-You-Wanna-Go" deal, which we used, in part, to explore the Caribbean. In the French West Indies, we had eaten our first Creole *budouin* sausages. Lying naked and asleep atop the sheets in a dirt-bag hotel on Antigua, we had been robbed, but not of our good times. On Barbuda, we had camped alone along the cliffs of a sharp limestone shore - catching fish and boiling snails, after a kind but distracted island potentate had dropped us there but forgotten to pick us up. We had worked our way between islands by loading and unloading banana boats. We had flown on a lobster plane - sitting on the crates, wincing, laughing and shifting our buttocks each time a spiny antenna poked our bottoms. And with our heels dug into a shell littered beach, we had dreamed how our lives might one day be colored by the yellow sunshine, deep blue sea and palm shaded green of the Caribbean. In fact, our current family caravan to the sea was not the first time we had tossed everything aside to go sailing. Diane and I had been down this road to the sea once before.

But before I back up to tell that story, I should explain how we found *Manta Raya*, the floating home that awaited our family in the French West Indies.

Gerard and Son

I was in St. Martin on the French side of the island, and I was captivated by a conversation between two people. It was the way they talked to each other and not what they said that arrested me. They hung their heads inches apart and stared into each other's eyes as if they were initiating a Vulcan mind meld. If they had been lovers, the closeness of their exchange would have been romantic. But they were a father and his teenaged son - a teenaged son speaking intimately and sanely with his father at a time in life when roaring male hormones tend to fray paternal bonds and "conversations" occur over distances no closer than a retreating son can still hear his father's angry shouts. But the father and son I was watching were not arguing; they were translating. The son was repeating for his father, in French, questions I had asked him in English about the boat we were aboard: a forty foot catamaran. The father, the son and two other family members (a second son and a mother) had lived and traveled in the catamaran for the past three years. The two men were talking intently, nose-to-nose; and from the few words exchanged, I knew they were communicating not only audibly but also in a sympathetic language of glances and gestures that only they understood. I knew they had developed this private language after years of managing their floating home together on the sea.

In that moment I realized I was seeing not what I had come to see but what I needed to see. I needed to reinforce my belief that a shell of fiberglass could somehow hold an entire family, their individual and sometimes chafing personalities, their caustic faults, their intense desires and their flaming fears, without melting and sinking into the sea.

I recall that afternoon in St. Martin starting in a haze of July Caribbean heat but ending in a cool café just off the water in the quaint colonial town of *Marigot*. Under the blades of a whirling ceiling fan, Diane and I cooled off, decompressed and enjoyed the niceties of good French wine and food. The turquoise bay, the sparkling sailboats at anchor and the stunning European beauties, who traipsed by wearing strapped sandals, pastel halter-tops and teardrop DaVinci sunglasses, were a seductive reinforcement to buying a boat in such exotic climes. But contemplating the buying of a boat and starting our voyage so far from the United States worried us, and Diane and I were composing a list of pros and cons – the con side beginning to tip the balance and engulf the pro.

One of the heavily debated and highlighted items on the list was my ethnocentric worry about launching a family cruise three thousand miles from the nearest marine hardware or boatyard that spoke English. When I rebuilt and refitted a boat (for any catamaran we could afford would need a serious facelift), I foresaw mind-numbing metric conversions and long, unproductive days squinting into a French-English dictionary for embarrassing phrases like: "What is the best paint to put on my bottom?"

As we pondered these questions in our idyllic café by the water, a smiling lady with short black hair joined us. She was the French wife and mother of the father and son, whom we had just met on the catamaran in the bay. Indeed, she was the actual owner of the boat, a *Catana 40*. Beatrice's boat was not one of the boats we had come to see in St. Martin, but a boat broker had mentioned the catamaran in passing; and we had rowed out into the harbor to take a look. And frankly, by the end of that hot day in June, she was the only boat we had come away admiring. She was clean, cared for and proven, for she had sailed to the Caribbean from France and then cruised throughout the islands from the British Virgins to Venezuela, a good deal of the time caring for Beatrice's family of four. Beatrice and her family had lived aboard and loved her for three years. And for us, this family liveaboard distinction made our cruising hopes more real.

After inspecting the *Catana 40*, we had visited with Beatrice, her husband Gerard and their two sons in their wide cockpit, floating on the beautiful blue water of *Marigot* bay. Gerard, a man of sudden passions, had jumped up, gone below and re-emerged with a bottle of *pastiche*. Yes, the boat and the family felt right. And now Beatrice, whose English was better than her husband᐀s, had dropped by the café to answer more of our questions.

For Beatrice, living aboard had been *"Bon! Ze best sing a family can do!"* And she proceeded to tell us tales of her travels through the Caribbean. But she stopped when the *garçon* topped off our cabernet and served us plates of conch roti on Creole rice with a side of golden fried potatoes. "Why," she asked, pointing to the plate of potatoes and struggling to piece together the words in English, "do you call zem 'french fries?'"

This question, I realized, was a small but illustrative example of what we would be facing, if we were to buy and refit a boat in the French West Indies. In fact, it was a metaphor for the cultural challenge of voyaging anywhere outside of the United States. As Beatrice, with a quizzical frown on her brow, stared at the steaming plate of *pomme frites*, I checked my first impulse to answer her with a flippant joke about Joan of Arc - the original French fry. Out on her boat, I had asked her husband Gerard if he had ever had a full roach main (a full and widely cut mainsail), and a bit indignant, he had told me that there had *never* been an *insecte* on his boat. Accordingly, I steered clear of subtle puns and opted instead for a diplomatic and "straight" reply. ·

"We call them french fries," I said, "because Americans love French cuisine. The name honors your country and the chefs who created this food."

The "french fry" diplomacy ended up being one of the first steps in our negotiations with Beatrice. Over the months it would take to complete our overseas transaction, we would take a crash course in international maritime law, bury ourselves in the translation of foreign documents and modify our sales contract over yet more bottles of pastiche. We would overcome many of the hurdles I had listed on the "con" side of our list, but we would also discover pitfalls we had not listed. In fact, we would be only half way through our far-flung boat deal, when, in the winter of 1997, an innocuous night at the movies would cost us $10,000.

On that night we were back in Flagstaff. We were just beginning to assemble our snorkeling gear and check off the first items on our growing list of liveaboard provisions, when the head of the Bundesbank - Germany's counterpart to Allen Greenspan and our

Federal Reserve - decided to go to the movies. Though it is not clear what happened at the theatre that night, my guess is that the film was disagreeable - perhaps a tragedy with too few laughs and a plot ending in financial ruin. Or perhaps the butter on the popcorn had simply gone off. Who knows? But when the head of the Bundesbank emerged from the theater, looking ill tempered and squinting into the lights at reporters huddled under the theatre's marquee, he made a gruff statement. He announced that he would no longer tolerate the steady decline of the Deutsch Mark against the dollar. Enough was enough. He then stomped off to his waiting car, where he must have sat back and allowed himself a brief smile. For without lifting a finger to fiscal policy, he had managed to shake the almighty U.S. dollar.

The next morning the dollar tumbled on the fear that the Bundesbank would raise interest rates. (It didn't.) And our catamaran, priced in French francs but intimately tied to the Deutsch mark and dangling on the end of the karmic money chain, became $10,000 more expensive. *Voila!* our first lesson in buying boats abroad, and not our last. But all of the lessons, despite the anxiety and antacids they engendered, would pan out. Bundesbluff or no Bundesbluff, the dollar would recover a bit; the boat would still be a good deal; and the players - sellers and brokers alike - would prove to be such decent and competent folks, that the transaction would be more fun than scary and more exotic than foreign.

In the book Under the Tuscan Sun, Frances Mayes wrote of buying and renovating an Italian farmhouse. A Chicago lawyer, obviously impressed with Ms. Mayes' aplomb and bravado, phoned to ask her a question. The lawyer was considering moving from the Windy City to an island cottage on the Washington coast and asked Ms. Mayes, in typical legalese, what she thought the "downside" might be. Without hesitation Ms. Mayes answered, "There is no downside."

And I suppose, in memory's whitewashing, there is not – at least not a downside any good coach should mention before urging a novice athlete to pole vault or fly off the end of a ski jump.

Despite all of the cultural differences, all of the sleepless nights of hashing and rehashing our foreign boat buying decisions and despite the voices that bounced about in our heads saying: "You idiot! What have you done?" we stuck with our decision to buy the French catamaran. But there was still one more thing we had to do before cruising: learn how to sail the boat.

Zen, Todd

It was still winter, and we were still in Flagstaff. The wind was cold, and snow blew about like confetti. For Diane, a botanist by training, winter is a season of mourning. To her the grey sky and shriveled brown plants of winter feel like a jail sentence. I took off from work, picked her up and drove to a local burrito wagon - maybe not romantic, but it was a date out of the house. As we stood in the gravel parking lot, ordered our burritos and shivered in the cold dry air, I handed her a card. Inside was a picture of the catamaran we were in the process of buying. We had put half of the money down on the boat, and the French owners were taking care of her in St. Martin. The picture showed our boat on warm blue water, and the card said "Happy Birthday - Come See Me." And we did.

The Great Escape and Boat Dream needed tactile reinforcement. I cashed in the last of my frequent flyer miles, and we packed our shorts and snorkels to visit our future home - this time as a family. From windy, frigid Arizona we stepped off the plane into a sultry Caribbean night. Tree frogs sang. Gerard and Beatrice were waiting for us, and despite a moment of consternation during which Gerard appeared overcome by the size and number of our American suitcases, we managed to cram our entire family road show into his little Paris commuter car – Diane and Sawyer in the back, Riley straddled between my legs and my head sticking out through the sun roof with my knees hiked up to my chin.

We were off, *allez!*, and as we whizzed by the neon lights of the island's casinos, Gerard talked steadily, sometimes in halting English but usually in blazing French. As he zipped around the mountain curves, he named landmarks and listed chores finished or not finished on the boat - all of which, in the groggy dream of a late night entry into a foreign world, were lost on me. Despite being stuffed into the car elbow to ear, Diane and the girls were nearly asleep when we arrived at *Marigot* bay. But by the seawall they stretched and began to take note. The surreal paint of our nighttime arrival suddenly gelled into a familiar canvas. Our family cruise was beginning.

The light from the lamps along the dock reflected off the water in shimmering crescents. Lured to this light like moths, black and yellow striped zebra fish swirled and spun in the clear water. Riley and Sawyer bent down to peer into the water, as wavelets swept past the dock's pilings in a soothing and familiar swish of motion. The damp night air smelled of the sea. As new as this place was to us, we somehow realized we knew it quite well.

Gerard loaded everything, all four of us and our heap of luggage, into his little rubber dinghy. We motored through the night until we found the catamaran, our new home, where we gathered under the salon light of the main cabin. Beatrice had left us milk, freshly baked french bread, marmalade and, bless her, dark roast coffee for the next morning. Gerard had taken good care of the boat for us, and he pointed proudly as he showed us how clean the catamaran was. We glanced about, and our eyes came to rest on the one blemish upon it: an ashtray on the galley counter. In a single sweep, Gerard scooped it up, announced that he was quitting "*fini*" and flung it out over the transom where only the sound of a splash indicated its disappearance into the dark night. Riley, intrigued by radical motions of any kind, dropped a marble she had managed to carry through three airports and four plane changes. It rolled across the cabin sole (floor), and I reached for it at the same time that Gerard tried to mash it (and my hand) with his foot. He thought a stowaway roach had boarded with our family. We were all nervous, excited and exhausted. Gerard said his farewells and motored off into the night, promising to return in the morning.

A new home creates a strange tension. We are not comfortable there, yet we feel we should be. There are unaccustomed dimensions and smells – strangers that we are eager to make familiar. On our catamaran, our new home, there were curved doorways, toilets with pump handles and motors that whirred in the night against a backdrop of other unfamiliar noises: birds calling, waves slapping, decks creaking and lines clanging.

Only time would make these new sounds familiar and bring them into our hearts; but on our first night aboard, our new home felt strange.

Despite being dead tired, I lay wide-awake beside Diane. I listened to the noises and stared at the ceiling just two feet above my nose. I was thrilled, and I was scared. "What were we doing? Where in the hell were we going? And how did the drip coffee maker work?" But after a while, rocked by the cradling sway of the boat, I drifted off to sleep.

The next morning we had just finished stowing our long pants and coats, when Gerard appeared at the transom. It was a brilliant blue day, and the four of us stood about smiling and blinking into the sun. Our blindingly white bodies must have made Gerard squint. In contrast to our snow-covered mountain in the Arizona desert, the warm and moist air of St. Martin was delicious. Gerard was all smiles. *"Bonjour. Comment allez vous?"* Had we eaten? Did we find the coffee? Yes, yes. It was a glorious morning. So now we sail, no?

We were not even out of the harbor before the girls felt seasick. But I had no time to help them. Gerard was teaching me to sail our new home, and I desperately wanted to learn everything he knew about the boat. We had raised the monster sail at anchor (it went up and up, Diane and I each taking turns at the winch and exhausting ourselves with the endless cranking of the thing). We let the wind back us off our mooring, and we headed out of the harbor into a fresh breeze. When we sailed clear of the north tip of the island, we were greeted by the winter trade winds and its roller coaster waves blown all the way across the Atlantic. The catamaran romped, and the kids disappeared below. Gerard was terse with his instructions, either because his English was lacking or because he too was preoccupied by the stiff wind and rolling waves. I watched his every move at the helm.

Around noon we left the rollicking ocean behind us and entered a cove around the northeast side of the island. The waves flattened and the wind died behind limestone cliffs. Gerard gestured briefly toward the engine controls - kill switches and gauges - and in French gave me what I supposed were instructions. Then he started the engines. *Varoooom!* And down came the sails. He lit a cigarette (the cold turkey flourish of the previous evening proving a ruse), and he strode forward to the anchor and windlass (a gear system for lowering and raising the anchor). He did not stoop to touch anything, but using his toes, loosed two pins and kicked the anchor overboard. We had not slowed as we approached the anchorage; and to me, the cautious American sailor, we were moving *very* quickly into a *very* crowded anchorage. Meanwhile, in a clanking whir, the anchor chain continued to peel off the windlass.

Gerard looked about - I suppose judging wind and current but perhaps checking the surrounding boats to see which of his buddies were about. He squinted and puffed on his cigarette. The anchor chain continued to unload until Gerard strode back to the cockpit, killed the engines and returned to torque the windlass clutch. The catamaran reached the end of her anchor tether, lurched and spun about like a teenager skidding through a gravel parking lot. Suddenly all was silent.

"So," said Gerard, "we are happy, yes?"

"*Oui*," I said, certainly happy to be anywhere in the warm Caribbean, though where I was at that particular moment, I had no clue.

"O.K!" said Gerard, as he stripped off his t-shirt and shorts, revealing his sinewy frame, "I see you tomorrow." Then he sprung from the deck and dove into the water, producing a tiny splash no larger than his brief, black bikini swimsuit. In a few strokes, he was gone.

For a moment Diane and I stood on deck in silence and watched the water where Gerard had disappeared.

Diane was the first to speak. "Do you know where we are?"

"No idea," I said truthfully.

"Do you think we could start this thing and sail it if we had to?"

"Maybe," I exaggerated.

"Do you think he'll come back?"

"I hope so."

Necessity is the mother and the teacher of invention. That afternoon we managed to lower the dinghy off its davits and into the water. We hooked up the outboard engine, made a run to the beach and had one helluva time playing in the sand and embracing what we could not have gotten our arms around back home - a warm evening wearing only our swim suits as we played together on a beach.

Gerard did return the next day. He appeared as suddenly as he had disappeared. He came alongside with some boisterous friends on a powerboat, and he was still puffing on a cigarette. Gerard, Diane and I pulled up the anchor together and sailed back around the island. I was rested and even more eager to learn, so my endless questions to Gerard found little pause.

Poor Gerard. He simply smiled, shrugged and puffed away on his cigarettes. But despite his air of nonchalance, he was a good instructor.

He had sailed the first day. We had raised anchor and were sailing together on the second day. And at the entrance to *Marigot* harbor, he turned to me, let got of the helm and said, "Now, Todd, you are ze captain."

I swallowed hard and took the wheel. The anchorage was crowded, European style, which meant moorings crammed together like eggs in a carton. Our boat, forty-three feet long and twenty-three feet wide, felt huge, and I felt as if I were steering not a sailboat but a basketball court. I looked up at the towering sail and wondered if I should not drop it and motor - the prudent approach. Sails, unlike motors, allow only certain angles for maneuvering and little room for error. I said as much to Gerard, and he shrugged. I took this as a sign that no engines were needed, and I swallowed again. We sailed on. As we approached our mooring, the area toward which Gerard vaguely gestured, I asked Diane to furl the headsail. She did this handily, but I was still nervous. Despite the dripping humidity of the Caribbean, my mouth was desert dry.

"Diane," I croaked, ignoring Gerard's nonchalance, "let's start the engines."

Diane went below. One engine roared to life - ah, sweet sound - but then nothing. Why hadn't she started the second engine? She reappeared looking quite pale. The port engine would not start.

A catamaran with one engine is a bit like a bird with one wing — wounded, not maneuverable and vulnerable. Without speed through the water to help its rudders dig in, a catamaran with one engine limps sideways rather than turn. It tends to veer and present itself broadside to the wind. Such drunken swaggering is not advantageous in an anchorage crowded with expensive yachts.

With the little time I had had at the helm, I barely understood how to maneuver a catamaran using both of its engines, let alone one. Meantime, either Gerard had not understood our predicament or was choosing a poor moment in which to reinforce his "you do," crash course, instructional technique. I asked him to go below and check on the errant engine. He shrugged and disappeared. Then I asked Diane to drop the mainsail. I was through bombing about the anchorage blown about by the wind and limping on one leg.

Diane raised the cam cleat to release the mainsail halyard (the line that lifts the mainsail up the mast) but nothing happened. The line was jammed in the mechanical cleat. I looked below. Gerard was bent over the engine controls and scratching his head. I looked ahead and aimed at the largest opening I could see between two boats. Then I jumped up on the cabin top with Diane, where I proceeded to crank on the cam cleat and curse its French construction. It was not long before I felt a hand on my shoulder and heard Gerard's voice.

"Zen, Todd, Zen."

Gerard reached around me, took the line and made a wrap around a winch. One jerk on the winch handle, and the camcleat released. The mainsail halyard came free, and the sail dropped to the boom in an elegant billowing furl. Gerard squinted at me through his cigarette smoke and gestured back toward the helm. I jumped down, took a deep breath, blew it out and brought the boat dead center over the mooring. Diane hooked the buoy and tied it off. Once again, all was still.

"O.K?" said Gerard.

I nodded my head. "*Oui.*"

"*Bon*! Now we celebrate, no?"

That night we ate delicious pizzas drizzled with olive oil and topped with romano cheese and arugula. When the wine disappeared. Gerard brought out two bottles of champagne; and when the first of these was drained, he fingered the concavity at its base and asked if we knew what its name was in French. "*La monde du désespoir,*" he said, eyeing the bottom of the empty bottle through its neck - the mound of despair.

It was a delightful evening, the kind that only a full day in the wind and weather can magnify. As tree frogs croaked and night birds sang, our girls smiled into their bowls of coconut ice cream. Gerard reached for my shoulder. "Todd," he said, and he turned to include Diane. "You and Diane will be fine. You are good sailors, no? Your new home; she is a good boat. Now you will get to know each other. Yes?"

The engine that had worried us that day had suffered from an ailment found on all sailboats - human error. We had hung a garbage bag over its kill switch and hidden its predicament. Still, this detail on a boat Gerard knew so well, had escaped him as well, and I figured there might be hope for us. Perhaps we *would* get to know our new home. But first there would be more lessons to learn – and our next test was at the "school of hard docks."

Dockside Trauma

In the early days of dings, gashes and assorted floggings we inflicted on our poor catamaran, I grew demoralized. The pinnacle of my exasperation occurred when we were trying to take on fuel and met a broadside gust of wind that forced us to donate several pounds of fiberglass to a barnacled piling. I cursed, shook my head and told Diane we simply *had* to work out a better docking procedure. Assessing our skills and our track record to date, Diane reflected that it might be easier if we perfected our repair procedures.

Resting lightly on the water, multihulls, especially high profile multihulls, are easily blown about by the wind. A sudden gust, and like fall leaf litter, they are off to the races skittering about in all directions. We learned this unnerving trait in Philipsburg, Sint Marteen, the Dutch side of St. Martin, where we docked according to my least favorite European convention: the Mediterranean Mooring. The Med Mooring is essentially a two point docking technique in which the bow or stern is secured to the dock and the opposing end of the boat is tied to an anchor or mooring out in the water. In this way, tons of floating real estate can be packed side-by-side, parallel parked if you will, as only a millennia old, densely populated society like Europe could dictate. The stability of the Med Mooring depends upon the mooring or anchor that holds the boat off the dock. Two moorings or anchors provide more secure holding. Our particular Philipsburg marina did not allow two anchors, and the one anchor we could use had to be set (secured) in a bottom scrubbed by recent hurricanes and littered with wreckage. Still, the marina was cheap, close to the marine supplies we needed to commission our cruise and just in front of an attractive, waterside restaurant.

After a week or so at the dock, we lost our apprehension of the Med Mooring system. The trade winds were generally on our nose, and they pushed us safely off the dock. We had settled into our new home. Diane and I were hard at work refitting our boat with sinks, alternators, new berths (beds) and sails. The girls played on the dock and befriended some kids from another boat. We were making a home. We were also trying to adjust to the heat. I read from an Israeli Army training manual that provided a work and rest schedule for acclimating to tropical climates (why and where I'd gotten the thing escapes me). But we blew out of the army schedule within days - sweating in the engine rooms and nearly passing out as we drug new mattresses into the berths.

One afternoon I left Diane and the girls and went shopping for a few refitting supplies. I returned with a shop clerk who helped me carry the new purchases with a hand truck. Once again I had prematurely emptied our accounts by paying something roughly equivalent to the gross national product of Bolivia for our refit. But money was not the problem at hand. The helper and I walked down the marina dock to find the wind blowing steadily and gusting mightily out of the wrong direction, toward, instead of away from the dock.

I stopped walking when I saw Diane out astern of our boat in the dinghy. She was peering into the whipping water; and she was so pale that she was nearly translucent. Seven-year-old Sawyer was also doing something odd: she was at the helm of our new boat vigorously working the twin engine throttles. It was then that I also noticed the spasmodic jerking of the dock, caused, I realized with a gut-wrenching pang, by our catamaran as it bashed its head against the timbers.

I dropped my fortune in diesel filters and caulking tubes and timed one of our boat's head butts to jump aboard. By this time Diane was also back aboard and had taken over the engine controls from dear Sawyer. She explained that neither our primary anchor nor a secondary anchor, which she had been trying to set, were holding in the gusting winds. Running both engines full astern was just keeping us from busting a new channel through the dock. I surveyed this situation with the calm and calculation of a novice catamaran owner, i.e. I panicked, and I decided that we would be better off letting go our dock lines and trying to motor around to the lee side of the dock. I had not taken into account that this maneuver would immediately enable the BLOWING LEAF PRINCIPLE.

Just as we loosed our lines and managed to come astern and a bit sideways to the wind, a gust picked up all 43 feet of us and sent us caterwauling toward the restaurant pier. At this point, many events occurred simultaneously: (1.) Diane tried to retrieve the stern anchors only to find they were entangled in two extraneous anchor lines and the rusted muffler off a 1952 Peugeot. (2.) The proprietor of the marina and restaurant rushed from his office screaming, "Don't hurt my dock! Don't hurt my dock!" (3.) We managed to wrap the growing spider web of anchor lines around our prop, killing, once again, the port engine and disabling our catamaran. And (4.) the elite lunch crowd, only mildly interested in our shenanigans up to this point, focused its full attention upon us. Some diners paused as if frozen, forks suspended in mid-air between their watercress salads and gaping mouths.

Careening sideways and tethered to a tangle of anchor lines, our catamaran behaved like a deranged dog on a leash run. Above the roar of our single, over throttled engine, I could hear the screams of the owner, the crash of silverware and the screech of chairs, as diners with better reflexes began pushing away from their tables. A few of the patrons, obviously fellow boat owners, made their way, linen napkins in hand, toward the edge of the dock. They were preparing to fend off our caterwauling approach (Bless them; but despite their good intentions, I only worried for them. Given our speed and trajectory; we were headed for a tremendous, splintery crash, and I hoped they would be spared.)

I have to confess (and please, dear Reader, do not think less of me) that I believe I closed my eyes. After all of our preparations and hard work trying to begin a new life on a boat, I just could not watch our dreams end so few miles from where they had been launched in a broken pile of fiberglass and wood topped with the cracked conch daily special.

But that is when the miracle happened. The wind paused. It hesitated as if inhaling for its next blow; and in that tiny moment our port rudder dug in. We began to turn. I opened my eyes to find myself face-to-face with the lunch crowd - not feet, but inches from the protruding pier. We ghosted, as if pushed by an invisible hand, past the dock and on to safety.

Ancient History

B efore Children (B.C.), Diane and I had learned how to sail on Arizona's Lake Powell. Consequently, we had learned how to respect the vagaries of Nature. We had also found ourselves relaxing on the water and having a damn good time. Sailing Lake Powell was a blast. We spent long weekends and eventually long weeks meandering in and out of the canyon coves and camping beneath red cliffs on Glen Canyon's sandy shores. And we began to dream of cruising on bigger water, Mother Ocean. But first we needed a bigger incentive, and before long our jobs gave us just the shove we needed.

We had been working for the same company, a company famous for a "new" business philosophy. The company was a Fortune 500 company voted one of the ten best places to work in America. It was founded by a stocky little fellow everyone considered a genius. He hired decent and creative folks, treated them as equals and let them work with as few directions as possible toward their own strengths, i.e., he let them do the things they loved to do until they either hung themselves or succeeded. He knew there was nothing more powerful than a team of good people given the freedom to succeed and the impression they are working for themselves. The Little Guru's company prospered.

Decker and Peters, the "sexy" economists of the day, wrote books about the Little Guru's enterprising management structure - which was very little structure at all. A joke at the time, but a propitious joke, was an article that came out in the *National Enquirer*. A story entitled "Company Has No Bosses" followed a piece about an alien dog that gave birth to a human litter. The article about our company was fairly accurate, which made we wonder about the dog.

The company had a founding principle that sounded simple but kept the possible pandemonium of minimal management in check: make money and have fun. And boy, were we having a blast. Working on high tech products with creative, gung-ho co-workers, mostly in their twenties and early thirties, was a bit like stepping onto the bridge of the Star Ship Enterprise with all exits leading to Fantasyland. We were inventing, building new and better gizmos and hiring yet more wunderkinds in our image. One of my interview questions for prospective employees was: "Do you feel that you lead a charmed life?" I never got an unqualified "yes" to the question, but given the company's outlook, it was an appropriate question, and we had a lot of fun asking it. We worked nights and weekends, and we loved (almost) every minute of it. The Little Guru's operating principle worked. We had millions in profits, and the bushel basket of money was growing, every year. We were young gods on Olympus. We wore shorts and sandals to work.

When a *Time* magazine reporter called to find out what was going on, one of my co-workers chuckled mysteriously and told him we were merely an extraordinary company run by ordinary people. "Oh, come on," said the cynical journalist, "surely you have some minimum skill requirements for your new employees." "Yes," answered my friend, "all applicants must be potty trained."

Ha. Ha. Boy, were we funny ... then. But I had not yet learned some of the tough lessons of big business. Eight years into the job and in the midst of developing two new products, a "friend" sued me for age discrimination. This was my first lesson, and it was painful, but I was to learn it was merely "business as usual," even if it were disillusioning, involving the spectacle of lawyers slithering in a pit of lies and delivering crotch kicks. Shortly after the lawsuit, one of our products failed - an event none of us had experienced before. And the Little Guru paid us a visit. I ended up having to lay off a good many of my friends and co-workers.

The easiest folks to fire were the ones who got mad. They shouted things like: "What about my family? My house payments?" or, "You lied to us! You told us we had a future here!" I had spent a week of sleepless nights anticipating these reactions. I had turned them over in my mind so many times that they had lost their jagged edges. Besides, as I began to fire my co-workers and friends, I was not really present.

I stood behind a sober face in an odd, emotionless world, where other people's pain could not reach me.

Then Verne, one of our machinists, peered into my office. "I know you're letting me go," he said. "That's O.K.... Truth is, I'm grateful." He asked permission to come in, and I gave him a stunned nod.

"When I started with you six years ago," he said, "I had problems, big problems, but you stood by me. You saw me through the drinking. You helped me get started with AA; and you didn't give up on me... even when I had my roughest times. I'm grateful for that. I mean it." And then, as an afterthought, as if Verne had not already delivered a buddahvista's sentiments of selflessness, he added: "Sorry your business didn't work out. If things do come around one day, I'd be honored to come back and work with you again."

Verne closed my office door, and I sat in silence – a silence in which something very subtle and very deep inside me twisted. The twist grew into a wrenching feeling that made me stand up and walk out of the office. I passed my secretary, who asked me whether I was all right, but I walked on in silence. I climbed into my old truck, turned the key and drove. I drove down the main street in town, past the fast food chains, the discount motels and the gas stations. The signs blurred. I stopped at a light and was a bit surprised when my disembodied fist rose into the air and started slamming into the steering wheel. That tightness in my chest, a very hard, tight and hurtful twist, tore. Tears washed down my face, and I felt them drip off the end of my chin.

That night Diane and I decided to take a sabbatical. We decided to go sailing and cruise the Caribbean. We considered farming in Idaho, but cruising won by a coin toss.

O.K., honestly, the decision to change our lives did not come that easily. Our jobs provided the motivation, but we also needed to overcome a few hurdles - obstacles I will call our *Cruising Fears*. But surprisingly, these hurdles proved to be a fiction compared with the real obstacles we encountered at sea.

The First Escape - 1988

Never mind that we were living in the middle of the American desert or that we had nothing but a bit of lake sailing and a few salty, nautical novels as references, we decided to move aboard a sailboat. We wanted to travel the Caribbean, and a boat seemed the proper vehicle. We kneeled on our porch amidst scattered charts (we called them maps then), a copy of Joshua Slocum's Sailing Alone Around the World and Katy Burke's Managing Your Escape. I held a plastic sextant pointed at a pan of water, while Diane read to me from a mail order course on celestial navigation.

We had our misgivings. Some of our friends praised our "bravery," but less tactful friends asked us harder questions like: Did we really know how to sail? This question had me up all night reading Chapman's by flashlight and practicing my bowline knot on lamp cords, drapery pulls and dental floss.

My first backyard sextant sightings put us just outside Duluth, Minnesota. My only encouragement was Jim Dickson, a blind sailor, who had just sailed across the Atlantic. Odds were, a friend told us, we would be able to manage at least as well.

If Diane and I had summarized our lists of pre-cruising fears, they would have looked like this:

My Fears:	Her Fears:
Find out I'm a landlubber,	Drowning,
Turn into a worthless bum, i.e.,	Dying,
waste away in Margaritaville,	Dying by drowning
Go broke	

Diane is claustrophobic and scared of the dark. For her, pulling a sweater over her head is a Stephen King nightmare. Would the ocean be that Great Cardigan waiting to slip its dark weave over her head? Could I keep the lights on? What reassurance did I, a lake sailor from Arizona, have to offer? A blood analysis would have detected not one ounce of saltwater in my veins.

Then there was the pointlessness of it all. At that time, the mid eighties, my fiends were leading meaningful and productive lives financing mergers and acquisitions, making generic drugs and managing loans for the S&Ls. Maybe my job was wearing me down a bit, but I was putting money away, and I had something to set my alarm for. What would happen when I became a worthless cruising bum? Would I sleep until the crack of noon and then wander aimlessly about the twisted docks of some abandoned seaport? Would my thick blood, which preferred an invigorating mountain clime, be drained by the mosquitoes, while I lay about, limp and fetid, like a slice of Swiss cheese?

But Diane and I persevered, one day at a time, and we tried not to listen to the nasty, nay-saying that bounced about inside our heads. Until one day rich with Autumn color, we climbed aboard our boat *Lucile's Sweet Thursday*, a Tartan 37 on the Chesapeake Bay. We had named the boat after my saintly grandmother and Sweet Thursday, the novel by John Steinbeck. The boat was our new home, but as soon as we pasted "Flagstaff, Arizona" on her rear end, we started getting some odd attention.

Certainly there were advantages to having "Arizona" printed on our transom. Displaying our homeport had much the same effect as a sign reading "Danger - Explosives." Boats that sailed behind us toward an anchorage changed course when they got within binocular range, while those already anchored shortened scope and left plenty of room lest our Wild West boat go loco and stampede the anchorage. At the dock, sailors wandered by, scratched their heads, chuckled, and sometimes stopped and adopted us like lost puppies (or refugees from a foreign, albeit less fortunate, country). The cruising community, good folks, but generally older and retired, were tickled by our hailing port; but what interested them more was how two young punks had managed to chuck it all and go sailing.

The white-haired cruisers did not realize we had willingly walked away from our careers. They did not know we had forfeited the income we were supposed to be saving or that we were losing money steadily as we made payments to the bank that actually owned our boat. But after explaining this bare truth, we noticed our honest answer brought only disappointment - a dimming of hopeful eyes.

I told my brother about this reaction, and he told me how to fix it. The next time I was asked how, at our tender age, we managed to "retire" on a boat, I offered this explanation: "We haven't really worked much ever since grandpa died." The effect was wonderful. There was relief, a conspiratorial smile or wink, and sometimes even a slap on the back. My brother's fabricated answer helped put the retired cruisers' world back in order.

In Savannah, I had a similar experience, and I should have seen it coming. We were seated around a long, checkered tablecloth in an old fashioned boarding house, where two sisters cooked delicious southern food. Smiling patrons, previously strangers but now seated side-by-side like relatives at a family feast, passed chipped bowls and plates filled with steaming corn bread and salty, southern ham. As the food circulated and we tucked in with darting forks and spoons, spirits rose; and our fellow diners, now filled with good food and good cheer, made efforts to get acquainted. Soon everyone's "what do you do?" story had been told, and our story – "crazy kids sailing their dreams into the Caribbean" – got a rise out of a fellow diner seated near the end of the table. He shook his head sadly.

"Yes," he sighed, "that's my dream too. I've got the boat picked out, and I've charted all the islands I'd like to see. But it'll never happen."

"Why not?" I asked.

Diane looked up from her plate, but I ignored her stare and kept my attention focused on the would-be sailor.

"Well," he said, "It's just too expensive; that's why... Plus, I've got *responsibilities.*"

"I don't know about the responsibilities," I said, pointing my fork at his chest, "but the money shouldn't stop you. We chucked our jobs, and we don't have the money, but we're making it work. There are lots of cruisers out there living on a shoe string and still sailing away into the sunset."

The fellow continued to shake his head, but he also began to fidget in his seat.

"Plus..." I continued, but then I felt a sharp pain in my shin: Diane's foot.

Outside on the cobblestone street, Diane educated me.

"Look," she said. "It's important for people to have dreams. But for some folks, it's also important to *feel* they can't live them. They're scared. Preaching at them doesn't help, and it isn't kind."

I stood, my brow furrowed. Diane was right, and she had once again demonstrated one of the reasons I tended to dance about her like a moth around a light bulb. She listened, and because she listened, she heard what people were saying, even if they had not *said* it out loud. And because she cared, she often ended up knowing more about people than I did. In fact, given the way I admired Diane, it was surprising I would find myself considering divorcing her just three months later. But we will get to that bit of the story in a moment. First we must dispense with the fictions of "Cruising Fears."

During one of our adoptions as landlubber immigrants from the sailing capitol of Arizona, we sat about a table set with all the excesses of Thanksgiving. We had been invited aboard a vessel named *Lordsway*, and we had been asked to hold hands for the blessing. As the captain, our host, led the prayer, I resisted the impulse to place a dollop of mashed potatoes in my palm. "Oh Lord," he said, "protect these children and their small boat as they venture out into your great and awesome ocean..." Squinting, I looked over at Diane, but her eyes were shut tightly. There were serious lines across her forehead. The captain, however, had opened one eye and fixed it on me. He continued: "Protect them, for they are young and know not of Your awesome ocean and the dangers which they are about to encounter." The turkey stuffing I had snitched before the prayer suddenly stuck in my gullet.

We met many sailors like the preacher, and they were full of advice - the scary kind. But I preferred the turkey and stuffing. We were to learn that advice given freely was worth about as much. Instead we relied on the tutelage and mentorship of more taciturn and experienced sailors. Plied by time or a few beers, they offered encouragement rather than advice, tales of crossings accomplished and dire circumstances survived rather than disasters at sea. It could and had been done. Seasoned sailors reassured us with stories of their own mistakes - mistakes they survived. And on rare occasions, and only when we asked, did they offer advice.

As we sailed we learned that the ocean was not a malignant force greedily eyeing our fiberglass hull, but a friendly, or at least, indifferent Lady who asked merely that we pay attention to her moods. We had never met the ocean before, but we knew her from our trips to the mountains and our hikes through desert canyons. She was a familiar presence that awoke a pleasant and reassuring rhythm within us.

This is not the case with everyone. Take my friend Lenny, whose job did not leave him much time to escape. He once took a flight and remembered, just as his plane left the ground and he looked out his window at the terminal shrinking below him, that he had left his car running in front of the ticketing lobby.

Not long afterward, Lenny was driving me down a desert road. The full moon had just risen, and we rode straight toward its enormous yellow face. "You know," he said wistfully, "there sure have been a lot of full moons this month."

I was startled and glanced toward my friend. But the moonlight revealed a sober countenance.

"This is the only full moon this month," I said haltingly, expecting an "Of course" or "I knew that" in reply. Instead I got a mildly surprised "Really?"

I proceeded to lecture on the phases of the moon, the various astronomical orbits, the lunar calendar, the origins of the word month, and I ended with "...and that's why, except every once in a blue moon, we have only twelve lunar cycles per year and usually one full moon per month."

"Gosh," said Lenny, shaking his head in amazement, "isn't that something."

I am not suggesting that everyone is as out of touch as my friend Lenny, when it comes to the natural cycles of Nature, but I will confess that as I write this, I do not know if the moon is full, new, waxing, waning or abstaining.

Still, I can think back to Diane's and my first night crossing of the Grand Bahama Banks, when Diane and I not only knew the moon was full, but were counting on exactly where and when it would rise. I glanced at my watch every few seconds and then scanned the eastern horizon, waiting anxiously for the moon to reveal our destination and the invisible sandbars through which we threaded our way. That night we knew where Jupiter was, because we had used it to confirm our position on the empty sea. We recited all the constellations we knew to keep ourselves awake. We traced their paths across the sky and named the major stars that could tell us where the heck we were in this world devoid of street signs, taxicabs and service stations. The moon's movement was tied intimately with the rising tide that flowed up on the banks and created the current through which we floated and for which we compensated our course. All of this made sense. All of it was intertwined into a natural pattern that moved us and gave us a place on the surface of the planet. This pattern, so easily forgotten under a roof or blotted out by street lamps, is reassuring. It reminds us that a motion much greater than our daily meanderings guides our planet and that a pattern more important than our alarm clock starts each day. And it carries on no matter how many full moons we think have risen each month.

But if Nature proved to be our boon, what about our other *Cruising Fears*? Did we doze in a Sisyphean dream? Did we turn into bums? When people think of cruising on a sailboat, I believe they picture the fictitious "yachting" couple. He, a chiseled and smiling lad in oxford shirt, does not have a clue how to change the oil in his diesel engine and he would not dream of pulling hairballs out of his sump line. She, with soft, breeze blown silky hair framed by the sweater wrapped about her tanned shoulders, is not a lady worried about roaches in her galley. She laughs and displays a perfect row of white teeth. Who are these people, and who does their dental work? We did not meet them when we sailed.

Diane and I met a few folks who tried to act like cruising bums, but I think they were faking. You cannot sleep all day with a newspaper over your face and survive on a boat. It took 16 trips with a 20-liter jug to fill our water tanks. Here were the instructions: Row a quarter mile into shore with the dinghy. Carry the jug a half-mile to the well at the schoolhouse. Wave and smile at the Bahamian children who are watching you instead of the blackboard. Pull four buckets of water out of the well and filter out all the water bugs. Carry the considerably heavier jug back to the dinghy. Row back out to the boat. Repeat.

Cruising was work and the rewards were...well, the rewards were unexpected. The children from the Bahamian school watched us carry our 16 jugs of water. They laughed and danced around us when school let out. That evening there was a conch fritter "fry off" and carnival, a fund-raiser to buy the school a "duplicator." The kids asked us to join in. Our backs were sore, our arms were a couple inches longer, but as we sat down with them to eat, we felt the deep satisfaction that comes from accomplishing the most basic work there is: staying alive. The conch was delicious and, beneath the warm glow of an island sunset, we made new friends. Not bad for an honest day's work.

Cruising gave us time, but it did not leave us with time on our hands. We had lists with a million repair, maintenance and welfare "to-dos." We could lose ourselves in boat chores. Often we had trouble putting down our wrenches and scrub brushes, when the real adventure was ashore in a Mayan ruin or beneath our keel in the delicious promise of spiny lobster.

So the secret of our "Cruising Fears" was that none of them ended up being real. The real challenge and the real danger, as always, was something we had not fretted about at all.

Imagine the couple that plans to make The Great Escape. They look forward to being on their own. They look forward to getting away, starting a new adventure and rediscovering their love for one another. But what they discover might be what they have been ignoring back home. Out There, no 9-to-5 jobs will distract them from one another. They will be alone in foreign lands, in a desert of ocean with no friends or relatives to soften the blow of their hard edges. All of their fears, their idiosyncrasies and foibles will be magnified. Their marriage bond will be heated to a critical temperature and stretched.

Not What But How – First Voyage
1988

If I had to name an external measure for sanity, it would be Diane. If I find her unattractive, undesirable, or worse, abhorrent, then I am surely off my nut. I chose Diane as a mate, because I found her first beautiful, then caring, joyful and good, and because she lifted me up and helped me walk a better path, one on which I flourished.

This said, about three months into Diane's and my first cruise together in the eighties, I thought we would have to divorce. I arrived at this critical decision because I could see no other solution to the growing anger, confusion, ugliness and poison I felt within me. I even envisioned our sad return to the States - Greek heroes who, having lost the Trojan War, return in disgrace. It would be difficult to explain our failed marriage to relatives, sell our boat and split our possessions. We would have to start over again, alone.

Not long before starting our 1988 cruise, a Buddhist buddy had pulled me aside. "Look," he told me earnestly, "My wife and I spent a year alone in a little cabin in Alaska. The cabin was at the end of a long road - a road that started where civilization had already ended. When you get out there in the middle of the ocean with Diane, remember that you're never really angry with each other. You're just scared." My friend was trying to prepare me for a waterborne version of cabin fever: boat fever.

In December, about two months into our first cruise, Diane and I were crossing the Neuse River. The wind was a freezing fist that gripped us through four layers of clothing. We had been facing black, fierce cold fronts, one after another since leaving the Chesapeake; and our dreams of cruising in idyllic tropical climes were disappearing along with the Hawaiian shirts and shorts we had long ago buried beneath the long underwear and foul weather gear we had been forced to don. As we silently bashed our boat through the grey wind and rain, the chopped sea across the shallow Neuse River threatened to shake our boat and our marriage apart. Diane, in a moment of weakness, made a few discouraging remarks about the weather, our general state of affairs, my attitude, the attitude of my relatives, my ancestors and the air I breathed.

"Look," I said calmly, remembering the advice of my Buddhist Buddy and glowing with the light of my secret knowledge, "You're not really mad at me. You're just scared. Heck, we're both scared. And the only person we can share our fears with is each other. It's just that our fears come out as anger."

Diane gave me a look that temporarily warmed my frozen face. "Okay, now you look, " she said. "You are not Freud, and Freud is not going to get us across this %*#1 river!"

By January we had reached the Bahamas, and we had grown very tense with one another. Cold fronts continued to move over us and through us in ceaseless waves. As we closed the hatches against the grey, cold sky and the sort of shrieking wind that drove pioneer peoples in the Great Plains insane, we felt like prisoners on our own boat. Back home, we had each left jobs where we had been in charge - setting budgets, hiring and organizing teams of people to get the work of making money done. We had traveled across the continent and on to Europe. Now, compared with the cramped quarters on our boat in a raging storm, even the private hells like the Dallas airport looked like paradise. In our corporate lives, we had been important members of teams. On the boat, there was just the two of us on the lonely, and sometimes terrifying, Mother Ocean.

Because I knew something (but not enough) about sailing, I assumed the traditional gender role of captain. But my command was a fiction of job security. Diane, equally unsure of but more honest about her sailing skills, simply allowed me the promotion. But I was a poor captain - not only inexperienced and insecure but often blustering to cover my inadequacies. I recall imperious silences and bursts of angry bravado. (Dear Lady Readers, never forget that men often display their depression in mean, false bravado). I steered clear of my own problems by staying busy. I lied and told myself I was the smart one, the capable sailor: "Pay no attention to the man behind the curtain!" Besides, anyone looking logically at the two of us would have to agree. We were sailing through the Bahamas. We were in paradise, right? And since I was "O.K.," what could be the problem? We were supposed to be having fun, damn it, and if we were not, then the problem had to lie elsewhere; and there were only two of us on the boat.

Meanwhile, Diane and I, though drifting apart, were (sorry for the pun) in the same boat: a scary new world of waves and wet learning. Her friends, her job and her world were also far away in Arizona. In a grocery store in North Carolina, where we had come up empty looking for Mexican food fixings ("Tortillas? Shucks, mam, never heard of 'em!"), I found Diane crying - a very rare occurrence for a solid and stoic lady. She was standing in the produce section before bins of lettuce, carrots and onions. Tears were trickling down her face. What, I asked her, was wrong? Wiping her cheek with the back of her hand, she pointed to a bin of elongated, green vegetables with crown-like caps. "I don't even know what those are," she answered.

This intelligent woman, avid gardener and degreed botanist had found herself stymied by a vegetable. The mystery vegetable had released the dam of her despair and turned the uncertainty of her new life into a river of tears. She had been undone by okra.

As Diane and I tried to create the fabric of a new life aboard our boat, I did little to help her and sometimes shredded the little self-worth she was managing to weave. Our rocking boat, the huge ocean and the storms were unnerving. Every time our anchor tugged, it pulled her from her sleep. While I slept, she spent long nights listening to the wind moaning through the rigging. If I did wake, I would find her on deck with a flashlight checking to see if the anchor was still holding. She was a timid sailor searching for her confidence, and I often made matters worse by acting as if nothing Diane did on our boat was right. I looked over Diane's shoulder, watched her perform the simplest tasks like coiling a line, and then snorted in disgust and redid the job. My busybody approach helped me feel necessary and gave me a whimsical sense of control over our new, uncontrollable world.

So, there we were, arguing about how to coil lines, where we should anchor, what we should eat and who had said what or done what to hurt whose feelings. Following our worst screaming confrontations, we would retreat to far corners of our boat (never more than twenty feet apart) lick our wounds and grouse about the damage we had inflicted upon one other. I could not stand being with the woman I loved. My world and our dreams of living on a boat and sailing to paradise were unraveling.

One afternoon, when we had each retreated temporarily to our own corners, I decided to escape by taking a bike ride with a couple we had just met, two of the only young folks we had discovered thus far on our cruise. I did not invite Diane to come along; or if I did, she had had enough sense to decline. I pedaled over limestone hills past green palms and big-leafed papaya trees along a turquoise sea, but I saw nothing. I was reliving past arguments, chewing on grudges and chipping at the ugly black wall of our impasse. Finally, on a cliff where my companions had stopped to take in the view, I stopped and turned to them. My chest was tight. I had to say something or burst. They were two good people, a husband and wife who had cruised together for years, folks with whom we would soon become the best of friends. But at that time, I did not know the couple well enough to burden them with my troubles. Still, my cistern was full, and I had to empty it, so out it poured - all of my troubles and complaints in a gush of confused words. When I had finished, there was a silence followed by a reaction I hadn't expected. The couple smiled. They even chuckled a bit. I was shocked, almost offended, and it must have shown, for the lady spoke quickly and compassionately.

"How long have you been cruising together?" she asked.

"Four months," I sighed.

Again, the couple exchanged a knowing glance and smile.

"It happens to everyone," she said. "Don't worry. When you are cruising together, a lot of things come up that haven't come up before."

"You're both good folks," added the fellow, "and you'll figure it out." Then he reached out and held my shoulder, and somehow the reassurance of his voice and the warmth of his touch took the storm out of my mind.

"And," said the lady, almost as an afterthought, "when you get mad at each other, get it out right away. Don't hold it in. Then once you've gotten it out, move on. You two make a nice couple, and you're gonna be fine."

Thank God for friends who have been around the bend.

A boat is a little pressure cooker in which our lives are simmered. When they reach a boil, parts of ourselves, even the parts we think we have outgrown or overcome but are really only hiding, come bubbling up raw and red to the surface. When we see these repulsive things, we can try to push them back down in the stew or we can scoop them up, hold them in our hands and know them for what they are. It is hard to call this boiling pot one of the gifts of life aboard a boat, but it is.

After the bike ride, I started thinking differently - not completely differently, after all, I am a stubborn man and an engineer, and my changes come slowly. But I realized this first: that Diane was more important to me than any other "thing" in my life - the boat, our tropical dreams, perhaps even my life itself. Realizing that, I knew I did not want to lose her, so I started by telling her so. That was step one. The second step was changing myself. That part took and will always take the most work. By listening to her - really listening - and realizing that no matter what I heard, no matter how much I might disagree with it or how much it might seem to threaten some silly part of me and make me want to destroy it, what I heard, because Diane loved me, contained an important grain of truth. That is one of the reasons I had married her, chosen her as my companion - for the Truths she always told.

But I must confess that I hate this, the work of self-discovery and change - figuring out which part of a problem I am responsible for and how I am going to change me to fix it. But Life sometimes gets like this; and it is messy, difficult work. At the time, as we sailed together toward the Caribbean, learning to sail was a breeze in comparison.

I stopped recoiling Diane's lines. I listened to her anger and her criticisms and realized that though they often came from her own fears (a fact I did not need to tell her, and a fact she needed to and would find out for herself), they were gifts. The nice part was that as I held back, as I quit interfering with Diane's sailing, she became the sailor she hoped to be. I found I could not only stop second-guessing but could rely on her as a shipmate.

She learned to do everything there was to do on a boat, from raising, trimming and reefing sails to kedging an anchor. The only boating realm I ended up reserving for myself was the engine room with its whirling gears and belts - a natural attraction for a boy who had been fascinated with erector sets. My last vestige of male pride was soaked with oil and smelled of diesel. Diane willingly relinquished it. She built her own repertoire of nautical skills, and her accomplishments became, as our daughter Riley would one day say, part of her permanent record.

So the real *dinero* of Diane's and my first cruise in the eighties was this. Being alone with each other and facing the greatest adventures, risks and uncertainties of our lives was no trip to the quick stop. But the challenges we *thought* we would face, our worries about finances, self worth and safety, were nothing compared with learning how to face one another and ourselves. What did we need to be happy? Which of our faults got in the way of this happiness? How could we learn to work together and get across the ocean safely? How could we remember to respect one another no matter how poorly we felt about ourselves? And how could we ever forgive each another and go on?

When I think about family, and I mean really sit back and reflect (O.K., meditate), a parade of images marches through my mind. For me the images of my wife and two girls cannot be separated from my own parents, my brother and sister, my grandparents and the chain of my relatives. There are moments of pure happiness, when my heart is knotted and drug away by these thoughts: my girls playing in soft grass, the dog galumphing about them in a frolic, their tinkling laughter, daisy chain necklaces, warm sun and young bodies leaping, blond hair flying - moments of supreme lightness. Then my own father holds me between his legs. A rope larger than my arm whirs by my ear. "It's all right," he says. "I've got you." And with an effort that must have put his back and legs in spasm, I am lifted, carried forward on my skis, the rope tow slowing to a stop as we gain momentum, match it's speed as we whoosh up the hill, the cushion and strength of my father carrying me. And scary moments: dropping our kids off for their first day at a new school, never knowing until then how our own parents' hearts must have ached with the caring and uncertainty, because they showed us only strength, hugged us, promised us it would be O.K. And moments that shame me: the moment of rage, when hands lash out and there is a startling slap or worse, awful, critical words that kill innocence.

I tell my girls that they should use me as an example – both good and bad.

It appears to be the fashion these days to revisit our childhoods and discover the wrongs our parents dealt us. And I suppose this is fine, as long the children, now adults, use the discovery to move on. But if revisiting childhood becomes another excuse for poor behavior, then we are only snuggling in our baby blankets and refusing to grow up.

One friend of mine had a rather rabid mother. At one point she came at him with a steak knife. Another time she tried to crush him with an automatic garage door. Another friend had a very rich, socialite mother. She performed her various society duties every evening. Although my friend's maid used to come into his bedroom to clean or turn down his sheets, he never saw his mother there. After her grand balls and dinner parties, she never once came into his room - not to tuck him in, not to kiss him goodnight. Both friends have some childhood issues with which they must deal. I hope they find not only understanding but also forgiveness. For those of us who make the trip back into our childhoods but get trapped there, musician Glen Frey wrote: "Worrying about your future, complaining about your past, I'd like to find your inner child, and kick its little ass."

We, and only we, are responsible for who we are.

Diane Scouting Coral Heads

The Slap - 1998

I have a confession my wife would rather I not make...heck, *I* would rather not make. The memory still shames me. But telling the Truth about family boat life means telling the whole Truth.

Not long after starting our family cruise, we sailed south to St. Kitts. We had a pleasant enough sail, but when we approached the island, its crowning centerpiece, Mt. Misery, sent wind and galloping waves straight into *Manta Raya's* snout. We reefed sails and in the process lost a winch handle. (Oops. Splash. Damn!) Bashing along at over eight knots with the hull pounding like a kettledrum, we tried motoring further off the wind to ease the strain. But the port engine, our ever-present Achilles' heel, died whenever we accelerated past an idle. We hoped to end our wild ride by anchoring at the town of *Basse Terre*, but white caps barred its entrance, so we staggered another five miles to Nags Head on the southern end of the island. When we limped into the protected bay, both girls were seasick. We dropped our anchor in silence and licked our wounds.

The next day I hardly glanced at the lush green escarpment of St. Kitts. Instead, I spent the entire day searching for the problem with *Manta Raya's* port engine. In the end I gave up. I hoped that cleaning the fuel lines, tightening all fittings and changing all filters had fixed the problem. I emerged from the cramped engine compartment reeking of fuel. The girls took to calling me "Diesel-Boy."

Perhaps it was the fumes, the frustration, the claustrophobia in the sweat soaked crevices of the boat or the skin the diesel fuel was eating off my feet; but anchored off St. Kitts I decided I was not having a good time. My voyage to paradise had become a cruising purgatory. And there in the heart of a Caribbean dream, I threw a self-centered, self-aggrandizing, full tilt hissy fit.

My tantrum had something to do with the broken diesel engine, which was doing a good job of sabotaging my move-fast-but-have-time-for-fun plans. I worried about the approaching hurricane season and its very real calendar deadline, and we were not making our way south as quickly as I wanted. I was also upset about the unsettling realities of family cruising. We were struggling with the novelty of living on a boat - a struggle that would not release its anxious talons for many months to come. Boating once again brought new roles for all of us – not the least trying were Diane's and my new roles as teachers, for *Manta Raya* was both home and school for our girls. There might have been dozens of "reasons" for throwing a fit, but honestly, no reason could justify such behavior. Today looking back, all of these "reasons" look like minor excuses compared with the one stark emotion that was again driving me wacky on a boat: my own fear - the simple but overwhelming realization that the trip was, for the most part, out of my control.

I washed the diesel stink off my body, as the girls got ready for a St. Kitts shore excursion – a process that, in itself, fed my fuming. A rancher I know says of his family, "They transport O.K., but loadin' 'em up is hell." Trying to get a family out of a boat, into a dinghy and onto shore is no different than trying to get a family out of the house, into a car and out to dinner. The endless readying, the back and forth between bathroom and bedroom, the summoning and tedious foot tapping can be frustrating, especially for a father. A father thinks: "Get a coat, grab your wallet and drive." A boat dad thinks: "Grab your sandals, get your money belt and dinghy in."

Though the kids were excited about a new island landfall, our shore excursion preparations for St. Kitts were moving along about as quickly as a space shuttle launch. I planned a relaxing evening in town and a trip up the mountain for dinner. It was Mother's Day, and I wanted to show Diane a good time, damn it! But the girls needed to load their backpacks with t-shirts, coloring books, dolls and beads (the important time fillers when mom and dad did boring adult stuff like shopping). They also had to pick out nice clothes to wear. After all, we did not get out that often. Then, after everything was packed, we still had to search for lost items - sunglasses, sunscreen, sunhats and other paraphernalia that had somehow disappeared over the past six hours.

After multiple trips up and down the steps of the transom to the dinghy, and after several aborted launches when crucial shore gear was suddenly remembered and retrieved, we were finally ready to go. But on the girls' last trip down the transom, I managed to get my fingers caught between the dinghy and the mother ship, where they were nutcrackered by the physics of wave, floating dinghy and the boat's immovable mass. My fault, I know, but I was still cursing when Sawyer untied the painter (bless her, she was only doing her job), and we shoved off.

Without giving Sawyer a chance to sit down, I jammed the engine in reverse, which threw her forward and nearly out of the dinghy. Worse, she almost bashed her head on the transom. Diane decided she had had enough of my temper tantrum, and she slapped me.

Diane and I knew that physical violence was a poor way to handle our emotions, and it had taken a team effort for us to avoid the wrestling, grabbing and shoves that had characterized some of our early romance. We had sworn off this bad sport not only because it sickened us, but also because we knew it would be one of the saddest examples we might show our children. Diane and I are both physical people. We love dancing, sports with bats and rackets and work with hammers and shovels. When we first dated, we played racquetball with such abandon that we slammed our bodies about until they were bruised and cut. The competition was fierce. I gave up softball after I watched Diane's easy stretch for outs at first base and her strong bat to center field. But our problem was not that we were competitive and physical on the court and in the field, but that we brought the same competition to our home.

I remember one confrontation (but who really recalls an argument rather than the emotion accompanying it?) when we were having a heated and seated altercation. Diane was hurling the heated words, and I was sitting on the john. As our argument reached its climax, I leapt up and charged across the hall. But my pants were around my ankles, and my charge was more of a waddle and hop than a coordinated attack. Diane saw her opening and gave me a tiny but accurate hip check that sent me sprawling into our humidifier. The top of the thing gave way, and I found myself neatly folded with head and feet pointing skyward and buns soaking in the cold water. Diane started to laugh, but seeing the dark look on my face, made a quick exit. Further violence was avoided.

After more incidents like the humidifier splash down, I grew depressed with our violence and decided to sit down with my Buddhist buddy.

"Diane and I are hitting each other," I said.

"Oh?" said my friend. "Well at least you are communicating. My ex-wife and I couldn't even muster up the energy for a good shout, let alone a fistfight. You, however, care enough to connect."

"I'm not kidding," I said, "and it's not funny. Besides, it's making me sad, and we've got Sawyer to think about now. It's gotta stop."

My Buddhist buddy agreed with me, violence was harmful, even against worms. He helped me first by applauding my resolution to stop my physical aggression, and then he encouraged me by telling me that my resolve would help me understand the roots of my anger. First though, he said, we needed to identify a warning sign, a yellow caution light that would help me predict when my violent tsunamis were coming. He asked me to recall the feeling(s) that preceded violence. And he asked me to describe how these feelings "looked."

I was befuddled for a moment. But then I recalled my anger. I felt it, and I saw something. I saw a red flash and then a whiteout of overwhelming emotion.

My friend told me that for a split second after seeing these warning signs, I would have an opportunity. I would have a choice. I could either be carried away by the flood of emotion and become "Todd the Terrible," or, recognizing the colors and feelings, step aside to "observe them." I know this process might sound odd, but it worked. Watching myself get furious was instructive, even amusing. My Buddhist buddy's advice and the ensuing heart to heart discussions I had with Diane ended in a pact to quit our angry physics. During tough arguments, we kept our mitts to ourselves.

But in St. Kitts, the colors of emotion had overwhelmed me. I had forgotten our pact and the lessons of my Buddhist buddy. I had let the anger carry me down a red and white, self-indulgent tunnel of deliciously wicked energy. And Diane had stopped me with one well-placed, solid, and head spinning slap.

The slap resounded off the beachside cliffs and spun my head around through a blur of green palms and white sand. The world flew by very rapidly until it came to rest on an empty, bright sea. My world, the one that had so recently been a solar system of my problems with me at the epicenter, shrank. It practically disappeared. What replaced it was a large world, the real world and its great blue sea. My family floated with me in a rubber raft. They were silent and staring. They were contending with their own fears. Behind us was an island full of people, all with their own problems - an island overflowing with humanity.

There was a long and embarrassed silence on the dinghy. Pretending to be busy, the outboard continued to hum and spit water out the side of its cheek. My face stung. It was red and glowing with heat - Mt. Misery erupting. When I finally turned and faced my family, Diane's face was white, her eyes dark and accusing. The girls sat silently, staring into their laps. I put the engine in gear and turned the dingy toward shore, but then I stopped.

"I'm sorry," I said.

But an apology is only a start. Recovery from red-hot emotion takes time. Once ashore, we stopped by the post office and bought stamps of colorful, tropical fish. We collected delicious fruits and veggies at the market. ("Dis one, honey. Iz dascheyne fruit. You eat him up, an' he make everyting right for you.") We took a taxi up the side of the mountain and into the green rainforest of fanned palms and chattering monkeys. We stared across the ocean at smoking Montserrat and wondered whether it would rain ash down upon us or allow us, like an indulgent bridge troll, to sail safely by. We ate a delicious meal and watched the girls consume and be consumed by coconut ice cream. We laughed and chased each other through a trellised garden. A peacock screamed at us and then mooned us with its haughty tail. I thanked my lucky stars for a family loving enough to forgive me and move on.

That night back in our berths, I do not know what the rest of my crew was thinking. But I was thinking of my resolve to pay more attention, to not let myself get to that red-hot place where a hard slap was the only antidote to my insanity.

Red Water, Blue Water

About a month before we left the U.S. to start living as a family aboard our floating home in St. Martin, I filled six glass vials with water. In two of the vials I dropped food coloring - red in one and blue in the other. Then I arranged four chairs to form the corners of a rectangle. While our girls danced about asking questions and the dog did its best to get underfoot, we wound rope (*line*, to you nautically inclined Readers) around the perimeter of the chairs to form an eight by ten foot rectangle. My wife and I seated ourselves, and then we invited the girls to join us. They crawled under the ropes and stood grinning and expectant. We had their full attention.

"Welcome aboard," I said. "This is your new home." Then I stood up and walked about creating imaginary shapes with my arms. "Here's the table, the bench seats, the sink, the stove, and the fridge. There's enough food and drink under those lazarette seats to last us two months, which is the amount of time we might spend offshore and away from cities and people at any given time. When we turn out of our berths each morning, we will sit right on top of that food to eat our breakfast. We'll go to school, play games, read books, entertain guests, celebrate the holidays and do just about everything you can think of in this space... Whaddya think?"

The girls, their smiles a bit diminished but still game, looked around at the rope fence, "It's kinda small," offered Sawyer.

"Exactly!" I exclaimed (my students were answering on cue). And I took out the glass vials. "Now," I said, handing the containers to

Riley, "what do you see?" Riley fingered and shook each tiny cylinder in turn. The dog edged closer sensing an event that, in my focus on the lesson, escaped me. "Let's pretend," I continued, "that the four clear vials are us. We go to school (I marched two vials off to their class rooms); we go to work (two more vials tottered away). But then something happens, and one of us gets mad" (I switched a clear vial for a vial with red dye). "So what happens to the rest of us?" The kids looked at the vials, waited a minute just in case there might be some sort of trick, and then hazarded a guess: "Nothing?"

"Exactly!" I shouted. "But what if we put these vials very close together?" (I brought the four vials into the palm of my hand) "What if we bring them so close together that they mix?"

And so, I asked Riley to open the vials, and that is when the excitement started - the spill of red dye on white carpet. Diane jumped up to get paper towels but did not manage to clear the turnbuckle rope. She tripped and brought down all four chairs. There was a tangle of arms, legs, chairs and rope that looked like a living room rodeo. There was confusion. The kids shouted. Diane and I stumbled about trying to separate human and animal parts from furniture and rope. I trounced on the dog's tail, and she yelped.

Calm was eventually restored, the stage was reset, but there was no need to continue the play. The point had already been made - drama within drama. As a family, we had an effect upon one another. In close quarters, we had a profound effect. Whether we taxed each other with red water rage or brought peace with our blue water calm, the tight living space that was about to be our home would be a new challenge. We would have no back yard where the kids could blow off steam with their neighborhood friends. For that matter, new friends would be few and far between. Mama and Papa would not be heading off to work or taking a break by hiring a sitter and spending a night at the theater. (I think the kids sobered at this realization more than we did.) Life was going to be different.

We discussed other heady topics that night (as we would during several family meetings on the boat). I remember trying to probe the origin of our anger - explaining that no matter where it was directed, its source was always ourselves, and its cause was usually our own fears. In the same vein, Diane warned that she would be a very protective mom, clinging tightly to the kids' life vests and growing short tempered in scary seas. And I apologized in advance for the dark spells I knew

I would enter as a grouchy captain. I tried to explain that when those times came, I would not be angry with the family but fed up shouldering the responsibility of boat and crew. But these warnings were understandably lost on the kids. After all, yelling is yelling, anger is anger, and poor behavior is just that... a hurtful and gnarly knot we must each unravel in our own time.

Gumby Boaters - 1998

Manta Raya Christening, Nevis, June 1998

Boat Christening

Gods of the sea, wind, sailing vessels, things electronic and diesel and the God of all things within and without us – thank you for this beautiful vessel. She has taken care of a good family before us, and now we ask for your blessing on her new name

*– old and new spirit merged, best of worlds, all thoughts, deeds
and actions – to protect and safely carry our family under her
new name Manta Raya. Please keep her rigging strong. Help her
through troubled seas. Guide her to calm waters. And help her
speak to us and teach us along the way.*

*New name, new sail, new family, new adventures. We
hereby place a golden coin (circa our last adventure aboard our
beloved "Lucile's Sweet Thursday") beneath the mast, and we
spill a treasured libation as offering to the sea, which covers the
earth and from which we came, squirming and gurgling, in the
beginning.*

*And so, now it starts – a new adventure. Everything before
was the past. Everything before us is yet to come. Now we are
here, on our new home Manta Raya.*

Je m'apelle nouveau Manta Raya.

*[Signed by captain Todd, first mate Diane and crew
members Sawyer and Riley]*

After refitting our boat on St. Martin, we sailed our family
catamaran south along the Windward Islands toward Venezuela. We
had learned a bit more about sailing our catamaran, not only through
misadventure but also during pleasant afternoon sails about the island
of St. Martin. In a family ceremony, where each of the girls placed a new
coin under the mast and we poured rum off the stern, we christened
our boat *Manta Raya,* Spanish for the grand fish she resembled. We still
had much to learn about sailing her; and as we headed south into the
windy Windwards, our passages would give us plenty of opportunities
to learn. The sailing was tough and bouncy, and we were often anxious,
especially since we were new to catamarans in general and *Manta Raya*
in particular.

Manta Raya felt big, unwieldy and sometimes dangerous. We did
not know if she were a better sailor than we – the critical trait of great
boats, which "speak" to their skippers. In calm or raging seas they tell
their captains exactly what sails, what speeds and what angles of attack
suit them. Great boats perform beyond their captains' expectations.
In a storm, when good sailors have done all they know to do and must
go below, they close the companionway hatch behind them and let
a great boat fend for herself. And a great boat brings her crew home
safely.

Manta Raya would prove to be a great boat, and she would teach us many things during the two years we cruised together. She would tell us, or to be more honest, we would finally learn to *hear*, how she wanted to sail. But at the beginning of our voyage, we were barely on speaking terms.

Here is Diane's log entry after our first passage, June 3, 1998, one day out of St. Martin and anchored in Gustavia Harbour off St. Barts:

> *Today we left St. Martin after one year of planning and the last five weeks of busting our bottoms at the Great Bay Marina in Phillipsbug, St. Marteen, Netherland Antillies.*
>
> *So this is the start of our adventure. Or was it leaving Flagstaff with our van groaning under the load of the U-Haul from Hell? Or was it when we boarded that plane in Miami with one-way tickets – no return? Or was it when we were shuttled under cover of night out to Manta Raya, then Toons Boat, by Gerard and Beatrice on their launch Betty Boop?*
>
> *Who knows, but it's all uncharted water now. It's so strange and scary trying to get used to this boat. More so than the last time. Why? Is it because the French West Indies ain't the Chesapeake, because the boat feels twice as big, because Todd has had to repair every system at least once, or because the kids are along as an added worry and distraction?*
>
> *I don't know, but I desperately look forward to the day when Manta Raya and I are in cahoots, and I don't have an anxiety attack every time we move her.*

At sea anxiety is an enemy so strong it can push queasy stomachs to the rail. In our family, we battled seasickness to varying degrees: Diane - rarely (thank goodness); me - at the beginning of rough passages after extended shore leave; and the girls - just about any time conditions got rough; though after paying respects to Neptune, they usually recovered, quickly. While on a particularly rough Gulf Stream passage during Diane's and my cruise in the eighties, we were both sick – so sick that I fell into a state akin to shock and was unable to move my limbs or speak. My paralysis was, of course, an unsettling time for Diane. But as much as I wanted to reassure her, I could not make my lips form the words "I'm O.K." Later a doctor told me my condition was a form of *Vasovagal Syncope*, or more simply, fainting.

He said I should not have fought the motion sickness, and that it was always better to toss one's cookies early and "clean the slate," as it were, so as to get on with the business at hand.

We tried all of the motion sickness remedies: Dramamine, promethazine, scopalamine, Idi Amin... We even tried acupressure wristbands, though I must tell you that when we were on a difficult passage across the Gulf Stream, also in the eighties, I radioed our dear friend and sailing mentor St. Frank, who was sailing ahead of us and also using the wristbands, to ask him whether they were working. Mine were surely not. I had already tossed my cookies, twice. St. Frank said his bands were not working either, even though for the last hour he had been pressing on them madly as if they were buttons in a stuck elevator. He wondered whether the wristbands were actually supposed to be taken internally, though we both grew silent thinking how that might be accomplished.

With our family on *Manta Raya*, bland, light diets and ginger seemed to help, but never completely. To this day, our girls cannot stand the taste of ginger in anything, not even cookies. It makes them seasick. Still, I believe the fundamental cause of seasickness is not the motion of the ocean but the anxiety that comes with it. There is nothing like fear to bring on barfing.

Before we left on our family cruise, I sat with an E.R. doctor, who was also a sailor. He was a practical and accomplished physician who prescribed simple medical solutions. I was meeting with him over breakfast as he wrote out prescriptions for our future floating medicine chest. As a sailor who had cruised the entire west coast of Mexico, he also knew, first hand, about the kinship between anxiety and seasickness.

"What about anxiety medication?" he asked, as he scribbled on his pad and tossed prescriptions at me. We were sitting in a coffee shop high in the mountains of Arizona, and the otherworldliness of our conversation thrilled me.

"Anxiety medication?" I repeated. "That's a great idea. Just as we're getting the poop scared out of, we'll pop pills, get blitzed and giggle our way to shipwreck."

The doctor, a patient and kind man, stopped his scrawling and looked up at me over his glasses. He was not laughing. "When you are at sea and things get rough," he said, "there is no reason to let fear overcome you. Fear is a wasted emotion."

Did we include the doc's anxiety medication in our medicine chest? Yes. Did we use it? By the time we tied the last bowline around the last piling of the last dock at the end of our cruise, the bottle was empty. And no matter what one's attitude might be about metabolic chemical adjustments, our take home was that the doctor's words rang true. There is no debilitating emotion like fear, and how we handle it is a hefty question.

Even though children might add yet more anxiety to the equation of cruising concerns, our girls (and perhaps the kid in all of us) offered an over the counter solution. On our rollicking passage between Nevis and Guadeloupe, not far south of St. Martin, I worried about the pounding the waves were giving to *Manta Raya's* underside. Each time a wave hit the flat surface beneath our pod, it sounded like a mallet hitting a kettledrum. The hull boomed, and the entire boat jerked and shuddered with a vibration that traveled to the very top of the mast. As we rounded the island of Montserrat into yet more wind and waves, I went below to check the bilges. As always, nervous energy was propelling me about the boat like a worried hen. I was preoccupied and feeling queasy, but I pulled up short when I entered the main salon and saw Riley. She was lying on the galley table, arms across her chest, and she had a wild look in her eyes. "Papa," she said, "watch this!" I waited, and when a big wave boomed against our bottom, Riley was propelled by the jolt. She flew into the air laughing hysterically.

Yes, we were Gumby boaters learning how to sail a catamaran, and at times we flailed – at times we were scared. But as we feared and as we flailed, we learned more about *Manta Raya*, and just as Diane and I had found on *Lucile's Sweet Thursday* in the eighties, we discovered help and encouragement along the way.

Late one night on Dutch St. Marteen, we visited with a commercial catamaran captain from South Africa. Every morning, with his crew washing down the deck and stowing sandwiches, sodas and beer in his sixty-foot catamaran, the captain would walk up the dock in front of us and welcome the daily gaggle of tourists. The tourists were lined up and waiting for an afternoon of snorkeling and a shopping on the chic island of St. Barts. The captain was our hero; a demi-god of sailing with a reputation for being a gruff but likable captain who ran a tight ship. We figured he must know all there was to know about multihull sailing. And when we finally built up the courage to invite him aboard, the captain surprised us by smiling and telling us he would be glad to meet us for a quick beer after work.

Late that night, after several quick beers, the captain was still aboard, and the kids were fast asleep. We had brought out all of our charts, from St. Martin to Venezuela, and the captain had circled all the best anchorages he could remember from his own voyages through the Caribbean. Each circle brought back memories and more stories. With each stroke of his pencil, we traveled further down the length of the Caribbean, where we hiked the green mountains and waterfalls of Trinidad and met the monkeys of Venezuela. But at one point, the catamaran captain suddenly stopped.

"Do you mind?' he said, reaching up toward our jib sheets and unfastening the cam cleat levers. "I can't stand seeing lines trapped like that, even here at dock. Never lock down running lines on a catamaran. These cats," he continued, looking over at his sixty foot charter cat and graciously including our *Manta Raya* in the gesture, "are big, fast creatures, and when something goes wrong, say you back a jib or mainsail, and the cam cleats are on, the the damned locks can freeze up on you. You can't get the bloody things undone. Then you're in the shitter."

With little encouragement, the catamaran captain gave us more tips, which all boiled down to one analogy that stuck with me long after our night at the dock: "You're not a heavy monohuller now," he said. "You can't muscle your way through waves. You're sailing a catamaran, and you've go to use your agility and your speed to move around the bastards. Forget George Foreman; now you're Sugar Ray Leonard, floating like a goddamned butterfly and stingin' like a friggin' bee." Despite the mixed metaphor, the captain's advice was sound. And he urged us to call on another catamaran sailing sage on the island of St. Barts: Randy the transatlantic multihull racer.

Randy was tall, almost albino, and he had long hair tied in a ponytail down his back. He might as well have been the goodwill ambassador for St. Barts, for he knew everyone. He got the best tables, quickest drinks and drew the largest crowd at every restaurant and bar on the island. He was a resort caretaker for a rich benefactor, and he lived in a beautiful home overlooking a calm bay, where we anchored after arriving from St. Martin. Not long after our anchor had touched down, Randy motored out on his fast skiff. Standing tall and wearing reflective sunglasses, he leaned into a tight turn and pulled up to our stern. "Beautiful cat," he said. "I'm guessing one of the early Catanas? Do you mind if I have a look?"

Many boats are beautiful – sleek Sparkman and Stephens designs like the *Swans* come to mind. But catamarans have never looked *beautiful* to me. Even though *Manta Raya* was slung low and swept back like a space ship (one sailor we met said she looked like "Darth Vader's attack ship"), like all catamarans she still looked more like a floating dock with sails than a proper cruising yacht. But Randy was a multihull racer, and his eyes were tuned and trained to appreciate multihull design. "She's a Lock Crowther design, isn't she?" he said. "I could see that from shore."

At sunset, Randy motored back to his palatial home and then quickly returned with freshly caught grouper filets. Instead of his usual carousing with island friends, Randy had graciously chosen to visit with us on *Manta Raya*. It appeared he had adopted our family. Over dinner we heard about his transatlantic races. We also heard about an unfortunate misunderstanding regarding certain cargoes he had once ferried about the islands - a misunderstanding that had landed him in jail. Randy was a U.S. citizen, and like many ex-patriots from the States, he had an easy way about him as well as a vague but interesting recall of his past. Why, for example, had he left his U.S. home?

"I had to leave Florida," he said. "Too cold."

With Randy's open ocean experience on catamarans, we could not resist asking him for advice. He responded by first offering warnings about nearby Montserrat. He told us not to sail to leeward (downwind) of *Soufriere*, the smoking volcano that occasionally erupted on the island. We learned later from one of Randy's friends that Randy had gotten caught trying to sneak downwind of the belching volcano when it erupted. The hot gas had melted the Dacron lines on his boat, burned his lungs and covered his deck with hot ash, which clogged his running rigging and ruined his winches and blocks.

The next evening after meeting Randy, we joined him for dinner in town. Between sips of fine wine and the parade of acquaintances who came by to pay their respects to "ambassador" Randy, we continued our catamaran conversation. At one point, relaxed by the wine, Diane and I confessed our catamaran cruising fears and our overall feelings of inadequacy. Would we, we wondered, ever learn to float like bees and sting like butterflies?

"Well, you're on a good boat," said Randy. "And she'll take care of you." Then he paused, as he contemplated his wine in the candlelight, and offered this encouragement: "God loves sailors, children and fools," he said. "It would appear you have all three."

The St. Whatevers

As we made our way through the Windward Islands, we began to learn how to sail and live aboard our boat as a family. Because we were racing the hurricane season (trying to get south of the historical track of named storms, i.e. the wind-fisted personifications of cruising angst) and perhaps because we had not yet shed our demanding first world agendas, we felt we had to move through the islands quickly. Besides, we had not come this far to follow the cruising herd within the well-traveled Windwards; we were on our way to South America, where we hoped to find "real" cruising away from the rum lines of conventional cruisers. We were eager not just to enter safer fall cruising grounds but also to leave behind the cruise ships, beach resorts, charter fleets and the unfortunate, jaded attitudes that tourists tended to engender in the *Saint Whatevers*. We were, we hoped, on our way to more pristine cruising grounds – clean water, healthy coral, and interesting and friendly folks, who might be genuinely happy to see us sail into their harbors. Still, though we felt rushed to get south, we did try to stop and smell the Frangipani along the way. We toured lush, green island hillsides and historic colonial towns by foot or on our bikes. We visited cool waterfalls, tropical arboretums and, Diane's favorite, small town markets.

Throughout the Caribbean, Diane, the curious botanist, spent a good deal of her time in the dusty markets searching out the Caribbean's oddest fruits and veggies. As smiling and indulgent vendors looked on, she would fondle, smell and taste sweet guava, starchy cassava, fragrant sapodilla, purple star apples, tart soursop and the oxymoronic ugly fruit, which looks like the gnarly, spiked end of a medieval mace, but tastes a good deal better.

Ugly fruit? Why did Diane spend her time searching out bizarre produce that would never make its way into the waxed and misted bins of United States' grocery chains? First, she is a lover of all flora; and second, the odd fruits and veggies were our passports to the Caribbean. By learning about them, tasting them, enjoying them (or hating them), we traveled one step further into the Caribbean. The markets and their odd fruits and veggies pulled us out of our white bread, apple, orange and banana routine and put us into the exotic Caribbean. Before our trip was finished, Diane would not only know the names of dozens of new fruits and veggies, she would also be able to ask for and buy powdered milk in six different languages. While we sailed south and honed our anchoring and navigating skills, we practiced our provisioning and "getting around in new places" skills. We were learning to think like cruisers.

As with our trips into the markets to visit with obliging vendors, with a little extra effort, we met along the way, even in the jaded *St. Whatevers*, nice folks. We knew from our voyage in the eighties that islanders would not always be thrilled to see us. And even if *we* thought of ourselves as caring and appreciative visitors, islanders in the *St. Whatevers* could not be blamed for taking us for charge card flashing, daiquiri swizzling, gone tomorrow tourists.

In Jamaica in the eighties, I once worked for over an hour to strike up a conversation with a Jamaican fisherman. He was standing at the end of a long dock and methodically flipping small white rocks into the water before following the pebbles with his net. I talked *at* the man for over an hour, prattling away about everything and nothing: the weather, his fishing, the price of bread…. all the while hoping that he would reply, in fact, say anything. I wanted to learn more about his world, and I wanted to find out, damn it, why he was throwing little white rocks into the water. For the first fifteen minutes the fisherman ignored me entirely. He did not even look my direction. For the next quarter hour, though he glanced my way occasionally, he did not speak. Still, I continued to smile and talk away. Finally, when he realized I was not leaving and that I was honestly interested in his work, he spoke. It took over an hour, but we became friends. And at the end of the day, dangling our feet over the water and sharing a beer and some jerk chicken, the Jamaican fisherman finally told me about the pebbles: "The fish, mon, dey tink, 'What is dis ting?' And dey comb to look. Den *BOOM*, de net, he comb and catch dem up."

With similar patience and effort, our family managed to find nice anchorages within the heavily sailed *St. Whatevers*. Bequia, a little over half way down the Windwards, may not have been a pristine cruising paradise, but it was certainly a beautiful cruising mecca. Bequia's harbor was crowded with boats from around the world. Water taxis, laundry launches and floating bakeries shuttled back and forth between shore and the horde of cruising boats packed into the harbor.

We arrived in Bequia early one morning after a long night passage. Despite the popularity of the anchorage, we were captivated by the lime green hills that draped down into the calm waters of the protected harbor. That evening we took a water taxi to a wonderful restaurant. After a friendly boat taxi dropped us off on the beach, we climbed a short trail up through lush palms and flowers for a delicious dinner of conch roti, grilled and lime marinated tuna and creamy calalou soup. Despite the cruising crowd, we had the place to ourselves and sat on a deck with a panoramic view of the harbor under a canopy of trees and dangling fragrant flowers. We finished the night with homemade chocolate ice cream – a nice way to spend one's fortieth birthday, no?

We also biked across Bequia and visited a Hawksbill turtle farm just off the roaring surf on the windward side of the island. A Bequian fisherman was rescuing turtle off the beach, and the little tykes swam about in shallow pools he had created in cement tanks. In the safety of the pools, the swimmers nipped at one another until they grew big enough to be released back into the sea. A fisherman saving endangered turtles? Bequia was no jaded *St. Whatever*; it was an island with a good spirit. Still, it was a popular anchorage, and to take a break from the fifty or so yachts gathered in the harbor, we made our way to a nearby island.

To find this getaway island, we used two "getaway" tricks: We got a copy of the local charter fleet guide, and we consulted our out of date sailing guide (our cruising bible from our first voyage in the eighties). The charter guide told us which of the islands were off limits to the charter fleet, and the Windward section of our sailing guide, written by outlandish sailing demigod Jon Byerly, described anchorages around these "out of bounds" islands. The island we chose presented a "considerable slog to windward" and an "anchorage prone to swell." It was perfect. The charter companies did not dare put it on their charts.

Our getaway island, like the Bequia restaurant, was delightful. We hiked a windswept mountain in the company of no one but wild goats; and we dined on fresh conch and lobster – all within a day's sail of the massed fleet at Bequia. After two months of wedging ourselves into crowded anchorages, watching our step to make sure we were not stepping on anyone else's anchor lines and taking nighttime showers hunkered down in the cockpit for privacy, we had an anchorage to ourselves – except for the lone fishing boat about one hundred yards off our stern. But just as we recalled from our days sailing in less jaded cruising grounds of the Northwest Caribbean in the eighties, instead of resenting our presence, the fishermen dropped by, chatted and shared a beer with us. Later, after returning from a hike ashore, we found a gift of two conchs and a lobster waiting for us in our cockpit. This was one of the reasons we were cruising. It was (and is) the experience and gift we wanted to give to our children.

Just south of Bequia was an island of an entirely different ilk. The island of Mustique was run, if not entirely owned, by big "F's" - fiscally fortunate and famous foreigners. When we biked Mustique's winding roads, we rolled past estates owned by Princess Anne, Mick Jagger and Sting. Iron fences and gated walls surrounded clipped lawns and flowering hedges. Mustique was a giant, private country club afloat in the Caribbean.

During our bike tour of the homes of the rich and famous, we befriended two lesser-known lads: Darren and his sidekick Junior. They were locals from the little town "on the other side of the tracks," and they brought their rusty bikes alongside ours just off a playground under the dangling flowers of a monkey tone tree. They wanted to be our "tour guides." Darren, though only seven years old, claimed to be an "expert guide." And guide us he did. He led us from hillside resort to beautiful white beach to bubbling, sulfuric swamp, all the while promising to end his tour with a feast at the "local pizza joint."

As the day wore on and the pleasant bike tour went on and on, the "pizza joint" became our holy grail. When our energy and spirits flagged, the restaurant was forever, "just over the next hill." Darren took us up and down so many rollercoaster hills that our sea legs first turned to rubber and then cramped. We nearly suffered heat strokes in the muggy heat. Sunset approached, sweat crystallized around our eyes and I could see that Sawyer, exhausted by the ride, was still pedaling but silently and in tears (Riley rode in a towing bike seat). I was about to give up on our little guides and bid them farewell, when we rounded a bend that, joy of joys, overlooked our anchorage. We were home, and according to Darren, at the "pizza joint."

We climbed off our bikes and tossed them against a mimosa tree beside a black BMW. I rubbed my sore bum and tried to straighten my back. We were starved. But when the sweat cleared from our eyes, I discovered that the "local pizza joint" was nothing of the sort. It was a posh, gourmet restaurant.

"You boys ever actually eat here?" I asked. Our guides responded with sheepish grins and whispered no's.

Inside we met the proprietor. With dangling cigarette in one hand and jiggling cocktail in the other, he looked us over and grinned – a good grin, I hoped. I told him the story of our epic ride and how his restaurant had become our holy grail. He raised his eyebrows and looked down at our tour guides. Darren and Junior, who had been chattering non-stop all afternoon, became very quiet and were lost in the contemplation of their feet.

"Well," said the dapper man, "my first guests won't arrive for another hour. I'll tell you what. You folks sit over by the windows, and I'll fix you up with something."

Wearing our grimy bike shorts and sweaty t-shirts, we sat down at a long table spread with linen and crystal. Out the big bay window was a white beach and a splashing fountain lit with gold and blue lights. Returning from the kitchen, our patron told us about his restaurant. Across the dining room from our table was the grand piano, which from time to time Phil Collins played. And in the middle of the room was Princess Anne's private table (I could not help but notice the throne-like chair at its head). We were living the posh life, and our little guides rose to the occasion. They were once again smiling and chatting away.

I glanced at a satin covered menu, which, from the rough French translation I could muster, contained nothing remotely similar to pizza. No matter, our dinner was special order. Our dear host brought rum and tonics for the adults and cokes with cherries for the thirsty kids. His chef improvised (I could hear him laughing in the kitchen) a feta cheese and rosemary pizza and a cheese and pepperoni pizza for the kids. The food was delicious; though honestly, after such a long ride, I think we would have been pleased to eat our cocktail napkins. We were a happy table in an empty restaurant, and we were lifted high by the epiphany of our unexpected adventure.

The next morning, Sawyer and I *walked* our bikes up the hill to the little town where Darren lived. We stopped by the police station looking for directions to his home, and the officer, leaning back in his chair on a rickety porch, narrowed his eyes.

"He's not in trouble," I said quickly. "We just want to give him a gift."

Still hesitant, the officer pointed down the gravel road toward a little shack over a limestone ravine.

The shantytown presented quite a contrast to our estate ride and gourmet restaurant. As usual in the Windward Islands, the homes were shacks pieced together with odd boards and rusted tin. Mangy dogs barked from beneath sagging porches, and roofs were patched with tar paper and cardboard. We found Darren's mother hanging laundry in the back of just such a home. When we introduced ourselves and asked if Darren were about, she too looked suspicious. For such a young fellow, Darren must have already built himself quite a reputation in the community. But when Darren's mother found out why we had come, she clapped her hand over her mouth and cried.

We left our bikes on the front porch. Sawyer's bike, it turned out, was perfect for Junior; and my bike, though a bit bigger, would soon be perfect for Darren. He would grow into it. With fifteen gears and knobby mountain tires beneath him, Darren (though I doubted he needed the notoriety) would be quite the young man about the island.

Grenada

We left Mustique and continued our way south through the windy islands toward Grenada - our first cruising goal south of the hurricane belt. We crossed our fingers and toes as we sailed over the underwater volcano *Kick 'Em Jenny* and around Grenada's southern tip. Maybe we had not completed a trip around the horn, but we had arrived in safer waters, and we had reached the haven together as a sailing family. As if in reward, we sailed the final forty nautical miles in five hours - time that melted away during one of our most pleasant passages through the Windwards.

We ghosted along the flat water off the lee coast of Grenada, while the wind and current patted *Manta Raya* gently on the shoulder. With the autopilot in charge, we ate lunch on the trampoline, watched dolphins jump off our bow and admired the scenery - green hills folding steeply down into a blue sea. We were at 12 degrees north latitude, an even dozen. We had sailed through the entire Windward chain of islands, 180 nautical miles in just over thirty days. Though this was a trifling of travel for any globetrotting cruiser, it was a good start for a liveaboard family just getting their feet wet on a new boat. For a month we had been on the move nearly every day. Finally, we could take a deep breath and simmer down. We had arrived.

We anchored off Calvigny Island in Clarks Court Bay in protected waters fringed by palm trees and white beaches. Riley, sensing a change in our cruising temperament, suggested we adopt the following daily schedule:

(1.) Eat breakfast.

(2.) Take a rest.

(3.) Parents read books.

(4.) Go swimming.

(5.) Run computer (generator) so the kids can play, while the parents do whatever they want.

(6.) Everybody helps to make dinner.

(7.) Read a book.

(8.) Go out on the tramp and look at the stars.

(9.) Everybody brush their teeth and hop in bed.

Over the next few weeks, Riley's proposed routine was not far from the agenda that filled our days. (Even folks living on a boat in the Caribbean need a vacation.) We turned away from our usual cruising duties of diesel repair, hull cleaning and home schooling to focus on novel pastimes like sketching Calvigny Island, a lush green island draped with red bushes and yellow flowers. When we got hot, we dove off the bow, climbed the anchor line and laughed as our voices echoed between *Manta Raya's* floats. Splashing about beneath the boat with the light shimmering on the emerald water and reflecting off the white hull, we were pirates in a secret cave, dolphins in a sparkling grotto.

Our mornings unfolded. They did not explode or unravel; they eased into gear with the gradual brightening of dawn and the first hoarse crank of a heron clearing its throat. Morning was private time for each of us. I took time to sit on deck, fill my lungs with cool, salt air, and scratch my head urging the blood into my brain. There were no alarm clocks and no ringing phones. Often there were no neighbors - only a cormorant perched in the mangroves and raising a dripping witches cloak of wet wings or a sober pelican regarding me sideways with a stern glance down its wizened beak. When the rest of the family lay sleeping, this was my time.

Riley was the first to stir. She would check to see if her sister were awake with a "hooty-hoo" - a secret language passed from porthole to porthole between sisters. But if her sister were still asleep (or feigning sleep), the morning would become Riley's and my time together. We would have some of our best conversations - surreal thoughts, from minds half awake and half dreaming.

"Morning, Papa."

"Good morning, Sweat Pea. How'd you sleep?"

"Good."

[Pause, in which I knew Riley was considering a revelation]

"You know why I love our dog?"

"Why, honey."

"I can take the queechies out of her eyes. I don't think you could do that with somebody else's dog."

"Probably not, honey..."

[And without pause...]

"You know the way some big people don't listen to kids?"

"Uh huh."

"I think they just don't know how to talk to kids...Maybe they're nervous 'causethey forgot how."

"Probably, Pea. Wanna go for a spin?"

"Uh huh."

We would lower the dinghy, and the noise would wake Sawyer, whose head would poke from her porthole.

"Where ya goin'?"

"Fishing, wanna come?"

Then the morning would become a morning for the three of us: the girls dangling their fishing lines to port and starboard, Sawyer half asleep but squinting and smiling into the sun, me steering with my foot and keeping both hands free to block the tips of the girls' poles from my eyes, as Riley, pontificated on the quality of the day, her night's sleep and whatever other thoughts happened to dart through her cerebrum.

Riley: "Look Papa. Vultures!"

[Indeed, vultures were circling overhead.]

Me: "What do you think that means?"

Riley: "I think we're dead meat."

We might catch a rock fish, we might catch a barracuda, or maybe we would lean together over the side of our rubber dinghy and stare through our glass bottom bucket - our voices echoing around the hollow circumference and our shoulders and cheeks pressed together to regard and be regarded by a stone crab, pincers raised and prepared to take on all three of us. Or maybe a pulse of color and a sudden swirl of blue smoke would surprise us, as an octopus the size of a cat would swoop into a hole the size of a quarter. Or maybe we would just snug the dingy into a lee shore and wade its shallows - the sea grass tickling our feet and swayed to the rhythm of lapping wavelets.

These were times to discover our liquid world, to float or walk in wonder. They were times to talk, or maybe they were times to say nothing and so say everything. For one entire morning, from breakfast until lunch, Sawyer and I sketched and painted an islet near Grenada. I recall every detail of that shore - from the rough cement and shell of the abandoned concrete dock to the soft orange drape of flame trees down the green hillside.

Was every day paradise? No. Sometimes, when tempers flared and the red water boiled over, we retreated to our own corners, ate our separate meals in silence, watched the waves or read a book, and tried to simmer down. But almost every day we ate all of our meals together - outside, in the wide cockpit, under a blue sky, watching the pelicans hit the water, recalling the best things that had happened to us that day and thankful that we were together. Then twilight gave way to the first stars, and we would lay together on the mesh of the trampoline with the cool evening breezes rushing up to tickle and cool our skin. The Dog Star would flash green and blue and sparkle white on the horizon like a jewel curried in sunlight. We would roll and wrestle like otters or tell stories about princesses and cowgirls, who, despite the odds and the pressure, always did the right things. In quantity, time can always become quality time.

One morning in Grenada, after setting Diane up with coffee and a good book, the girls and I took a spin with the dinghy around the bay. Both girls had fishing rods, and before long, the prayer of every fishing father had been answered. Sawyer, trolling over a rock ledge, had caught three fish. Riley, with a little minnow lure on a fixed reel, was not having any luck, but after I convinced her to let her bait "swim" through the water rather than "leap" through the air, she managed to catch a small baitfish. She then used the baitfish to catch a nice grouper. At the time, in a bow to animal rights, we were dispatching our catch using "anesthesia" rather than the customary bludgeoning. I poured some rather awful brandy into the fishes' gills to painlessly and bloodlessly finish them off. Later that morning, as we ate our breakfast of mangoes, papayas and muffins, Riley related the fish story to Diane, who recorded it in the log. And though it appears that some of my fishing expletives may have become confused with fishing nomenclature, the following is an excerpt of the tale:

Now, O.K.... My sister and me went fishing with my Dad in the dinghy. My sister caught three rock bastards, I mean sand divers. Two were

too small, and we threw them back in the water. I didn't catch anything for
a while, but then I got a baby fish I used to catch a medium grouper. We
put wine and beer down their throats, and they got drunk and died. Papa
cut them up, and we'll eat them for dinner.

For several days in Grenada we explored no further than our own anchorage and its watery playground, but when we did come ashore, there was some not so ancient history to learn. We met a cruiser who said our anchorage had seen less tranquil days. Just where *Manta Raya* floated, he had seen a cruise boat strafed by gunfire.

"Someone shot at a boat?" I asked in astonishment. "Was anybody hurt?"

"No, not really," said the cruiser. "The shots were fired in the water around the boat. It wasn't really anything serious. It was the early eighties and the communists had armed the locals, mostly kids, who were up there in the hills 'on watch.' But there was nothing to see, so the kids got bored and decided to try out their guns."

Indeed, even on idyllic Calvigny Island, the pastoral island we had been sketching in green pastels, we found evidence of trouble. In the midst of beautiful ornamental palms, we found an abandoned hotel, vines growing over and into its broken windows, great stone fountains filled with muddy water and croaking frogs. On the hotel's walls, odd gouges appeared in regular patterns across the surface. I had seen these marks before – once on the Reichstag building in East Berlin and again around the columned, front porch of an antebellum mansion in Nashville, Tennessee, my childhood home. In each case, the gouges were made by bullets. "Bury the silverware, Ma. The Yankees are coming."

The U.S. invasion of Grenada, or Operation Urgent Fury, had occurred 15 years before our arrival. We remembered Reagan had invaded the tiny island, but when we tried to recall what we really knew about the invasion, we drew a blank. Why had we sent troops there? Was anyone hurt? At the time, had not the invasion of the tiny island seemed almost laughable? After all, who in the United States even knew where Grenada was? As we stared at the bullet holes in the hotel wall, we suddenly felt odd, spooked actually. We were standing where something very real and very dangerous had happened. Yet back in the cozy United States, Grenada had been an unreal affair that simply played across our television screens. At the time, Grenada had seemed as real as Gilligan's Island.

The reality of what had happened and why it had happened depended, as always, upon whom you chose to believe. At the time of the invasion, the White House cited communist threats, Castro influence and the construction of a military airport (shades of the Cuban Missile Crisis). But some journalists and liberal academicians took a different view of the invasion. They believed Grenada's strategic value in the spread of communism was questionable (110,000 impoverished people living on 133 square miles of mostly vertical mountainside). The liberals also pooh-poohed the military airport and the claim that the U.S. needed to rescue American medical students on the island (One might even question whether we should encourage medical diplomas from the Caribbean). While some of the workers building the Grenada airport were Cuban, Canadians, Finns and Grenadians were also employed.

What was the truth? Would we ever know? Should we have cared? As a family, when we sailed out of our home waters into foreign lands, we wanted to help and not hurt the people we visited. In return for being allowed to visit, the least we could do was show our goodwill. Before folks even got to know us, we certainly did not want them to dislike us for the things our country may or may not have done before our arrival - a nasty bit of discrimination that sometimes took sustained smiling, explanations and apologies to overcome. Since 1987 we had made a practice of flying not the Stars and Stripes on our transom but the setting sun, Arizona's flag. We were proud of our country. We just wanted to be judged for *who* we were, not *where* we were from.

Up on a hill above our anchorage, we stumbled upon a little restaurant and bar. As we looked over the bay and sipped our cold beers and cokes, the proprietor and his French wife shared their opinion of the conflict with us.

In the first place, claimed the husband, U.S. Rangers had been landed on the wrong side of the island. If rescuing the medical students were really one of their objectives, they were unreasonably forced to cross difficult sections of the island to reach St. George, the capitol, where the school was located. This was, the restaurant owner felt, at the very least a costly mistake. In fact, added his wife, the commander of the U.S. ground troops had stopped at their bar on his way to St. George with a very odd request. The commander had asked to use their phone. Apparently his radio was not working, and U.S. ships offshore were shelling his men. The commander had called the United States and spoken with an AT&T operator, who had then connected him with the ships. He had yelled quite a bit, and the shelling had stopped.

The human results of the invasion? U.S.: 19 dead and 116 wounded. Grenada: 49 dead and several hundred wounded. Cuba: 29 dead and over a hundred wounded. "An unnecessary and sad mistake," said the restaurant owner's wife, shaking her head. "The whole affair, the entire invasion, could have been avoided with a little talking."

This was as much as we learned, and frankly, as much as we wanted to know about our country's invasion of Grenada. When we eventually made our way into St. George, we strolled through the market and walked beneath a large banner hung across the main avenue. It read: "BIENVENIDO (welcome) CASTRO." Right or wrong, our invasion of Grenada had apparently not diminished the island's affections for the bearded man from Cuba.

Margarita Woo Woo Breakfast

All of our dreams about cruising on a sailboat in the Caribbean were captured in the romance we felt when dreaming about sailing to Venezuela. While still in Grenada, a trip to a Venezuelan embassy served to further our dream. We drove up a winding road through Grenada's lush green mountains to a large house overlooking a blue bay. Red bougainvillea bushes bloomed at each end of a long wooden porch, where wooden shutters were pinned open to let the cool mountain breezes pass through floor to ceiling windows. Inside the house, the long blades of ceiling fans cooled a big room filled with red leather and mahogany furniture. The flowering trees without and the bookshelves within gave the room a musty smell of spice and nut - the aromas of tropical adventure. Once inside, Diane and I showed our passports to the polite and officious secretary and filled out the many elegantly stamped papers for our visas. We were Humphrey Bogart and Ingrid Bergman in *Casa Blanca*. We were voyaging to a new continent.

Our sail to Venezuela, with the trade winds at our back, was delightful. A night passage brought us shooting stars through a sky balanced with a sunrise astern and a new moon ahead. We stopped in the remote *Los Testigos* islands, named the "witnesses" by Columbus, who must have needed supporting testimony for his discovery of land in the Americas. In *Los Testigos* we trudged up a three hundred foot sweeping dune of white sand and "skied" down to the clean, blue ocean. Riley said she "flew." Our family befriended our first Venezuelan, Cucha, wearing a sun visor and floating on a blow-up raft with her kids. Chucha drifted by our boat, and we invited her and her children aboard for cookies and lemonade. The next day Cucha's father took me spear fishing, and Cucha's brother-in-law, the head of the *Guardia Costa,* Venezuelan Coast Guard, extended our stay past the normally allowed limit, allowing us to re-anchor in a more secure anchorage near the Guardia station. At anchor we rode out the sandblasting winds of a tropical wave (weather depression), a gritty reminder that we were still vulnerable to the whims of hurricane season. A few days later as we sailed on toward the island of Margarita and radioed our thanks to the Guardia station, we felt that Venezuela was indeed proving to be the friendly, getaway cruising ground for which we had hoped.

As we approached Isla Margarita, Diane was on deck with the binoculars. "Wow," she said, "Cliffs. You should see this...big white bluffs....no, wait a minute... They're not cliffs; they're... high-rises!"

We anchored with over a hundred other cruisers along the open west shore of Isla Margarita, Venezuela. Margarita, we were to learn, was a duty free island, where well-healed Caribbean Latinos and world cruisers in search of first world provisions flocked like pigeons to a corn field. Our fellow boaters, afloat in everything from triple-decker power yachts to ancient, wooden sloops that spouted non-stop bilge water, were packed in tight rows. The holding was poor in grass and sand, so we put out two anchors for *Manta Raya* - the extra anchor not so much to secure our footing as to keep us from swinging into adjacent "parking spaces." But despite the crowding, the Trades blew steadily and held the entire fleet lined up and facing the beach... until August 28th.

On that morning, Diane and I woke to an odd motion and even odder sounds. Our boat was leaping, not lightly and momentarily as if to a passing wake, but steadily and increasingly, as if at sea and facing an approaching storm. We heard shouting, then a piercing scream that jerked us from our bunk and pushed us on deck. There we saw a nightmare as surreal as a Salvador Dali painting tipped on its ear and flung into a desert sandstorm. Were we really awake?

The sky was the yellow brown of a Kansas tornado. Stinging sand and spray blew into our faces. We were at sea with a flotilla of boats, each leaping and crashing over cresting waves. Isla Margarita was gone - at least that is what we thought until we turned and saw the crashing waves on the shore behind us. An empty dinghy skidded past and a lounge cushion, as if jerked by an invisible string, bounced along the wave tops and leaped into the air to perform a triple gainer over our boat. Now we were wide-awake.

A storm had blown out to the island from the mainland bringing freak gale winds and waves from the open roadstead to the west. The entire fleet had swung on its anchors, fouling one another's lines and banging about like tin cans behind newlyweds. Folks were in their dinghies trying to reset anchors. Some had already pulled their anchors and were limping about in circles, and others were blowing toward shore, where one boat lay crippled on its side, shuddering sickeningly each time a wave careened and geysered off its hull.

We started our engines to take the strain off our anchors and managed to veer to port just as a French motor yacht drug by to starboard. To be heard over the wind, Diane shouted in my ear. She wondered whether we should raise our anchors and head out to sea. What had been our windward position at the front of the fleet was now a leeward position behind an armada of boats - all jerking at their anchors. In the storm, the fleet was a tentatively leashed football team preparing to tackle and carry us to the beach. I looked at the bow of our boat, first dipping then vaulting out of the sea in a thrust of spray, and I decided that sending my true love forward to release the anchor might only add personal tragedy to property loss. We stayed in the cockpit, worked the engine throttles, clenched our teeth and stared forward for a very long time. Then the storm passed.

In the aftermath, there was moaning, the sort of eerie wailing one might associate with wounded after a battle. Folks were in the water untangling their anchor lines, wedging their boats apart and retrieving floating paraphernalia. We launched our dinghy and motored about returning bits and pieces of floating detritus to shell-shocked owners. Things looked grim, yet the neighborhood would survive to tackle another day of shopping.

When we returned to our boat, we drug the dinghy aboard and dropped ourselves into the cockpit. We were exhausted, and we felt as if a long day and not the bare start of morning had passed. That is when Sawyer's face peered out the companionway. She was rubbing the sleep from her eyes, yawning and stretching her hands toward the brightening sky. She smiled and asked in a voice as free from trouble as a canary's song: "What's for breakfast, Papa?"

Boat School

When we sailed on from Margarita to Venezuela's mainland and its nearly landlocked gulf, the *Golfo de Cariaco,* we were surprised to come upon a land we already knew. Sharp cactus and dry scrub on white, pink and red hills reminded us of Arizona's deserts. The blue water lapping at this discordant dryness was like the flooded Grand Canyon, damned to make Lake Powell. We had traveled 3,000 miles to be back in our home state sailing the lake where we had first learned to sail aboard our little O'Day 22. But unlike the bare sandstone cliffs and long dead Indian ruins we would have found under Arizona's flooded canyons, the *Golfo's* saltwater held all the bounty of ocean life – colorful blue and yellow butterflyfish and little coral *Christmas Tree Worms* - shaggy drink umbrellas in shades of pink, blue, white and orange that disappeared into grey tubules every time we drew close.

After a few hours of uncomfortable windward slogging, as we tried to make our way east along the *Golfo's* northern shore, we came to our senses and pulled into a protected inlet, a fingered bay called *Laguna Grande.* The water flattened, the steep desert hills glowed with the backlit warmth of an approaching sunset, and the parched wind dried our sinuses, lips and eyeballs. Yes, we had been traveling for over four months to be beef-jerkied by Venezuela's version of our home state. Still, this was an empty anchorage, and we were surrounded not only by the serenity of solitude but the security of a practically landlocked anchorage. We hiked, swam, rested and, for a few days, nearly forgot about the mighty Ocean.

With our windward slog out of the hurricane belt complete, Diane was able to concentrate on boat school. A new schedule of academic courses, reading and artwork filled each day. And though the girls sometimes fought this new discipline and we all struggled with our new roles as teachers and students, the routine added some structure and depth to our liveaboard lives. Diane and I began to feel we were fulfilling (and not neglecting) our roles as parents, and the girls demonstrated the wonder of young minds - eager brain cells easily filled with knowledge.

Of the bonding experiences on a boat, home schooling may be the most telling and the most testing. Home schooling is that time when moms and dads, alias captains and co-captains, don yet more vocational caps to become teachers and principles. Every aspect of teaching: the discipline, the patience, the progress and the frustration, are added to an already full family life afloat. If, dear Reader, you are a parent and you have ever felt yourself to be an overbearing parent, home schooling is where you might throw your prodigy and your progeny overboard.

Everywhere we sailed during our cruise, boat moms and sometimes boat dads disappeared each morning. They went below and hit the books with their kids. School was out when we heard the scream and splash of kids released from their daily brain building. At one liveaboard anchorage off Aruba, we knew morning home schooling was finished when we caught the flash of newly released students zipping by our portholes. The kids were nearly airborne with the joy and freedom of their after school sport - windsurfing.

While in Venezuela, everything on our boat was labeled. Sawyer was learning to spell, and Riley was learning to recognize words and link them with objects. Our sink had a "sink" sign, and the engines each read "engine." It was always a bit of a fright, when, still half asleep, I looked up each morning and saw the word "mirror" pasted across my reflection. Our boat was hung with signs that not only taught spelling but also practical boat handling. "Port, starboard, forward and aft" were the four directions in our school, while "engine shutoff" on at least two occasions proved critical. "Fresh water" and "salt water" signs were not just instructional. Except for a few unfortunate lapses, they kept mom and dad from making regrettable morning cups of coffee.

Home schooling took patience and, if not divine intervention, at least assisted professorship. At liveaboard anchorages, boat moms and dads welcome new cruisers with an important question: Just what did the new arrivals do back in the "real" world? Doctors and nurses were drafted to teach biology and chemistry. Engineers had to dust off brain cells and present lessons in physics. Languages were taught according to an arriving boat's ensign. And writers were asked to teach literature and compositions, while answering such grammatical conundrums as what words might be proper to end a sentence with.

But the majority of subjects were taught by the *maestros*, mommy and daddy, who conducted school in the tiny classroom of the family boat, where real world lessons were always close at hand. Natural sciences took on new reality. The girls did not read about pink flamingoes; they held the food source, brine shrimp, which give flamingos their day-glow, pink colors, in their palms. They learned about predators by staring into the silver eyes of sharks. And meteor showers taught them more than a bit about astronomy. One night in *Laguna Grande*, as meteors flamed through the sky, we examined the constellation Orion through our binoculars and found the nebula on his belt – another galaxy, just like ours, so far away. Both Riley and Sawyer were blinking with confounded comprehension. Sometimes, as the girls laughed and splashed about our floating school room, fluorescing plankton mirrored the sky and coated their skin with phosphorescence so concentrated that the girls' skin looked as if it were covered with cool, green, glowing lava. And in the full web of life, there was no ecological laboratory exercise more instructional than the barter of an endangered animal from a fishermen. The girls helped us release a frightened but relieved Hawksbill turtle back into the biggest underwater classroom on the planet.

But as we taught school during the hot, blue baked days and piercing starlit nights in Venezuela's *Golfo de Cariaco*, something else pulled at us and gently but persistently pleaded for our attention: civilization. This is the *yin* of the *yang*, when seclusion calls for society and society's niceties. Life on a boat, at least for those with tight strings securing the bags of their cruising kitties, can begin to feel austere. Even heavy spenders, if they go offshore for long periods of time, eventually have to search the pantry for something else besides canned food. At times like these for cruisers on an extended voyage, the definition of "luxury" degrades to simple pleasures like fresh fruits and veggies, bread, paper towels and beer served at under eighty degrees Fahrenheit – eventually, luxury is having any beer at all. A pizza and a night at the movies are lusty, impossible dreams.

Before we left the Windward Islands, we met a cheerful couple who also lived on a Catana Catamaran. With this basis for camaraderie, we immediately shared our cruising plans and philosophies with one another. In order to build the cruising kitty for their voyage, the couple had been working for West Marine. Before this "refinancing" interlude, the couple had been cruising for almost six years.

"When we quit cruising and went to work," said the male half of the cruising couple, "it took me a year to forget I wasn't on a boat. We would be in somebody's kitchen. They would drop an ice cube on the floor, and I would go chasing after it on my hands and knees." 'Hey, hey,' they'd say. 'Settle down, big fella. You're not on a boat anymore.'"

More than the ice, the fresh veggies, fruits and other niceties of liveaboard life, cruisers who take long sabbaticals from society, whether they realize it or not, need the sanity check that society offers. And herein lies a cruising paradox: Cruisers want to get away, but they also need human interaction; otherwise, they go a bit off their nut. Boat fever infects anyone left alone on the sea for too long. Even though Joshua Slocum, the worlds first solo circumnavigator, blamed bad mussels for an hallucination he had crossing the Atlantic (during the delusional episode, Joshua had a long discussion with the pilot of Columbus's' *Pinta*), any cruiser left by himself out on Mother Ocean will eventually get wacky. There are times when all cruisers feel disoriented, lost and perhaps insane - all of us. Throwing ourselves out into the great blue yonder, on a boat, in the middle of the ocean, or worse, into a troubled, foreign country, can be a raw experience with no friendly buffers to take the sharp edge off insanity.

All cruisers exhibit one symptom of insanity: they anthropomorphize Nature. When cold winds, waves and rain rake their deck day after interminable day, Nature becomes a malevolent warden. It locks them in the jail cells of their own boats, and these cruising hermits come to believe that their bunks, cabins and cockpits comprise the entire world. Or worse, they begin to think that the odd ideas and nagging voices produced by their company-starved brains should be taken seriously. Their world can become an odd place. Cult ideas and conspiracies become plausible. Alone at sea, these sailors can become a bit odd.

On the *Golfo de Cariaco*, even with family around me, I found myself muttering about broken boat parts to disinterested pelicans and complaining about worn rigging to blinking seagulls. Our Spartan boat life and our regular routine of schooling and boat chores needed juxtaposition. Even on our extended sabbatical at sea, we needed a vacation from our vacation. We needed to get away amongst and not away from the things of mankind. Even if the only outcome of our visit ashore might be a reaffirmation that our life at anchor was better, it was a visit we needed to make.

Medregal Village

We had heard about a possible cruising haven near *Laguna Grande*, a resort of sorts, where our cruising wants of water, food and laundry might be had. So, picking a morning when the howling trade winds carried a little less bite, we pushed eastward toward *Medregal* Village.

For cruisers frequenting posh resorts and marinas in the Med, along California's southern coast or Florida's Gold Coast, *Medregal* Village would look... well, pitiful. But to our desert weary and solitude-sickened family, the little resort looked like paradise. We anchored in an open roadstead in front of a collection of beach huts and tin buildings. About a half dozen other cruising boats dotted the water about us. The boats hailed from France, Denmark and Germany, and as we circled the tiny fleet to pick a nesting spot (much as a dog sniffs and circles a spot before deciding to rest his rump), I was particularly intrigued by a beautifully swept, two-masted, wooden schooner that looked as if she had been transported through time straight to our anchorage. She was, it turned out, a classic, wooden boat reconstruction. Her owner was to play a part in our future Venezuelan adventures, but for now we simply admired his boat, its elegance and its grace, from a distance. We found ourselves a spot a bit removed from other boats in the anchorage; after all, we were looking forward to but not entirely ready for civilization (and probably never have been). In no time, like kids rushing for the playground at recess, we had boarded the dinghy for a look-see ashore.

We tied off to a spindly dock, whose planks angled and swept like waves that only a drunken sailor could navigate. A gravel path led up a hill to a cloister of cabana guest rooms, a restaurant set with tidy plaid tablecloths and a palm-thatched bar beside a clear pool set in cool blue tile. Around the resort was nothing but desert and dry bush. We gawked at the tiny resort like country hicks arriving at the Ritz. The girls, of course, were hysterical with newfound possibilities. They were already begging us to take them back to our boat to get their swimsuits.

"*Buenos Dias*," came a voice from behind us, and we turned to greet a petite lady, all smiles and an apron. She was the owner's wife, and her husband, who was off shuttling some sailors into town for supplies ("Oh," I thought, "tell me this is not a dream too good to be true!") would be back later that evening. Would we care to use the showers or get some water for our boat? They were complimentary, of course, courtesy of the resort. Or perhaps we would enjoy some freshly baked breads and sweet rolls? (The warm, yeasty aromas had already reached us from the kitchen. Pavlov style, they set our saliva glands awash). And laundry? The resort would be happy to wash our decade of dirty, salt encrusted clothes. (Diane and I glanced at one another, sharing the look of lottery winners). Meanwhile, would we like something to drink – perhaps a lemonade, an iced tea or a cold Polar beer?

For the crew of Manta Raya, *Medregal* Village proved to be the perfect respite. After months of "camping" aboard our floating RV, the clean laundry, freshwater showers, freshly baked breads and meals ashore were wonderful. The girls spent happy hours splashing about in the pool, while we sipped cold drinks and pretended we were rich gringos on vacation in the Caribbean. We rode our bikes along the sandy road that the hopeful resort owner had plotted for future development. His resort, his development plans and his spectacular sunset stunt of flying over the fleet in a rainbow colored ultra light plane, were extensions of the man himself. They spoke of his full-blown yet tenuous dreams – dreams one can find throughout the Caribbean. The resort owner was a Paris expatriate, and his dreams, like the dreams of all who venture outside of the cookie cutter world, were at once appealing and quite far-fetched.

Late one night (anytime after sunset is late for boat folks), Diane and I sat exhausted but happy in the open restaurant. The resort had thrown a "Cruisers' Party," and the twenty or so liveaboards from the anchorage now sat about the pool. The kids were nearly asleep in our laps. We had danced ourselves into delirium, twisting and stomping to the music of James Brown. (*Hot-ah!*) Our fellow cruisers, also with eyelids at half-mast, were gathered in little clusters sorted according to language and inclination. Our bellies were full of delicious seafood paella the resort owner's wife had prepared for us. The balmy evening breeze was idyllic, warm and yet cool enough to sweep the beads of sweat from our foreheads. Smiling, Diane fingered the little bib of paper towel with which the bartender had wrapped her rum drink. The towel was damp - full of the dripping Caribbean humidity it had been designed to collect.

"Sure," Diane said, "you *could* call this paradise. But look how our drinks sweat."

For the remainder of our liveaboard cruise, this late night reverie was our new mantra. When our motors quit, when our toilets siphoned back into the boat, when storms tossed us and saltwater soaked everything (even our beds), when cabin fever nearly drove us to violence, and when provisions dwindled to unappetizing cans of pale, green peas, we would recall the *Medregal* Village night and others like it and attempt a smile. Lounging by the resort pool that reflected the bright Caribbean stars, we had no way of knowing that an impending boatyard prison sentence would nearly destroy our dreams and send us back to the U.S., tails between our legs. But even then, when our ability to complain would become infinite - our every utterance a litany of complaints - if we had any spunk left, we would recall this night. We would remember how all facets of the world, every star in that black night and we along with them, had felt. We would remember that, all else aside, we were a lucky family, together and afloat on a warm sea. And perhaps one of us, the one with just enough blue water left to spare, would end any complaining with a rejoinder: "Yeah, and our drinks sweat."

Which reminds me of a joke:

An American tourist compliments a Mexican fisherman on the quality of his fish and asks how long it took him to catch them.

"Not very long," answers the Mexican.

"Well then, why don't you stay out longer and catch more?" asks the American.

The Mexican explains that his small catch is plenty for him and his family, so the American asks what he does with the rest of his time.

"I sleep late, fish a little, play with my children, and take a siesta with my wife. In the evenings, I go into the village to see my friends, have a few drinks, play the guitar and sing a few songs ... I have a full life."

But the American interrupts, "I have an MBA from Harvard and I can help you! You should start by fishing longer every day. Then you can sell the extra fish you catch, and with the extra revenue, you can buy a bigger boat. With the extra money the larger boat will bring, you can buy a second one and a third one and so on until you have an entire fleet of trawlers. Instead of selling your fish to a middleman, you can negotiate directly with the processing plants or maybe open your own plant. Then you can leave this little village and move to Mexico City, Los Angeles, or even New York City! From there you can direct your enterprise."

"How long would that take?" asks the Mexican.

"Twenty, perhaps twenty-five years," replies the American.

"And after that?"

"Afterwards? That's when it gets really interesting: When your business gets really big, you can start selling stock and make millions!"

"Millions? Really? And then what?"

"After that you'll be able to retire, live in a tiny village near the coast, sleep late, play with your children, catch a few fish, take a siesta, and spend your evenings drinking and enjoying time with your friends."

A Classic In Venezuela

ach dawn anchored off *Medregal* Village, I would come
on deck and gaze at the classic, beautiful wooden sailboat.
Sketched in the morning mist, it was an apparition. The tall,
slightly canted wooden masts spired from an elegant hull. Tarred
rope rigging stretched between mizzenmast, top gallows and a
boom that carried the eye in a tapering sweep to the stern and back
to a time when sailing ships still spoke to mariners.

The owner, I learned, had built the boat back in the tidewater flats
of the Chesapeake's Eastern shore, where such a boat fit the hometown
heritage. He had cast the bronze blocks and wrapped canvas boots
around the base of each varnished mast. He had crafted the entire
beauty himself, and for the past seven years he had let the Caribbean's
thrashing hurricanes sweep to the north, while he rode his elegant and
timeless reproduction safely in the southern swell off Venezuela.

I wanted to meet the boat's owner. I figured whoever had crafted
such an ideal and had spent so much time in Venezuela had to be worth
knowing; and in truth, I itched to get aboard his historic vessel. But
the Owner was a hard man to corner. He rarely came ashore, and when
he did, he skirted human contact like a contagion. When I finally did
catch him on the dock, he refused to meet my eyes, glancing instead
back and forth between his wooden dinghy and his beautiful boat, as if
desperate to make his escape.

"You're on that French catamaran," the Owner finally offered.
"Gotta admit; it's the first cat I've ever seen that wasn't godawful ugly."

I took the Owner's comment as a compliment.

"When you came in to anchor," he continued, "I was afraid you would break my face rule. I figured you were French."

And what, I asked, was the "face rule?"

"It's simple," said the Owner. "If you can make out someone's face, then they're too close. I hate that damned society crap, you know: somebody shows up and shows their damned puss, and you're supposed to be cordial… howdy, waving, all that polite shit. It bugs the poop outta me. I always move if I can see somebody's face."

O.K., maybe the Owner was a bit gruff around his hermit edges, but I liked him. We managed to cross paths at the dock a few more times, and I learned more about him. He was an accomplished physicist, and he had earned his cruising kitty by inventing a machine that carved "hand-made," wooden decoys. Anyone who has ever driven the shoreline roads of the Chesapeake Bay might be interested to learn that the Owner is responsible for most of the wooden geese and ducks perched in front yards. The Owner made a fortune on decoys – not to mention the wooden cutouts depicting sturdily built women bending over and showing their bloomers. With the money from his decoy business, the Owner built his classic wooden schooner and sailed away.

Despite his hermit tendencies, one day the Owner deigned to visit us on our plastic catamaran. And eventually, knowing all the while how desperate I was to see his handiwork, he invited us aboard his classic, wooden reproduction, which was everything I had hoped she would be. Diane, Sawyer, Riley and I sat amidst teak and forest green canvas cushions. The rigging creaked, and the slapping waves barely moved the great oak hull. The wooden boat reminded me of every sailing book I had ever read and every pirate movie I had ever seen, from Moby Dick to the "Red Pirate." There in the Owner's cozy cockpit beneath the great wood mast, he told us more about his boat and his life in Venezuela – more, perhaps, than I ended up wanting to hear. After all, eager young ears were, between wolfing bites of pretzels and swigging root beer, tuned into the adult conversation.

"Yep, I was married for a spell," said Lee. "The wife came with her own crew of kids, and we tried our hand at boat schooling. The older kids took to the routine pretty well, but the youngest boy was a wild little cuss. He was mad about being away from home, mad about not being with his dad, mad at his mom for divorcing his dad and mad at me for breathing. About a month into the boat schooling, I stopped in the middle of a math lesson, took that boy and loaded him into the dinghy with all of his books. I rowed ashore and dumped everything but the boy in the dumpster. Then the little monster wanted to know how he was supposed to finish his schooling, and I told him not to worry, he'd already flunked, school was over, and he could take the whole goddamned grade over just as soon as I could get his little butt back to the United States and throw it ashore."

My girls were wide-eyed.

Thinking to turn the conversation to less inflammatory topics, I asked the Owner for his recommendations on Venezuelan destinations.

"Been to *Mochima*?" he asked. "Prettiest little harbor on the coast… of course, the shooting last year has kinda cooled folks on the place a bit."

Before I could derail the conversation again, the Owner continued:

"Why some father would come on deck in the middle of the night, spot some Venezuelans bolt cutting his dinghy, shine his goddamned flashlight in their eyes and start wrestling with 'em is beyond me. Of course the dumb s.o.b. got shot in the face! He was lucky he lived - lucky they didn't do worse!"

Riley's eyes were hubcaps, and I was contemplating an exit strategy, but the Owner, the taciturn hermit, was proving, once he got started, to be quite the talker.

"Of course, I had a bit of a problem in *Mochima* myself. A few years back I was anchored in one of those beautiful little bays varnishing my deck, which takes a good bit of time, as you might guess. Motorboats were buzzing by me every morning, and I guess some cruisers were being held up in the anchorages around me, but I was lost in my work, so I wasn't paying much attention, as usual. Anyway, one afternoon these fellows stopped and came aboard my boat. They tied me up in the cockpit and pistol-whipped me, asking for my money. But I kept my trap shut, and those fellows rummaged through my boat until they'd taken pretty much anything with an electrical cord on it. But do you know those fellows never went into my galley? I guess their mommies had told 'em to stay out of folks' kitchens, and that's where my money was hid – right under their noses, wads of bills wrapped up in a coffee can, because you know, you should always carry a wad of funny money, like all that worthless Caribbean currency, so those fellows will think it's a fortune, even though it doesn't amount to fifty bucks. Inflation has made these Venezuelans crazy. But those fellows weren't that bad really.

Heck, I asked one of 'em, the one who was guarding me in the cockpit, to loosen the ropes around my wrists, because they were making my hands numb, and he did. In fact, we ended up having a pretty nice conversation. No harm done."

Yes, the Owner was eccentric; but he was also straightforward and honest. It turned out he would be right about many things; including warning me against the debacle that would take place if I chose to use a Venezuelan boatyard. My family had sailed to Venezuela hoping it would be our cruising dream destination, but we were about to learn that dreams could go bad in a heartbeat. The Owner was the first warning. The second warning was the flies.

The Flies

"Sometimes the Light's all shining on me
Other times I can barely see"
Truckin' by the Grateful Dead

WARNING TO THE READER: You are about to enter an area of intense whining, and yet I urge you to bear with the story. I am not fond of whiners - their drinks always sweat. And I hope you will find little of this weakness elsewhere in the book. On *Manta Raya*, we hung a sign so that it was conspicuous over the main salon window. Perhaps you have seen one like it: the word "WHINING" in big black letters covered with a red circle and diagonal slash signifying "PROHIBITED." When the girls complained about boat schooling, we pointed to the sign (though this flourish was generally ineffective). And when I groused about the *friggin'* diesel engines - wiping my hands of the oily mess and cussing under my breath - the sign invariably came into focus and warmed my cheeks. After all, wherever we were, there we were; and the whining was no better than a self-indulgent distraction that exaggerated the problem at hand and delayed its resolution.

But whining is an important part of our cruising story, for it tells how a particular setting can force the play of characters – even in "paradise." Every family reaches a point when its true character is pried out into the light. That point can be despair. And while whining may be little more than a relief valve – the sound of steam escaping from the boiler of bad fortune – it does provide serviceable solace. And at this particular point in our story, the steam of bad fortune was about to whistle like a gale.]

The worst part was the flies. They were everywhere – crawling over the ceiling, doing push ups on the galley table and humping each other in groups of twos and threes on top of our dishes. With impunity they crawled about on our girls' lips. There was nothing we could do about them. They were everywhere.

We were used to having bugs about our boat, and we always expected more flying and crawling critters while anchored or docked around the detritus of civilization. Biting *nosciums* sometimes drove us underwater; and, when we surfaced, sent us scampering and yowling like madmen, beating ourselves as we fled to the safety of the cockpit door. (I once examined these minuscule monsters under a magnifying lens. They were little more than spindly legs and tiny wings attached to giant mandibles. Horrible.) But unlike most anchorages, where we were able to close up the boat and barricade ourselves against the bugs, the stifling heat of an airless boatyard in Venezuela was about to offer us no respite. Closing up the boat would be death by sauna. Leaving it open was submission to the Lording of the Flies.

At night, when the frenetic flies would finally come to rest on the cabin ceiling, all four of us would massacre them with fly swatters until the cabin floor was dotted with their black carcasses. One morning when we could not find the fly swatters, Riley grew indignant. She was sure the little devils had stolen them.

The flies were in a boatyard, and the boatyard was in Cumana, Venezuela. And if there are, as the astrologists believe, "energy longitudes" on the planet, Cumana must have been our black hole. Yet somehow Cumana was a city we were fated to endure... I guess. We (I) felt we needed to repair a bent rudder shaft and cover *Manta Raya's* bottom with new paint. At this point in our cruise, *Manta Raya* sailed with a nervous tick - a sashay and shudder that emanated from her port rudder (again our Achilles' heel). The rudder had been bent in a mishap which only Gerard the former owner could have explained and which, frankly, I did not want to hear. Gerard, anxious to sell and a bit *laissez fair* about maintenance, had not always kept *Manta Raya* in tip-top shape. The paint on her bottom had nearly disappeared and only with regular scrubbings could she be kept clean of a carpet of underwater vegetation. Gerard loved to sail, but he was lax to the point of negligence about the mechanics of a boat. He would, for example, change the oil in *Manta Raya's* diesel engines, but not the filters. The anal engineer in me shuddered, and I worried about *Manta Raya*; I wanted her to be mechanically perfect... or perhaps it was our trip, our safety or my ability to captain that I wanted to insure. Whatever the reason, I decided *Manta Raya* needed a haulout and repair – a trip to the boat spa, so I arranged a trip to a boatyard in Cumana.

While on their fall hurricane watch near the equator, cruisers are *supposed* to hang in boatyards. They are supposed to soak up the sunshine in the safety of the small latitudes, while they watch the named storm beasts roar harmlessly by to the north. After listening to a radio report or watching the swirl of a tropical eye on a poolside TV, they are supposed to say things like, "Whoa! There goes a big one... headed straight for St. Badluck ... pity the poor bastards up there."

The equatorial boatyards also tout cheap work. So, while the cruisers wait out and watch the hurricanes, they can fiddle about detailing their boats. Mostly they have their bottoms painted (and it doesn't hurt a bit!). All of the cruising rags tout the cheap labor in Trinidad and nearby Venezuela. Cruisers are supposed save big bucks on boat work, while they lounge beachside or poolside and savor a warm winter in the tropics.

A friend of mine has a saying about saving money: "If you want economy, you have to pay for it." This and other warnings about going on the cheap should have played in my ears before we sailed to Cumana. The Owner, a six-year, Venezueala veteran, had also warned me: "Haul outs obey a mathematical formula," he had said. "To calculate the actual time they will take, simply multiply the time you are told they will take by π." While these friendly boatyard warnings should have made me hesitate, the spooky stories about Venezuela's mainland should have made me turn tail and sail away.

The same sailing rags that wrote about incredible boatyard savings also warned about robberies and rough treatment of visiting liveaboards. Venezuelans were appearing uninvited on deck, and they weren't carrying gifts from the welcome wagon. On a road trip from *Medgregal* Village to Cumana to arrange our haul out and do my customs and immigration dance, seasoned cruisers who joined me on the long van ride peppered me with advice. As we neared the city, their warnings reached a fevered pitch: "Remember," they said, "stay on the main roads, no backstreets... better yet, maybe one of us, preferably somebody big, should go with you."

But I politely declined their offers with a self-assured bravado that I hoped hid my growing unease. Though I was nervous, I had been in tough cities before, and I knew the ropes - even the frayed and sometimes menacing ropes that barely bind civility in many third world countries. I planned to walk through Cumana's "valley of death" with swift determination. I would conduct my work in daylight. I would be decent but businesslike - polite but officious. I would wear simple, dirtbag clothes and carry no backpack or wallet. I would hide money and passports inside my hat. (Only later would I learn that thieves riding buses liked to lean out and pluck hats from startled pedestrians.)

Don Street, a cruising guide writer and intrepid Caribbean sailor, saw Cumana for what it was back in the eighties: **Warning**, he wrote, *Cumana is a rough, tough seaman's town. Females should not wander around alone, nor should they wear jewelry, especially necklaces, as even in broad daylight, Cumana has some bold and fleet-footed snatch-and-run boys. At night, travel only via taxi; do not walk.*

When our gang of gringo cruisers arrived in Cumana and began unloading in the growing morning heat, I looked about and wondered whether Mr. Street had not been a bit too optimistic. Since the eighties, Venezuela had fallen on hard times. Her oil boom had busted. Inflation had been astronomical, and most Venezuelans, even the diehard stoics, were shaking their heads. As I looked about the city streets, posters pasted over open sewers and on crumbling walls told of an upcoming election. An army officer and supposed Castro sympathizer (Chavez) was running against the incumbent president. The election promised to be very heated - that was, if the people did not serve notice and storm the presidential palace before the polls opened. Even I, Mr. Bluebird's on My Shoulder, sensed a peculiar unease - a tight note playing above the usual tension of poor, third world want.

At customs there was the usual long wait, though no one else was there to occupy the officials' time. I made the usual runaround visits to multiple offices "down the hall," where brow-furrowed bureaucrats examined my paperwork as if it contained coded instructions for insurrection. Still, the folks I met were pleasant, and no one asked for "extra" monies or "donations" (a fact that later amazed my fellow road trip cruisers).

But then, as the heat of the day slowed my pace and my gaze wandered off the straight and narrow path of the business at hand, I began to see more signs of things gone wrong. There was the usual garbage heaped about the streets, but near the crumbling *Ave Aristedes* bridge and just in front of the shack homes stitched together with cardboard and discarded tin, was something else: a dead dog, eyes glazed and vacant, belly bloated. The flies swarmed. I hurried past the stench and over the bridge and toward the paltry dry goods stores, advertising little more than dust in their display windows. Finally, I found what I had been searching for. I came to a *panaderia*.

In Latin America, a *panaderia* or bakery is a special treat. In the cool of the evening or just before dawn, the *panaderia* is busy with the work and delicious smells of fresh baking. Crusty loaves of bread emerge from great ovens. Crisp cookies are sprinkled with cinnamon sugar, and moist cakes are coated with bright frostings. Éclairs, Danishes and cinnamon rolls line silver trays behind glass cases; and the warm, delicious scents pull pedestrians off the street.

I made a point of stopping at *panaderias*. Standing before the shop in Cumana, I thought about my girls and what their faces would look like when they saw the sweet surprises I would bring them. But there was something odd about this *panaderia* - a novel spectacle at its entrance, a spectacle I had never seen before in any Latin country, and one I now realized was at the entrance to most of the worthwhile shops along the street. Before the door of the *panaderia* stood a guard, not a plain clothed, bored security guard halfheartedly watching for shoplifters, but a serious and heavily armed guard. This guard wore two broad belts across his chest loaded with shotgun shells. The barrel of a sawed off shotgun rested in the palm of one hand, and the forefinger of his other hand encircled the trigger. No kidding. In Cumana, men with big guns were guarding bakeries. In Cumana, apparently a 12-gauge slug was the only thing that stood between the people and a lawless cinnamon bun free-for-all.

I stopped and stared. The guard stared back briefly, but his alert eyes moved on. I was obviously no threat. I hesitated. What was the proper greeting for such a fellow, and for that matter, every armed guard we were to meet in Venezuelan banks, groceries and liquor stores? *"Bueno canon, senor* (nice canon, sir)." Though we were not to see these fellows in the touristy cities, where polite police were available in quantities to assure the suitable flow of otherworld dollars, in Cumana, the *policia* were apparently no match for the desperate thieves. With a quick *"Buenos tardes, senior,"* I slid past the armed gentleman and into the panaderia. The guard said nothing, but continued to stare past me at the crowd on the street. Oh dear, "Yea, though I walk through the valley of sawed off shotguns..."

After the *panaderia*, I hurried on to my last appointment: the boatyard. It was getting late, but I still had one more disturbing spectacle in store for me. At the entrance, or rather the wall, surrounding the marina, I found a rope dangling from a steel door. Seeing nothing else, I pulled on the rope and waited. As I looked about I noticed shards of broken glass protruding from the top of the wall surrounding the boatyard. I waited, then at eye level, a small panel slid open, and a face appeared. An armed guard asked me my business, and using my poor Spanish I stammered out something about an appointment. But before letting me in (a gringo wearing cutoff shorts and sandals and no weapon more lethal than a Swiss army knife), the guard picked up a phone and spoke to *someone*. Then he nodded, the panel swung shut and finally the huge metal door slid aside. I was in.

The boatyard was huge. Giant cranes swung over railroad tracks that led past steel warehouses painted with warning signs about chemicals and flammable liquids. There were fishing trawlers, passenger ships and tugboats; but what worried me immediately was what I did not see. Except for an eighty-foot power yacht covered with tarps, there were no pleasure boats. The yard was filled with towering hulls, great rusting behemoths braced with iron beams and honeycombed with scaffolding. It was a working boatyard for steel boats, and I nearly turned and left right then at the thought of frail, plastic *Manta Raya* swallowed in the tangle of metallic industry.

But I saw the sign for the office and climbed iron steps toward some windows that overlooked the yard. Inside, after more broken Spanish explanations, I was ushered into an office where a busy man, Victor the yard manager, sat squinting over some blueprints. I shook Victor's hand and, glancing down at his desk, saw what looked like the blueprints for the turbines and screw propellers of a battleship.

Victor's eyes were shy, but they also showed the strain of middle management. With a sheepish smile he said "hello," in English, and I explained who I was and why I was visiting. Victor's brow furrowed; something was not clicking, so I rambled on until I realized he was not following a word I was saying. Mike, Victor's boss, the man who owned the boatyard and the man with whom I had arranged our haulout over the phone, spoke fluent English. But Mike was nowhere to be seen. In fact, Victor informed me, he would not be back for a week - a week during which the yard was to work on our boat.

I paused, another bad omen and another chance to back away, but still I pressed on. After all, what could go wrong? We had a simple job to be done, bottom painting, and since I had gone to the trouble to schedule the work, by God, I would make sure it happened. I switched to my weak suite, Spanish, and reached into my pocket to pull out the cheat sheet of Spanish terms Diane had prepared for me; and Victor, to his credit, pulled out a pocket translator. (The translator, though useful, was mute when confronted with words like "waterline," "rudder shaft" and "epoxy resin.") So we stumbled through a plan for the haulout. A date was set, I think; and the job was understood, I suppose. And yes, most importantly, there would be blue bottom paint, *azul pintura*, on hand for the job. We shook hands, and Victor appeared happy. Though thinking back, I believe he was simply relieved to be done with me. I climbed down the cement stairs, shook my head once more at the naked industry and swirling dust of the boatyard and walked out the great iron door. As I passed the guard, he smiled. "*Via con Dios*," he said. Go with God.

Back with Diane and the girls at *Medregal* Village, I passed out candy bars and other "big city" goods that I had collected from behind the barbed wire protection of a marina - the domain of a small, privileged class of Venezuelans, who drove about anonymously behind the tinted glass of shiny black Suburbans. Apparently even Cumana had its elite wealthy. I decided not to be too specific about what I had seen in the city. After all, we would be in and out of Cumana in two to three days, tops – just a quick commercial in a commercial port. There was no reason to start my family worrying.

In a few days, we said our goodbyes to our fellow cruisers, pulled up our anchor and headed toward Cumana.

Cumana

E ntry into any new port is a bit tense. As they feel their way to safety along an unfamiliar shore, arriving boaters must make out new, three-dimensional landmarks and match them with their two-dimensional charts. There is much scanning of the shore-line by binocular, and there are many anxious trips to consult the charts. In a big port, there is the additional challenge of commercial traffic - tugs, boat taxis, fishing trawlers and cargo ships going from A to B as fast as they possibly can, on what to them, is a routine workday. Understandably they do not care about white-knuckled novices, newly arrived yachties sailing about in their tinker toy, plastic boats.

As we scanned the shoreline of Cumana and tried to pick out our boatyard in the forest of cranes and industry, the commercial traffic buzzed about us. Boats sounded their horns and threw up jostling waves. After months of quiet anchorages and lonely passages across empty seas, we were, excuse the pun, at sea in all the confusion. We were country bumpkins in the big city, hicks merging onto the L.A. freeway, and our hearts pumped *muy rapido*.

Diane did her best to locate the boatyard by radio, as I tried to dodge the traffic and yet keep us close enough to the bustling shoreline to spot the tracks of the boatyard railway. We hoped to be pulled up these tracks - yet another novel experience for the crew of *Manta Raya*. After a tense wait during which we played several rounds of boat dodge ball, Diane got an answer from the boatyard. Sure enough, with our binoculars we could make out two small figures jumping about and waving at us from between the metal sheds and beneath the tall derricks on shore. The sight of the bouncing men was, oddly enough, reassuring.

Diane radioed for instructions; and bless her, she spoke in Spanish. Using a foreign language face-to-face and on shore is one thing. There are visual clues: smiles, frowns, finger pointing, and the rubbing together of thumb and forefinger to signify "expensive." But staring into the blank face of a radio, there are no clues. And Spanish radio transmissions, like English radio transmissions, are filled with coded verbiage. For example, it took us ten minutes to realize that the oft-repeated word, *adelante*, meant "talk." In radio jargon, *adelante* was the Spanish equivalent of "over." Without it, a Spanish radio conversation could not proceed, as both parties try to figure out whether a transmission is concluded and whether it is time to respond. Eventually, in the boatyard, there would be lots of Spanish terms that we would never decipher, and we would simply have to skip over them, hoping they were not critical terms like "eye protection" or "flammable." On the radio and under the duress of ship port slang, Diane rifled through her dictionary to decipher one enigmatic transmission after another. The vision of her struggling with that radio reminded me that I should never think of a foreigner in the U.S. struggling with my language as either slow or stupid. I was grateful that Venezuelans, like all American Latinos, were charitable enough to help us stumble through their language.

With the radio lesson in progress, I continued to dodge boat traffic. For extra difficulty points, I surfed a fine line between the current of the *Manzanares* River and a shoaling bottom, which I could not see. The hustling boat traffic was disgorging from the brown river along with flotsam of logs, dead animals and a mystery scum, which hid the bottom. The river's current pushed *Manta Raya* sideways toward the shallows, where obvious wreckage like boat masts, concrete blocks and twisted iron refuse was slapped by the oily waves. The wreckage looked like battlements guarding the shore. There was a thin "safe zone" between these defenses and the steady stream of river traffic; and I tried to hold my position there by jockeying both of *Manta Raya* engines like a berserk backhoe operator. Just as I was congratulating myself on keeping a balance between the jagged shore and boat traffic, the accelerator cable for our old Achilles' heel, the port engine, snapped.

The throttle cables on a catamaran are a simple system. With them a boat can be slowed, turned and reversed with ease; but it is imperative that both cables work. Otherwise, one finds oneself helpless and spinning out of control like a duck shot through the wing.

We slid sideways and away from the tooting horn of a river taxi filled with blank-faced Venezuelans. It appeared that *Manta Raya* had found a new skipper who favored a beach invasion through the jagged iron and cement battlements. As Diane shouted "What the hell's going on?" and the radio operator on shore responded "¿Que?," I threw the one good engine we had into full bore "flee" and threw the rudders over to head back out to sea. *Manta Raya* rounded just in time to miss a derelict piling, and with this momentum, headed back out into deeper water.

Away from the shore and idling in a slow circle, I tried to slow my heartbeat and think what to do next. Looking back, I realize that it is times like this when our children learn the most about us. They learn, in fact, more than they can learn from a lifetime of well-intentioned lecturing. I tell my girls that this learning experience, the chance to witness their parents in a real life drama, is a gift. But in this instance, my gift, my real life response, was that I got mad, and I got busy. I raced back and forth between the engine and the control levers and refused to talk to anyone about what was happening or what I was trying to do. Now, as I sit calmly before my computer screen, I see what a horse's ass I and perhaps all people are, who think they are "in control" simply because they keep their lips shut. And I also recall a story about a good friend, a fellow sailor, who found himself in a similar situation, scared and clueless at sea.

My friend, then a novice learning to sail, was in the San Francisco Bay. The Bay offers big waves and big currents, and Bay sailors learn big sailing lessons. My friend's crew, which was also learning how to sail, was composed of his wife and his mother - both good-humored and adventurous women. My friend was below deck performing some sort of manly deed, when his wife, who was steering at the time, called out to him. "Honey," she said, "we appear to be sailing backwards."

"Nonsense," thought my friend, as he threw down an oily rag and came topsides. He was smirking and preparing a witty response, when he looked about and realized his boat was indeed going backwards. His boat was also, he noted, headed for a rear end collision with a rock jetty. He frowned at the water; he studied his sail trim and he glanced back at the growing rocks. Then, maintaining complete silence, he busied himself by jerking lines, changing sail trim and, just in case, firing up the engine.

My friend's wife became frustrated by this flurry of activity without explanation. She wanted to know what was going on. After all, she too was there to learn about sailing, and at the moment she particularly wanted to learn what to do when sailboats sailed backwards. "What," she finally asked," are you doing?"

My friend said nothing, but his wife persisted. "Will you please," she pleaded, "tell us what is going on?... Just tell us what you're thinking. We'd rather hear anything than stand around like useless idiots."

My friend stopped his frantic activity and regarded his wife. His mother, a lady who loves the Truth, was now listening intently from the companionway, and she too was interested in what her son would say.

"You want to know what I'm thinking?" asked my friend.

"Of course," said his wife.

"O.K., he said, "I'm thinking: 'Oh shit! Oh shit! We're going to die."

Back in *El Golfo*, I couldn't have expressed my thoughts more clearly; yet with my family standing about me, I too continued to bustle about in silence. I was searching for an answer to our dilemma, and it was not coming to me. The steering cable had snapped just below the lever. I could see it, like a draw string sucked inside a pair of shorts, and there was no way to get at it. Even if I could grab it, there was no way to reattach it to its vital control arm, for it had broken off below its bayonet fitting. We were, as far as I could tell, screwed. On one engine, *Manta Raya* could not negotiate a flat lake, let alone the busy port of Cumana; but I refused to give up on my boatyard plans, the plans I had cemented so solidly in my brain.

Then, as I focused on the broken cable, the demon plan wrecker, I thought of yet another friend. Back in Arizona, in the middle of the desert on a highway where Navajo Indian mud homes called "hogans" sit under redrock cliffs and sagebrush bounces across an empty highway, there was once a roadblock. It was a fruit and vegetable checkpoint, though I'm not sure exactly what desert agriculture it was designed to protect. Still, it was there, a lonely block hut in the middle of the desert, where folks were required to stop and answer questions about whether they were carrying out-of-state fruits and veggies, often while smacking on delicious Gala or Macintosh apples from Utah.

My friend, riding a motorcycle across this particular stretch of lonely desert, had snapped the lever off his clutch cable. Being a resourceful fellow, he had jury-rigged the thing by clamping its free end with vice-grip pliers. Though awkward, he could, by yanking on the pliers, get his bike out of gear. As he neared the roadblock, he slowed and pulled on the pliers. But unfortunately, just as he came up to the roadblock, the vice-grips slipped, the bike slammed into gear and he was launched past the startled checkpoint officer as if he had been shot out of a cannon. He shot through the roadblock doing a screaming wheelie that he later describes as "awesome." And given his performance, he knew there was no need for a curtain call. He rode on through the desert.

As we motored in circles off the coast of Cumana, my friend's wheelie story, as odd memories are want to do, popped into my head. I went below and found my vice grips. I fastened them securely to the port engine cable, and before long, we were once again motoring in front of the boatyard and listening to incomprehensible Spanish instructions on the radio.

By this time the boatyard workers had decided they were dealing with imbeciles. They abandoned their shoreline waving, trudged up the shore to a shed and reemerged with a tiny rowboat, which they immediately launched. Two of the workers jumped in and began to paddle toward us; one man used a real paddle, though it was broken off near the blade, and the other used a board. It was not long before they were swamped and swimming. They clung to the overturned keel of their boat, which was barely buoyant. Now we needed no radioed instructions. We knew what to do. We motored alongside the men, hauled them out of the water, emptied their rowboat and secured it astern.

Our wet guests introduced themselves as Antonio and Rafael. Though they smiled sheepishly; we knew better than to make light of their accident, for they were Latin men, and their sense of dignity had to be honored. Despite their shivering, they did not need a towel, thank you. But, yes, a cup of coffee would be nice.

With the help of Antonio and Rafael's directions and their rapid-fire communications with workers over our radio, we were soon hovering near shore. Lines were thrown from the railway ramp; and, from nowhere, a voice suddenly shouted "Ola!" Startled, I looked over the side to see a mustachioed face smiling from the water. It was Antonio #2. Broad shouldered and thick to his father's wiry frame, Antonio #2 handed up another line, saluted and dove out of sight. I admired the man, if nothing else, for the bravery he displayed in the murky and questionable water. When he re-emerged, he gestured with an emphatic "thumbs-up," and we began moving up the railway ramp. The cable that towed us squealed around its rusty spool, the water began to drain away from *Manta Raya,* and up the ramp we climbed.

I am not acrophobic and neither is anyone in my family, but the novelty of our growing altitude silenced the entire family. I felt a peculiar churn in my stomach, and Diane grabbed rambunctious Riley by the back of her t-shirt so forcefully that a swirl of wrinkles and a mound of fabric became a permanent topographical landmark on that particular shirt. We were on solid ground, but we were thirty feet in the air. The capricious buoyancy of our watery world had vanished behind us, and our sudden solidity and height off the ground felt very wrong.

Manta Raya in Boatyard Bondage, Cumana, Venezuela

The Boatyard

About one week (notice: not a few days, as planned) into our high and dry, boatyard debacle, the owner Michael appeared in his boatyard. Michael was the reason we were in the boatyard - he and the recommendation of a sailor. The sailor (let us call him Jim) had once come to Michael with his own sailaway dreamboat. Jim had sailed to Venezuela from North Carolina, fulfilling a lifelong dream of escaping the daily toil of a construction job. He had sailed into the Caribbean sunset with his honey. But his dreamboat had rusted, sprung her ribs and, like his dreams, had begun to come apart. So he had limped into the boatyard where Michael and Michael's family had taken him under their wings.

Jim had told me this story as we had sipped cold Polar bears in the palm-swishing breeze on the beach at Isla Margarita. He had told me what a decent person Michael had been and had warned me that Michael's Cumana boatyard was one of the few yards that could handle *Manta Raya's* vast beam. What Jim had also said, but more obliquely, was that the boatyard had an industrial aspect and that the town had a "rough and tumble" nature. What Jim had not told me was just how low his fortunes had sunk, when he had landed in Michael's boatyard. That story I had to hear from Michael himself.

Once again I climbed out of the heat and swirling dust of the boatyard and climbed the long stairwell into the tower of the boatyard's air-conditioned offices. Michael was busy, and I waited outside his office, grateful for the cool air that chilled my sweat soaked t-shirt and soothed the swelling of my dusty sandaled feet. From behind Michael's door, I could hear the staccato of highly emotional Spanish answered by the low hum of a soft and even reply. Before long the door flew open, and a tiny, red-faced man rushed by, blueprints roughly folded and jammed beneath his armpit. Through the door I could see another man seated at a desk and scratching his head. He appeared to be chuckling. I rose and entered his office.

"Michael?" I asked.

"Si," said the man, and he rose, still smiling, and extended his hand.

I introduced myself.

"Ahhh!" said Michael, switching to nearly flawless English, "the catamaran family."

"I hope I caught you at an O.K. time?"

"Yes, yes...just the usual Latin business - lots of emotion, a bit of shouting, and in the end, all is well."

A broad smile of amusement returned to Michael's face, and I realized that, despite our boatyard debacle, I liked this man. We talked a bit about *Manta Raya*, her unexpected and extended repairs. And Michael shook his head in sympathy, but having reviewed our problems, he agreed with the repair plan, which would call for much more time than we had originally planned. He would work up a new cost estimate. There was nothing more to be done.

I liked Michael, his wry smile and his air conditioning, so I remained seated in his office and tried to think of a way to prolong our meeting. I recalled Jim, the man who had sent me to Michael's boatyard in the first place.

Michael again smiled his broad smile, but this time he closed his eyes and shook his head. Did I know why Jim had been in the boatyard? Yes, I said. Hadn't his steel boat needed repairs?

"That boat," said Michael, "needed a new boat. Her ribbing, bulwarks, everything was *kaput*."

I learned how Jim's boat had to be rebuilt from the keel up. The work to repair her had been extensive, and in order to make the project affordable, Michael had allowed Jim to live in the boatyard for free. He had even taught Jim how to weld, charging him only for materials.

"One day," said Michael, "Jim sat right where you are sitting now. He didn't think he could finish the job. His marriage was in trouble. He was ready to give it all up. He was in tears. (I felt a shiver. Was it the air conditioning?) I hugged him and told him everything would be O.K. And in the end it turned out all right...despite the earthquake."

"The earthquake?" I croaked.

Michael studied me. Apparently he was surprised Jim had failed to mention this part of his story, and I began to wonder just what other trifling details Jim might have left out.

"When it happened," said Michael, "Jim thought the dozer operator had hit his boat. He was below welding when the shaking started, and he came up shouting and waving a crowbar. But he saw what we all saw: the cranes swaying back and forth and the boats rising up and down as if they had all gone to sea."

"You were here too?" I asked.

"Yes, right in this office. I looked out those windows (we both turned and gazed out the big windows that fronted his office and afforded a wide view of the boatyard and the sweeping bay), and I watched the booms falling and the boats tumbling over. The water in the bay drained away until all you could see was mud to the horizon. Then it rushed back in and filled the yard with fifty years of god-awful muck, sewerage and dead fish. Oh god, what a mess."

"And what did you do?" I asked, wanting, and yet not wanting, to hear the rest of Michael's story.

"Well, I got up from my desk and moved away from the windows. They were bulging and looking like they might shatter, so I moved to the center of the room. But then the bookcase fell over, and I had to jump back here to keep from getting smashed. The windows started popping – bang, bang, bang! - like rifle shots, and I got under my desk. That's when the floor gave way right about where you're sitting."

I looked between my feet at the solid concrete floor and felt dizzy. I also felt the impermanence, of everything.

"Oh god, what a mess!" Michael repeated, rubbing his forehead. "Anyway, we got things back together. We sent Jim on his way. He left a happy man. I'm glad you got to meet him."

"Well... Michael," I stammered (and I know I must have been blinking my eyes as fast as the blades of his whirling fan), "I suppose the chances of another earthquake like that one are pretty slim."

Once again Michael grinned his big grin. "Hell, it could happen any day."

"But...," and I struggled to grasp the sense of this man, living in such a place, grinning about something as horrible as an earthquake, but

I also began questioning my own sense and sanity - for hanging around the very same place and including my family in the gamble. "Why would you stay here? I mean, knowing what you know?"

"I grew up in Chile," said Michael, chuckling. "That quake was nothing."

When we look back at our time in the boatyard, we can almost feel nostalgia. We were, after all, a family together on an adventure, no matter how sordid that adventure became. And memory has the grace to ease painful memories. There were good things about the boatyard. We made friends with the yard workers, who stuck around after work, shared a beer with us and shyly laughed at our Spanish. There were evenings, which despite the industrial setting, still left us awed and staring at the warm glow of the sunset on the gulf - billowing purple storm clouds, spent and hung in a fiery sky over a blue sea. But as I glance through the entries in our log (few and far between - another indication of the tight-lipped times we were enduring), there is evidence all was not well.

As the Owner of the wooden ship reproduction warned, the "pie factor" determined our boatyard prison term. The bent rudder shaft on our port engine (of course) was "kaput." In our log the "two-to-three day job" turned into a ten-day job, with the original time estimate crossed out and drawn over in ever darkening and uglier numbers. "We learned today," reads one entry, "that the *pintura del fundo* [bottom paint] applied by the previous owner was not done right. It must be removed with hand scrapers and sandpaper one inch at a time." And later: "I wouldn't have wished this on one of my worst enemies...WE GOTTA GET OUTTA HERE!"

Every day we worked alongside the boatyard workers. In the dead, still, tropical heat, we installed a new port engine cable, sanded wood and fiberglass into irritating spicules and changed oily hydraulic fluid. Shouting to be heard over the whine of sanders and the roar of bulldozers and jet pumps, Diane took her Spanish to new levels every day. I can still see her standing before the boatyard shop - a pretty gringo lady in a straw hat in the midst of group of rough and tumble Venezuelan boatyard workers. She is pointing at a small screw: "*Si, senor, necessito tornillos, pero solamente con ocho millimetros prefundo y quatro millimetros aya. Comprende?*" [Yes, sir, I need screws, but only eight millimeters long and four millimeters here. Do you understand?]

Diane is not Miss Mechanical. She can make the toast, but she cannot fix the toaster. And that is all right. Otherwise she would dump me and my tool belt for a brainless boy toy. Wonderful marriages teeter on these balanced extremes. So when Diane translated boat parts and intricate mechanical repairs, even though she had to climb the ladder between me and the parts shop many times to get it right or, despite her lack of interest, had to bend intently over a piece of paper with my hand drawn schematic upon it in the middle of a huddle of sweaty men, I was grateful and very proud of her.

At night, when the day's heat had barely released its grip and we lay sweating and exhausted in our bunks, giant turbines would scream to life, and spotlights would blaze the darkness into daylight. The wee hours, it turned out, were the only hours cool enough to sandblast the gargantuan rusted iron hulls around us. Through most of the night we tossed and turned with crushed pillows about our ears; and in the morning after such a night, we would emerge to drifts of gritty sand. Each day a new beach was sandblasted onto *Manta Ray's* deck.

"We wash the dirt and sweat off each night," reads the log, "in the steamy closet called a bathroom." Riley, the young porpoise she was, still shakes her head in disgust when she remembers how hot it was and how she could not go swimming in the polluted brown water that flushed into the gulf. The boatyard had a bathroom, of sorts, a claustrophobic cubicle with rusty toilet and drizzling showerhead, where we took our breaths in gasps in order to avoid the stench. On weekends, there was no running water, so whatever went into the toilet was an accumulating deposit, so we foreswore showers. This daily constitutional challenge could not have come at a worse time for Riley, just four years old at the time. Ever since we had arrived in Venezuela, she had overheard talk of *banditos* and shootings; and Riley, who is tough on the outside but an astute observer and an impressionable softy inside, became incontinent. In the turmoil of the boatyard and surrounded with an unsafe world, she retreated to the safety of her infancy. As parents, we worried and felt miserable – guilty, bad parents. Despite our pasted smiles and our efforts to keep up the daily routines, as we shouted over the noise of sanders and grinders to conduct school, we knew we had put our children in a tough place.

Manta Raya's perch thirty feet in the air made us feel alternately safe and cutoff. After repeated reminders and soft urgings, Riley would sometimes admit the need to use the restroom. Diane and I would rush to the ladder. One of us would descend below to steady her descent, and the other would help start her down the ladder from above. After carefully negotiating the dozen or so rungs to the ground, it was still a good walk to the uninviting bathroom - a distance Riley remembers today as "twenty miles." On one occasion, in the middle of the night after accomplishing this high wire descent, Diane spun around at the base of the ladder only to stare into the barrel of a sawed-off shotgun. The night watchman, with nerves jangling from too much coffee or some other adrenaline-pumping drug, had taken Diane for a trespassing thief. Diane danced with her hands in the air and her knees pressed together, miming the need for a bathroom visit and spewing all the Spanish she could muster. The night watchman was soon spewing apologies, but by then, as on most of our bathroom expeditions, Riley would simply look up at her mother and announce: "I don't have to go anymore, mom."

Poor Riley. More than a year later she confessed to us that her berth, not twenty feet away from where we slept, felt to her miles away. She recalls sweating in her bed, too scared to take off the covers and too scared to come to us or call for help. These were trying times.

Why did we not get a hotel and escape the boatyard blues? Well, later we did, when we had to return to Cumana to redo our boatyard repairs (Fear not, dear Reader. I will not drag you through that ugly *deja vu*.) But in those early trying days in Cumana we were scared - scared of the city with its tales of bus traveling hat nappers and muggers, scared of the cockroaches and dysentery that lurked in the seedy hotels and scared for our beloved *Manta Raya* and ourselves. Every few days, tools and construction supplies would disappear from the boatyard. Despite the shotgun-toting watchman, thieves climbed the fences or waded around the beach barriers to scavenge the yard. Even though "boat sitters" slept on the luxury yacht next to us, they would wake with expensive electronics and tools missing. Cumana was indeed a nasty hellhole.

[O.K. Let's get this over with. Here comes the crescendo of the whining tirade:] Two times each week, in order to keep produce and dairy products cold on the boat, I walked two miles over broken concrete and along barbed wire fences to an ice plant, where I stood in line with truck drivers and waited for an eighty pound block of ice. I packed the ice into a backpack and humped it back to the boatyard, where we stowed whatever portion had not melted and drizzled into my shorts along the way. The boatyard was next to a tuna processing plant, the

smell of which, when the wind was right, drifted down upon us warm
and rancid like the smell of death. Besides Diane's excursions to find
food and my trips to get ice or find hardware, we hazarded only one or
two walks into town as a family. (We simply had to get out off the boat
and out of that industrial boatyard.) But our trips were disasters. We
searched for a "lighter side" of Cumana at the city's produce and flower
market, but we found such bedraggled produce and wilted foliage
beside a "park" filled with broken playground equipment and reeking
of urine, that we never attempted the excursion again. Sawyer fell into
a gaping hole in the "sidewalk" and pierced her foot on iron rebar.
With her riding on my back, we returned to the boatyard expecting to
celebrate the one thing that would have rewarded our perseverance in
the "shadow of the valley:" our first coat of *pintura del fundo* [bottom
paint] and a new rudder shaft. With these hurdles behind us, we would
have been within one day of a blessed departure. But when we arrived
at the boatyard, Diane gasped. The bottom paint was not blue, as I
had arranged with Victor, but sh-- brown. In fastening the rudder
shaft, the workers had split the c-clamp that secured it to its hydraulic
drive. Instead of a bent rudder, we now had no rudder. The part would
have to be replaced, and in third world Venezuela, that would mean
fabricating it in a machine shop. To top off all this good news, our new
poop brown hull was oozing water. Despite new epoxy undercoats and
primer coats applied to the meticulously sanded hull, blistering, the
abhorrent leprosy of boat bottoms, had appeared. Water was dribbling
out of tiny pustules in *Manta Raya's* side just as the last vestiges of hope
were leaking out of our hearts.

I look back on those days and see myself trying to be the father
I wanted to be for my family. As parents, what we hide from our
children and what we share with them is a tender balance. This was
not the Caribbean adventure we had hoped for, but Diane and I kept
up appearances. We conducted school each morning. We made regular
meals, and despite the flies and the *eau de tuna*, we ate dinner together
out in the cockpit each evening. With her dictionary in hand, Diane
somehow talked the *panaderia* owner out of precious ingredients, so
that she could bake a cake for Riley's birthday. We tried to greet each
day with optimism; and faking it, I'm afraid, was better than giving in
to the reality. We pasted smiles on our faces and patted the workers on
their backs, and each day Diane waded through the fiberglass and paint
chips around our hull to serve them lemonade and crackers.

One day I waited three hours in a Cumana bank line to get a foot high stack of *Bolivars*, Venezuela's inflated currency. The line never moved. While I waited I wrote in my diary, and I read a book, or two. Standing in the endless, silent line, I tried to make friends. I worked up the courage to spin some poor Spanish, and I talked with the folks around me in line. Their faces lit up. They were shy, polite and friendly, but when we ran out of things to say, or more realistically, I had plumbed the depths of my Spanish, the vitality in their eyes would once again turn dull. They would return to their lost and patient resignation. My family had not been singled out for mistreatment. The Venezuelans lived this way all their lives. Their resignation was palpable and pitiful. We were the privileged and lucky ones – comparatively wealthy gringos. We would be leaving. We had no right to whine.

Near the end of our stay in the Cumana boatyard, I managed to find a working phone, and after several attempts, an operator patched me through to my parents. My father answered. At the sound of his voice, and I had to close my eyes to quell the emotion.

"Hey buddy! Good to hear from you. How's yer ol' potato been?"

"Fine, dad, fine. We're getting close to getting out of here. The work on the boat has taken a bit longer than we thought it would. It's been a little trying."

A pause. "Everybody O.K?"

"Oh yea. The girls are hanging in there...We're even thinking about heading home. We have some long passages ahead of us, but we're looking north..."

Another pause. "Your mom will be glad to hear that. I wish I could help you with the passage, but I'm not sure I'm up to that sort of thing these days."

"No problem, dad. How are you doing?"

"Fine. I just mowed the yard [I could smell the sweet scent of freshly cut grass]. It looks good. We've had a wet spell [I could smell the moisture, the waxy magnolias and the pink and white dogwoods]. Your mother is at church helping with a supper. I'm headed there after a bit. [I could taste the sliced country ham and russet potatoes with dill and butter.]

I ached. I wanted to be a kid again. I wanted to quit my job as a father. I wanted to play ping-pong with my dad and watch the Wonderful World of Disney on TV. I wanted my mom to tell me to wash my hands for dinner. I wanted out of all the planning, the worrying, the hoping and pretending, my struggle with life in Cumana.

"You still there?" asked my dad.

"Yeah, dad, yeah... Dad?"

"Uh huh?"

"You've been a really good father. Thanks."

"Hey! What a nice thing to say! Your mom and I are proud of you and all the things you are doing. We always have been...You sure we can't do anything to help?"

"You already have, dad. We'll call you when we get outta here. I love you."

"Love you too, buddy. Hug that family for me."

"I will."

The click of the receiver severed a very fine and precious thread. It hurt. But it also helped. Within a few days, I had most of the boatyard workers gathered around *Manta Raya*. We were back at the ramp, in the ready position, lining up in the birth canal, ready for a new beginning and a return to freedom at sea. It was drizzling rain. We must have looked like a wake - a grim ceremony under a grey sky. Over the past few days, I had worn my safety glasses and stood by workers in the metal shop, while a crude but serviceable rudder attachment was fashioned. I had wedged myself into the aft rudder compartment and carefully tightened the thing into place. On the last turn, I had sprung up like a jack-in-the-box and hugged the startled workers.

But even at the ramp, the work was not finished. Antonio #2 was standing next to the port hull. While someone held a plastic sheet over his head, he was feverishly curing a gunk of epoxy by toasting it with a hair dryer. This sort of last minute repair in the rain was not, by a long shot, a procedure recommended by the epoxy manufacturer. But we could not have cared less.

As we slid into the water and fired our engines, the workers waved. I believe a few of them even cheered. I would like to have thought that we had made some friends, and no doubt there was a feel of camaraderie in the group, but there was also relief. *Buenos Suerte* (good luck)! *Bien viaje* (bon voyage)! *Vayas!* (get the hell outta here?). *Manta Raya* was free once again.

Passage with RT – First Voyage 1988

My father served in the Navy during World War II. He sailed into Pearl Harbor just days after the Japanese attack. He tied off on the sunken mast of the USS Arizona. He fought at Okinawa. Though these days I can get him to talk about a few of the grim details of those adventures, he prefers to talk about gentler war memories.

Like the time he went crab fishing with his skipper. As the two men fished, the skipper suddenly shouted. He had lost his engraved lighter - a present from his fiancé. The skipper was devastated, so the fishing trip was cut short, and my father reluctantly pulled in his line. But there was a crab on the end of the line, and the crab held my father's bait in one claw and the skipper's shiny, silver lighter in the other.

My father will also tell how he and a Navy buddy rejuvenated a bombed out jeep. With the windshield gone, they made their own tropical breeze by driving around and around a tiny island. And as they drove through the palms all night, they drank a flammable rum concoction and sang.

I call my father "R.T.," just as his friends do. I suppose I use the familiar term in part because I think of him as my buddy. And though he is from the rolling farmland of central Ohio, I also think of him as a sailor. So I was pleased that when Diane and I asked R.T. to sail with us in the eighties, he signed up for a three-day passage across the Gulf of Mexico.

Long ocean passages are sleep deprivation experiments with ocean angst and seasickness thrown in to sour the pot. Samuel Johnson likened boat passages to jail, only you can drown. Diane and I were the only crew on our little sloop (we had no autopilot or wind vane steering in those days, so watches were spent, as in the days of yore, at the helm). Three hour shifts over several days and nights meant neither of us slept more than a few hours at a time. By the second day out, we were usually brain dead, or as a friend of mine says, "bread dain." We looked forward to having R.T. as a third crewmember, for we would get six to eight hours of rest - sweet slumber between watches. But the help R.T. ended up giving us was not the help we had expected.

Diane and I were anchored off Isla Mujeres near Cancun, Mexico on the final leg of our 1988 Caribbean Cruise. Our planned passage from Cancun to Key West, Florida was to be the end of our trip and our first step back in the United States in nine months. R.T. arrived with my mother and my sister. It was a delightful family reunion and a fitting celebration for the last leg of our journey. But during the celebration, we made a day sail and snorkeling trip out to a nearby lagoon, and I surfaced after an encounter with clown fish to see my mother waving to me as the current drug her out to sea. As I swam over to help my mother, I noticed my father was also struggling – he was hanging upside down by one leg, trapeze style, over the side of the dinghy.

After we had collected everyone from his or her mishaps and put ice on R.T.'s rapidly swelling knee, we sat about the cockpit and laughed at ourselves. But I could not help but feel uncomfortable. As liveaboards, we were used to minor calamities when landlubbers visited, but these particular landlubbers were my parents. For the first time in my life, I had had to rescue and take care of them. They were getting older, and up until that time, I had not stopped to notice.

In fact, the next day when R.T. hobbled aboard, his knee in a bulging bandage, I wondered if I had not made a mistake asking him to crew for us. Ocean passages are physically demanding and emotionally trying, and I wondered if, like a negligent parent, I had put R.T. in a difficult and dangerous situation. Then to add to my worries, only an hour out to sea the winds picked up and the seas began to leap. With the mighty Gulf Stream running counter to the blow, our boat began to buck in the galloping waves. She flung herself into a flipping twist (my favorite) that sent torrents of water over the deck. In order to handle her in these conditions, the helmsman or helmswoman had to stand bow-legged with both legs braced against the cockpit seats, while gripping the wheel and steering pedestal. Then, by peering over the dodger to negotiate the wave troughs, the helmsperson would get just enough warning to duck down when a crashing wave leapt over the dodger. Otherwise, he or she would end up with a face full of saltwater and a torrent of cold water down their necks.

Just off Mexico in the straits facing Cuba, we entered miserable seas that proceeded to get worse. It began to rain. I was not paying attention to how long I had been at the wheel, but I knew I had gone past the end of my watch. R.T. was next up to bat, but honestly, I did not want to put him at the wheel. The companionway hatch slid open, and R.T.'s head popped up.

"Say, Sport. Isn't it about time for my shift?"

I shouted something in the affirmative into the wind and told R.T. to ask Diane to help him suit up. It took another half hour to get R.T. dressed, but I knew this was reasonable for a first timer. Preparing for a stint at the wheel of a bucking boat was no easy chore. He had to pull the full suit of foul weather, farmer john pants and suspenders over his existing clothing. Then he had to secure the jacket and hood. Next, he had to step into his harness, a spaghetti of loose lines and straps, which with its many attachments and leads, was like a cobweb snare ready to trip and send him to the floor, even in flat calm water. But eventually R.T. managed the full suit of armor, including the bulging life vest that went over the entire mess.

Diane came topside to sit with me before R.T. came on deck, and the look she gave me told me we shared the same concerns.

"How's he doing?" I shouted over the wind.

"O.K., but just when we had him rigged up, he had to take everything off again to use the head."

Yikes! More proof I was becoming a retro parent – we were dressing a toddler.

When R.T. finally emerged from the cabin, he was a sight. His glasses were crooked and fogged, and the multiple layers of gear, harness lines and life vest, made him look like a blimp escaped from the hanger. He pulled himself along the cockpit seats clanking his harness behind him. This did not look good.

Still, I slapped him on the shoulder, welcomed him to the helm and asked him whether he was ready. "Sure," he said, and I detected neither enthusiasm nor insecurity in his response. I began giving instructions for steering and course, all the time reassuring him (and myself) that if he had any problems whatsoever, Diane or I would be ready to help. (I had already given up hope of getting any rest.)

It was time to get the show on the road. We had to hook R.T.'s life harness tether to the steering pedestal, so Diane and I bent down to find the line and clasp. What we both saw started us laughing. R.T. had zipped his tether up into his fly. It was hanging out of his pants. We laughed so hard we could not breath - a laugh just this side of lunacy.

R.T. just smiled and wedged himself in behind the wheel. I stood beside him to make sure he was comfortable. But honestly, I was unwilling to leave him alone. For a while, he concentrated in silence on his steering and his timing for ducking bow waves. But when he got the swing of the helm, he started talking.

He talked about nights at sea on the Pacific on his LC10 troop landing craft. He talked about storms and tropical islands. And he talked about a nervous lieutenant who went ashore for a reconnaissance with him and several other more experienced sailors. The lieutenant, like the rest of the shore party, was scared, but he was also a *putz*. He stumbled, and because he had left the safety off his gun, it fired. Everyone hit the dirt. Then, after a pause during which the sailors realized from whence the "enemy" fire had come and after they had checked themselves to see if they had been hit (and, as R.T. said, "changed their shorts"), they made the lieutenant walk in front – the safety secured on his gun.

Warmed by this story, R.T. also told jokes, like this:

A fellow in a bar finds himself standing next to a pirate with a peg leg, a hook and an eye patch. After a few drinks, the fellow can't stand it any longer and has to ask the pirate how he got his peg leg.

"Well," says the pirate, "I fell overboard, see, and before me mates could haul me back on deck, a shark came along and bit me leg off."

"Oh!" says the fellow. "That's horrible! And the hook?"

"Well. I was boarding a boat, and some swab took a saber and cut me hand clean off."

"Yikes," says the fellow, "that's terrible! But if you don't mind my asking, how did you end up with an eye patch?"

"Oh that," says the pirate, "a bird pooped in me eye."

Astonished, the fellow asks, "Bird poop made you lose your eye?"

"Aye," says the pirate. "It was me first day with me hook."

R.T. scanned the dark sky and heaving waves. But he was smiling. And though I could not see his eyes behind his salt-flecked glasses, his words were enough to make me let go of my last bit of worrying. Looking straight into the storm, he said, "Is this great or what!"

I clapped R.T on his shoulder and wished him luck. Then I went below, dove into to my berth and passed out for six hours of solid, death-like sleep.

When I awoke, the sea was still rough, and I looked up through the companionway, I could see that Diane and R.T. were at the helm and smiling. And R.T. was still telling stories. I was inspired, and I moved to the chart table to see if there were any way we could change our rough luck. The answer was obvious. It was time to give up.

I talked my plan over with the crew, and we agreed. We changed course. Instead of taking weather on the nose to Key West, we bore off and steered north toward Fort Myers. The wind and waves eased to our beam, and within an hour we had worked our way out of the rough grasp of the Gulf Steam. As if to bless our new course, the sun popped through breaking clouds and warmed our smiling faces. It was glorious!

Diane went below into the war torn cabin and scrounged up some breakfast. R.T. and I toasted one another with glasses of orange juice. But as soon as the acidic liquid passed my lips, I knew I had made a mistake.

I do not think the stuff even made it past my throat before it backed up and exited with considerable velocity. I spewed like a fountain. My crew was silent as I wiped my lips with my sleeve. But R.T was the first to speak: "That's gotta feel better!" he said. And it did. For the second time on our voyage, we laughed – quite long and hard.

At dawn the following day we sailed through Florida's Boca Grande entrance and made a surreal landfall. Venus and Jupiter were bright diamonds hung above petticoat clouds lit from below so they glowed chartreuse and orange in the rising sun. There were delicious, warm land scents. Diane presented R.T. with a commemorative shirt that read "Cancun to Key West," with the "Key West" crossed out and "Boca Grande" written it its place. We hugged one another in the cockpit, and later that day after checking in with U.S. Customs, we indulged our welcome home food fantasies with cheeseburgers and chocolate milkshakes.

To this day I do not know whether R.T. ran his life harness through his fly by accident or on purpose.

Mochima

O.K., It might sound trite, but for every dark and stormy sea, there really is a ray of light leading to a sheltered anchorage. *Mochima* was our first anchorage after the Cumana boatyard, and despite some of the foul play that had recently taken place there, it was a beautiful getaway anchorage.

We threaded our way through a narrow channel leading inland. Lush green hills folded down to meet the winding channel, and blue swallows swooped in and about our rigging. Like trapeze acrobats, one swallow would hold a feather in its beak, drop it at the apex of its swoop and pluck it up again before it could flutter to the deck.

As we rounded the last bend in the channel, a vast bay opened up before us. Cool rain clouds moved overhead and cast contrasting shadows over the water. *Puerto Mochima* was four miles up a deep, winding channel and protected in all directions by steep hills. We gawked at the countless protected coves and inlets where we might anchor, because such a secure paradise rarely presents itself to wandering sailors. A description of the bay of *Mochima* from the 1867 "Guide to the West Indies" reads: *To these advantages may be added that of free ingress and egress with the tradewind, altogether making it the best harbor in this part of America, and indeed, one of the best in the world."* Yes, we had arrived.

Sure, we had concerns. This was the bay where a father had been shot trying to stop nighttime bandits. It was also the spot where our friend, the Owner, had been tied to his mast and pistol-whipped. But we were not scared. I think we were too happy to be out of the Cumana boatyard, a bit calloused to the rough poverty we had seen in Venezuela and too relieved to get back to cruising to be concerned. We anchored, got out our scrub brushes and began washing away the accumulated grime of our boatyard internment. With each cleansing douche, dirty water rinsed over the scuppers and a bit of our black mood washed away. Before we could complete *Manta Raya's* re-baptism, the clouds broke and finished the job for us. In the downpour, we danced around the deck like lunatics - shivering in the cold and laughing as we hugged one another. We collected sixty joyous gallons of fresh water in the downpour, and this gift from heaven would repeat itself many afternoons in *Mochima*.

The days were idyllic. We got back into the rhythm of cruising. In the mornings we swam or hiked through the jungle. We chased Blue Morph butterflies as big as our two outstretched hands. We made minor repairs, read books, and one afternoon we rigged a line to a six-gallon water jug. We pulled the jug behind the dinghy like a boogie board, and Sawyer rode the fishtailing jug wide-eyed but managing to jump the wake. In the afternoons, lime green parakeets launched themselves from one side of the bay and flew, quite poorly, chattering and squawking, as they flittered over our mast to the opposite shore. One evening we slept out on the tarp, making up stories until we fell asleep in a giant family bundle under our blanket. At four AM we woke to see the constellation Orion swirling overhead.

With Halloween coming up, Diane decided a pumpkin was in order. She got out her Spanish dictionary, wrote down what she thought would be a few helpful words and dinghied the girls into the little town of *Mochima*. In town, there were several false starts, as the locals scratched their heads, offered cut up pieces of squash or directed the girls to dead ends, where more locals scratched their heads. To complicate the expedition, Diane met blank or suspicious stares when she tried to explain why she needed an entire pumpkin – you know, the ritual carving, lighting and display of a scary visage… crazy. *loco gringos.*

Finally, giving up, the girls started back toward the dinghy, but a lady with whom they had just spoken re-emerged from her home, whistled and waved at them with a pushing motion of the palm of her hand as if to say, "Keep going, head on down the road." Diane and the girls smiled, yelled *"gracias"* and returning the goodbye wave. But again the lady whistled, and this time when Diane turned to face her, the woman was waving quite frantically. "Get going and good riddance," she seemed to be signaling. But Diane studied the "move on" wave and thought it odd. Perhaps this "move along" wave meant something different in Venezuela. Diane pointed to herself. The lady smiled and pushed even harder with her "move along" wave, so Diane and the girls walked back to investigate.

Sure enough, in Venezuela the "move on" wave actually meant "come back." Diane found her pumpkin...well, not a pumpkin really, but a big squash. And once it was onboard, we hollowed it out and made a decent, grinning jack-o-lantern. Lit, it must have looked a bit scary from shore and confirmed every suspicion the locals held about the odd, *Norte Americanos*. But the pumpkin incident left us wondering. In Venezuela, just how many words, symbols and signals had we misinterpreted? If you did want someone to move on, should you wave your hand toward yourself and call them back? Worse, should we be smiling when we were angry or scowling when we were pleased?

Despite the idyll and the recharge Mochima offered us, we also had some tough family conferences. For us, Venezuela had proved to be rough around the edges, and wondering whether we had the chutzpa to continue, we discussed a run straight home to Texas or Florida. We had freed ourselves of the boatyard blues, but we also felt a bit beaten, and we felt the need for a change of scene (or perhaps a change of approach.) At the time we could not know that our next offshore passage would give us exactly what we needed. But before we headed to sea, we would have to provision, and that meant dealing with yet one more coastal Venezuelan town.

Los Aves (We Fly Away)

Were we in Naples, Florida? No, hurricane Mitch, an extra-tropical storm, or so the weather folks called it, was near beautiful Naples at the time. So the plush resort where we found ourselves, with its clear blue sky, pool and palms, could not have been in Florida. We were tied up to the Bahia Redonda marina in Puerto La Cruz, Venezuela. Still, with its grand, kidney shaped pool and fountain, snack bar with frozen chocolate bars (just ten paces off our foredeck), restaurant with fried calamari and workout gym with showers, it sure felt like Naples.

When we left Mochima we sailed straight to Puerto La Cruz and the Bahia Redonda marina, our last mainland stop and our last provisioning stop before getting the "heck outta dodge" and back on the open ocean. But even though Puerto La Cruz was, unlike Cumana, a tourist destination, it too would prove to be a quirky place.

During our short stay in Puerto La Cruz, we provisioned at the oxymoronic "Makro," a giant warehouse of foods and household goods. Since inflation had turned the Venezuelan Bolivar into so much funny money, I carried great wads of Venezuelan cash to the store, one stack in my hip pack, one in my money belt and one stuck under my hat. Walking out through the intimidating loops of razor wire that surrounded our resort marina, we passed directly into hovels of desperate poverty. While gringos and rich Venezuelans continued to drive about behind the black-tinted windows of their black, air-conditioned Land Cruisers, the average Venezuelans drive old, swaying and smoking cars, ride bikes or walk. The Venezuelan oil boom, after just beginning to create a new, stabilizing middle class, had blown up. And it appeared the Venezuelan people's hopes had burst with it. Many blamed the government, and we were exiting the mainland just two weeks before the national election, which was becoming understandably tense. Already there were rumors of strikes and possible riots.

When we made our foray to the *Makro*, I learned that an older cruising couple, who had chosen to go there by bus, had been mugged. At one of the bus stops, a group of toughs had boarded the bus and surrounded the couple. A knife had been pulled, the wife had screamed and turned to the other passengers for help. But the Venezuelans had shaken their heads and put their fingers to their lips, urging the wife to be quiet. When the thugs pulled the husband off the bus and began pushing him about, the bus driver simply drove on, while the wife continued to scream. Later the couple was able to find one another and returned to the marina. Now it was not clear whether they would be joining the rest of the cruisers for their scheduled charter bus tour of Angel Falls, including a night at a naturally constructed eco-tourist lodge featuring a gourmet Venezuelan cooking class. The mugging had taken some fun out of their tour.

Despite the conscience-disturbing dichotomy of our plush marina, we had to, as red-blooded *Norte Americanos*, enjoy the place. Hell, the girls were thrilled to play at the pool with their newly found gringo friends. And it was easy for Diane and I to clean the boat, do laundry and stow, as the saying goes, ten pounds of Makro supplies in the proverbial five-pound sack. Frankly, being U.S. gringos came naturally. And yes, we even enjoyed the cruisers' potluck, where we met lots of nice folks - sailors holing up for the hurricane season or resting up before resuming their passages toward the Pacific and perhaps around the world. In fact, it would have been easy to give into the place (we were certainly lulled by its Sisyphean dream); but we were cruising, not hiding out in *Xanadu*, and it was time to move on. Our first step would be toward Venezuela's offshore atolls.

Coral atolls are incredible gifts from Mother Ocean. From the depths of the sea, they rise up into a ring of islands and reef that are, for the seafarer, safe havens and oases. Barrier coral flattens ocean waves into calm ponds, and within the circle of protective coral, the island's beaches and turquoise lagoons look like scenes from *South Pacific*. In fact, most of the world's coral atolls are in the Pacific, but there are a few of the treasures in the Caribbean – one or two we had visited off the coast of Central America and a few more we hoped to see off Venezuela's coast. So, one early morning in November, we woke at 0400, cast off the dock lines and ghosted away beneath the yellow lights of the Puerto La Cruz marina. The security guard whistled, we waved and once again we were on the ocean. The twinkling lights of the city gave way to the Big Dipper and the Southern Cross at either end of a dark blue Caribbean sky. There was a good wind, but the seas were lumpy, and Riley came out of her berth and up on deck for repeated "ablutions" to Neptune. There were dolphins, and the dolphins scared up a flock of flying fish, some of which flew and were "netted" by our trampoline. As the big-eyed bullets with wings flopped about in the net, we smelled "tuna." Diane took the girls, though they were seasick and sleepy, in her arms out onto the trampoline. The girls rescued the flying fish and then held one another. Then they stared out into the sea and wondered what our next destination would bring us.

We made our way to the first of Venezuela's remote atolls, *Los Roques*, a beautiful oval of white sand and green islands. By afternoon when we arrived, the Caribbean Christmas Winds were carrying us on a downwind gallop. Great hillocks of waves pranced and peaked about us, picking up Manta Raya's skirts so that she raced along the crest of one wave, fell back and then was lifted onto the shoulders of the following wave. Diane had first spotted the atoll by its blue and green reflection off the clouds that floated above it. The *Roques* entrance was a skinny, white-knuckled entrance that took us out of the galloping seas and into a wide open, calm pasture of turquoise water.

With our arrival at Los Roques we were back – back to the pristine and open waters that had captured Diane's and my souls a dozen years before. Remote beauty was one of the reasons we had returned to cruising, and now we could share it with our children. But the first "Out There" demonstration I shared with them was also a Rhyme of the Ancient Mariner.

We had anchored near the entrance to Los Roques, and we were staring out at the wide-open ocean with only a thin line of coral breaking the incoming waves. The wind hummed through the rigging, and *Manta Raya* tugged at her harness like a scared filly. Despite the beauty and the relief we felt being at sea again, we also felt a familiar, raw nerved angst, the same angst that sent so many western plains settlers to the loony bin. Yes, we were *Out There*, and the ceaseless Christmas Winds and endless sea from horizon to horizon was reminding us just how far out we had come.

Sawyer and Riley with "Larry" the Lobster, Las Aves, Venezuela

Still, I wanted to show the beauty of the place to my girls, so we loaded up the dinghy and motored to some nearby coral. But so as to not damage the fragile coral formations, we cut the engine and paddled through the pillared formations that looked like volcanic lobes of cauliflower. We were having fun playing hide and seek in the labyrinth, when I spotted a lobster, a big one, and was instantly overcome with lobster lust - thoughts of sweet, white meat and melted butter dancing in my head.

The lobster was in season but "out of bounds" - way out of bounds, because Los Roques is a national park, and spear fishing is not allowed.

But I rationalized that if I were to capture the thing with my hands, I would not be breaking the law. Clever lad.

Riley had taken to carrying a stick onboard Manta Raya. She carried it everywhere, and we called it "Riley's stick." I had her use it to coax the lobster out of the rocks and into our dive bag. But the thing's powerful tail swept through the water, and, *whoosh*, out of the bag it came to hide in a tinier crevice of rock, where I proceeded to work for thirty minutes, prodding, poking and coaxing from various angles, until I was able to grab it by its monster tail.

I knew the lobster was not coming out. It was wedged into a crevice I could barely get my hand through. But I found myself in an interesting position, namely: I was holding the dinner end of the deal. So without thinking through the consequences, I twisted my wrist, tore the tail free from the lobster and rose from the water triumphant – that was, until I noticed the bright orange ornaments dangling from the beautiful brown and green tail. They were little eggs the poor mama lobster had been trying to protect.

For a fellow who talks as if he were a charter member of Green Peace, I felt like an ecoterrorist, an earth rapist. With the ocean's coral reefs disappearing and the lobster population in severe decline, female lobsters, like the one I had just rendered, offered the only hope, and I was holding not only a precious female's severed body but hundreds of her mutilated young. Infanticide.

There were many lessons to be learned from my act of greed, not the least of which was that I ought to have respected Venezuela's efforts to protect endangered reef animals. By using a snare and my eyes instead of a spear or my fist, I would have seen that the lobster was a mommy, and I could have released her. But seeing that things were as they were, I did the only thing I could do: I confessed my sins to my daughters, and I never again hunted without remembering this lobster, the albatross that to this day hangs about my neck.

The next day we ghosted over shallows and anchored off another small island in *Los Roques* called *Carenero*. It was the weekend, or so we were to learn, since we had stopped keeping track of days, and the distance from our offshore atoll to the metropolis of Caracas turned out to be not far enough. In the little anchorage, which should have held two to three boats, six other yachts joined us, including a sixty-foot, wooden yacht classic, with a high bow and a long, narrow and low stern that swept the water. I expected Marilyn Monroe to appear any moment to execute a perfect swan dive. No wonder, since the yacht was built in San Diego and was a sister ship to a yacht once owned by John Kennedy.

But the weekend brought us more than Caracas luxury yachts. It brought us a new friend. When we met funny, smart and competent Sue Ann, her smile was the first thing that reached out to us. A Virginia girl with a big personality, she was sailing with her husband and daughter. They planned to sail around the world. At the *Carenero* anchorage, she simply grabbed us and invited us aboard. In her cockpit we learned of her circumnavigation plans. (At the time we thought, "Around the world. That's nice.") But over the next two years, as we followed Sue Ann's travels through her ham radio updates, she and her family did just that, with only one interruption. Sue Ann had to make a brief visit back to the States for a mastectomy – her second.

Sue Ann had been diagnosed with and treated for breast cancer before we met her; but of course, she told us nothing of this in *Carenero*. Instead, she simply invited us aboard and baked us a cake - a chocolate cake with cream cheese frosting – and an unbelievable treasure in such a remote anchorage. She threw Diane a birthday party that went late into the night. And the next morning, Sue Ann returned - this time paddling over to *Manta Raya* on an odd, triangular float.

"Hey," she shouted, "Did you hear about the agnostic, dyslexic insomniac?" Diane and I looked at one another and shrugged. "He stayed up all night wondering whether there really was a dog."

I asked Sue Ann what the heck she was sitting on, and she answered with a command to action. "Let's hook this bad boy up to your dinghy and have us some fun!"

The picture of Sue Ann laughing as she skittered along skipping the wake behind our dinghy - a blonde smile in a blur of water and spray - is a permanent entry in my right-stuff-scrapbook-of-the-mind.

When we left the protected *Los Roques* and sailed on to the even more beautiful and even more pristine *Los Aves*, we left the last of mainland Venezuela and the last of the weekend yachties behind us. On the way, we caught our first deepwater ocean fish: a Cero tuna - wonderful barbecued with a soy sauce marinade. Our catch was a good omen. We were getting into fertile water. The real beauty, the real cruising, lay just ahead inside the next atoll,

The *Aves* are really two atolls – *Barlovento* and *Sovento*, windward and leeward. They are, or ought to be, every cruiser's pinup poster of

Holy Grail cruising. I can still picture Diane, slender and tan, standing high on the mast step, wearing her baseball cap and Polaroids, so she can survey the waters of the shallow reef. It was a little after noon, and the high sun showed us gold and emerald coral just below our hull. To starboard the tallest mangroves I have ever seen towered over an island swarming with birds. Ahead there was nothing but calm, clear water and a distant reef that swept the entire horizon and muted the assault of tradewind driven waves. A blue, cloudless sky blended with blue, spotless water. We had arrived, and we were free.

There were only a few fellow cruisers in this remote atoll - the hearty type of cruisers who venture out beyond the normal cruising routes. We chose an anchorage near the mangrove island with a lone fishing boat, as we always trusted fishermen to know where to rest peacefully through the night. In the quiet, under the stars, we slept like babies. I was grateful to be away, finally, to be cruising once again… the way we had dreamed back before the cruise had begun, to be floating in a warm and empty place. And while we slept, the Magic of the place began to work upon us.

In the morning it was "Gentlemen, start your engines!" Still, the motor-like buzzing I heard was no rude awakening. Though it sounded like the "brrrrrrrr" of weed whackers in full dandelion frenzy, it was the morning call of the red-footed booby bird. We had anchored next to their rookery, and just in front of us, a narrow channel led into a sixty-foot tall mangrove – a "bird sanctuary." After a quick breakfast, we dinghied in to see what the fuss was about. It turned out the birds were "revving their engines" as they prepared to get their morning catch and feed their white, frumpy, puffed up and squinty-eyed chicks. The baby fuzz balls sat in nests hung throughout the mangroves. It was a busy nursery. Larger, by fluff, than their parents, the baby boobies were bizarre looking birds only a mama and papa booby could love. We were so captivated by the birds, despite their strong aroma, that Sawyer and I went back to the boat for sketchpads and spent the morning drawing them. What we were able to put down on paper was nothing compared to what we saw and what we took away. It was a miracle of winged life, and the recording of it, together, was intoxicating.

By afternoon I was ready for a swim. My Lloyd Bridges sea hunt lust, despite the albatross lesson, was unquenchable. So Diane and I headed out with Sue Ann to see if we could scare up some dinner.

The ladies dropped me off on one side of a coral island, and went on to scout the other side by dinghy.

Swimming in a warm sea through a coral garden filled with colorful fishes is about the most sublime feeling I know. The water moves across my body like a caress, and there is a delicious sensation, as fins kick and a wave of power moves over and through my body – a fluid motion through a weightless world of water. There along the coral wall I dove and spun like an otter – just for the fun of it, until I spotted the lobster.

The lobster I saw made my albatross lobster look like a shrimp. The behemoth was hunkered down under a large coral outcropping, and I had to poke and prod him, first to determine his sex ("Excuse me, but would you mind showing me your privates?"), and then to work him out into the open for a shot with my spear.

After a few round-the-mulberry chases, I managed a clear shot – adrenaline beating the drums in my ears, and I had him! But there was a problem. Though he was now on my spear, he was so big that with each powerful thrust of his tail, he was literally pulling me through the water and back toward the rocks. If I were not careful, I would lose him and earn yet another demerit on my Ancient Mariner report card – this time not only for killing but also for losing one of God's sea creatures.

I thrust hard with my fins and made my stand by bracing myself against the rocks and lifting the monster out of the water, where I figured his thrashing tail, beating in thin air, would provide little purchase. Only I could not quite get the monster clear of the water. Under his weight my spear bent like a bow, and his thrashing tail beat the water into a froth.

I had to get help. So I supported the spear between my armpit and elbow, ripped off my mask and managed a quick but piercing whistle before falling back into the water and resuming my wrestling match - Tarzan battles the giant lobster. The next time I surfaced with the monster, I was happy to see Diane and Sue Ann on their way around the reef.

I hooked one arm over the rubber gunnel of the dinghy, and with Diane's help, hefted the lobster into the boat. As he hit the floor, both ladies moved back and lifted their legs into the air, Sue Ann blinking and whistling. "Holy cripes!" she said. "It's a sea monster!"

I pulled myself into the dinghy and lay on my back panting beside the lobster. We were both exhausted, but only one of us was dinner.

"Looks like we're having a party," Diane said. "And we'll need to invite company."

As the sun began to set and the sky warmed to amber and red, we made the rounds to our fellow cruisers' boats. Sue Ann invited sailors from Switzerland. Just that week they had rescued crew off a midnight wreck on the reef. Their Swiss flag – a red and white cross – was appropriately reminiscent of the Red Cross. They asked if they might bring along one of the shipwrecked sailors, a young lady from Australia, still smiling but with a bit of a dazed look of shock in her eyes. Diane and I invited an Italian couple and their children who had anchored not too far from us. Poor as church mice and happy as clams, they were thrilled to get the invitation. They would bring wine, for no matter how much they had skimped on beans and rice, there was always wine. We also invited new friends Ross and Katy off their steel cutter - Ross so calm and decent, like an earthbound Buddha, and Katy so kind and smiling. They had always dreamed of sailing this far to the Southern Caribbean; and now that they had arrived, they were in bliss. Could they bring a big plate of cookies they had just baked? Oh yes.

Counting our own kids and Sue Ann's family, we had the makings of a hefty party. As dusk settled about the anchorage, the dinghies began to arrive. They tied up to our stern in a long line. Smiling faces came aboard with delicious treats – tropical rice with mango and raisins, freshly baked bread, golden conch fritters (for Diane had also caught conch that day) and more steaming white lobster drizzled with butter than the entire anchorage could eat. Because not only did we serve the behemoth I had caught, but also a lobster Sue Ann had speared. The first lobster she had ever caught.

I found out about Sue Ann's accomplishment late that evening, and I felt a moment of shame. I had been so taken with my own catch that I had not noticed Sue Ann's moment of glory. When I apologized, Sue Ann's proud blush and hug told me all. She too felt the grace of the festivities.

The spontaneous fellowship of cruisers gathered on a tiny boat in the middle of a Mother Ocean is a miracle. The soft laughter of adults on deck, the giggle of kids below, the music (sweet strains of Mark Knopfler's guitar), the light tropical breeze and the piercing stars above all mixed together to overwhelm us. We sang. The Italians started with "Under the Boardwalk," and there was no stopping the grin that spread across my face. I had to hug Diane. I had to squeeze Riley's arm and kiss Sawyer on the head. We had truly arrived back in Mother Ocean's arms, surrounded by empty Nature and the good will of friends. For that moment and many more to come on our cruise, the world was right... as it, of course, always is.

I know now that a person can own acreage and surround himself with Nature so that he keeps himself just far enough away from his fellow man to be a good neighbor. And I know he can own a boat and let it take him to places where the math works out about the same. In these remote places, life moves at the right pace, and we can flow along with it, or as writer Marjorie Kinnan Rawlings urges us, we can have "some small place of enchantment to turn to."

After about a week in the *Aves Barlovento*, most of our newfound cruising friends had moved on. Our cruising stores were running low - water and beer for example – and we reluctantly turned our eyes to the west and toward civilization. But before we embarked for the next populated island of Bonaire, we opted for one more secluded stop in the *Aves Sovento*.

Like its sister atoll, the leeward atoll was fringed with coral reef. There were mangroves, swooping frigate birds, white sand beaches and shimmering blue waters painted with splashes of green and gold coral. Once again we sailed out of the trade wind waves and into the smooth blue water of a sheltering reef. We anchored over a canyon of coral, where waves crashed just off our stern but we rode calm and upright. We were living on the edge in a fluid painting by Matisse.

For the next few days we kept to ourselves. We read, snorkeled and swam. We ate conch with marinara sauce and risotto. And while the reflection of the full moon slid and sparkled on the water, we told nighttime stories out on the trampoline. The girls were probably growing weary of the wilderness, but their papa was in heaven. I swam through the coral and thrilled at the rhythms of water and wind. I lost track of time. It was hard to turn my attention to what might lay ahead. I could contemplate the first world enticements of the Dutch Islands like Bonaire, but the long and unfathomable passages that lay beyond were too much. Just where were we headed? Should we sail further west with the wind or north toward home? I tried not to think. But as the days passed and our canned fruits and veggies disappeared, we gave into the inevitable. We pasted Trandserm® Scop patches on the girls and fueled up the engines for our next passage to Bonaire.

On our last night at the leeward Aves, we moved through a dead calm to an island near the western end of the atoll. As we motored, Riley pronounced that motoring with our sail covers on was like wearing a hat in a restaurant. Were we, I wondered, raising a sailing purist?

Just before dawn I woke to the stars and looked north to the Big Dipper. In November at the equator, the Dipper was an early morning player. And just as the Dipper faded beneath the pink and orange tinted clouds of dawn, Diane and I quietly raised the sails. Once again, we were on our way.

Precious Cargo

When Diane and I cruised as a couple in the eighties, we learned that most of our pre-cruise fears - like dying, drowning and dying by drowning - were unfounded. After three and a half years of being tossed about by wind and waves, we had to confess that, as scary as it was being Mother Ocean's chew toy, it was more likely we would meet our end on one of America's crowded highways. Still, adding the precious cargo of our children to our seagoing cargo weighed upon us heavily.

Before offshore passages, we would lay out our children's life vests and safety harnesses. We would pack the "abandon ship" bag: sunscreen, water, glucose rations, compass, chart, fishing line, playing cards (Hey, the boredom could kill you!) and rehearse for the umpteenth time the steps we would take if we were to capsize or sink. Who would carry what where? But despite the practiced preparations and the rational arguments we made about the probability of our safety, my wicked imagination would always play out a brief and chilling fiction of screaming children, water and confusion.

One of a dozen passages we eventually made together comes to mind. To prepare for our midnight departure, we sounded the shoals leading away from our anchorage by dinghy. Then we entered all the waypoints (or destination marks) in our GPS, calculated a safe and over the shoulder sunlight landfall, so we would have a good view of any shoals when we arrived at our destination, and drew a course line on our charts over the deep and fathomless ocean. Given all this preparation, we were a bit surprised, not an hour after getting underway, when the depth finder echoed a bottom - a steadily shoaling bottom. Seventy-five feet. Sixty feet. Fifty feet. We luffed, re-checked the chart and our GPS position, squinting into the darkness and straining to hear the rip of waves over sand or coral. But there was nothing.

Complaining to one another and Father Neptune about the impossibility of the depth readings, we inched forward - wretched and slogging in wallowing waves, until the kids, not quite asleep, came on deck and forced us to keep our whining to ourselves. Together we watched the depth sounder - thirty feet, twenty-five, until I thought I would scream. But as suddenly as they had come upon us, the "shallows" disappeared. The depth sounder pinged an infinite bottom.

Was it a mid-ocean, uncharted shallow? A sounder infarct? A great school of fish or a pesky whale beneath our keel? We will never know. Conjectures now are about as useful as our complaints were then. Later during the same night passage, since the kids were already awake, we settled back in the cockpit, girls in our laps, fingers interlaced and arms wrapped around dear chests. We stared up at the stars, where we could just make out the nebula in Orion's belt, and we told stories - ancient Greek and modern contemporaneous stories - about people, their weaknesses and their heroic deeds. And despite the earlier scare, at that moment it was good to be at sea, together.

Kids, though a responsibility and a worry on long passages, can also provide relief. On a long, upcoming passage, Diane and I would tag team for three days of three-hour watches. Tempers would flare. Not only would we lose perspective, we would not be spell able to spell the word. At that critical time, when our acid stomachs and tempers would threaten to boil over, Sawyer would emerge from the cabin. She would hold two lengths of carefully woven yarn. Her presents would be two worry bracelets - colorful strings with knots where we could place each of our worries. When the bracelets break, she would say, our worries would fly away. We would be free. I would waste no time hexing my knots and snagging them on a cotter pin. Bless that child.

Strawberries

Not far off the *Aves*, we began to lift and fall to a slow, heaving swell. Sawyer rolled out of her berth, and despite the Transderm Scop, went straight to the stern rail. But before long, she was "at her desk" for school – an admirable, solid girl.

We were on passage again, and I made my usual ship survey: horizon, sea, sails and compass. Though we were in the famed tradewind belt, there was hardly a breeze. The high white bluffs off the northern end of Bonaire were visible off our bow, but at our slow pace it would take us at least six more hours to get there. I decided to fire up the engines.

With little wind blowing from astern and our motors chugging at full throttle, there was now no relative wind, and we "sailed" in a breathless envelope. Even at 0900 (nine o'clock in the morning) we were feeling the heat, so I considered putting up our shade tarp. But in order to raise the tarp, I would have to drop our mainsail - the only equipment left that identified us as a sailboat. Up to that point, I had always left the mainsail up during passages, just in case the wind came or the engines failed – a belt and suspenders approach to motor sailing. Besides, if I dropped the mainsail, Riley, our budding sailing purist, would notice.

As I pondered my next move, I realized my dilemma was bigger than a question of mere seamanship. The issue was what sort of sailor I really was. After all, *real* sailors would have waited for days or even weeks for a decent wind to blow them to Bonaire. Hearty square-rigged sailors would not have had a choice. In the doldrums of the Horse Latitudes, they threw equine ballast overboard until they were able to move with the light breeze. In our case, I supposed I would have to toss the kids.

But at that moment I realized we were not *real* sailors. In fact, I had known we were not *real* sailors since we had been getting ready to embark on our first cruise in the eighties. I had been at a dock on the Chesapeake installing an outdoor stereo system, when a passing sailor (a purist, no doubt) had remarked: "Got a little motorboater in ya, huh?"

On our passage to Bonaire, I lowered the mainsail. But I wondered where my degenerate sailing tendencies might lead. Would I end up barreling along at twenty knots on a Bertram power yacht and flinging hors d'oeuvre toothpicks on the pitiful little sailboats that wallowed in my wake? The Truth was (and is) that when I sailed, I was always more interested in the "there" than the "getting there." Though the sailing was sometimes fun, we were not weekend sailors out for a picnic. We were a cruising family trying to get somewhere, and we wanted to get there (and off the open ocean, with all of her awesome majesty) as quickly as possible.

Also, we were not hardcore liveaboards. Despite our long stay "roughing it" out on the Aves, we were not the type to eat hard tack, drink tepid rum and pee in a bucket. We were looking forward to Bonaire's first world, civilized delights. We liked the *yin* of the outdoors contrasted with the *yang* of civilized amenities. So when we arrived in Bonaire's *Kralendijk* harbor, we went straight past the line of cruising boats "parallel parked" along the shore and swung into the marina. We squeezed our wide hulk between a fifty-foot Swan and a forty-five foot Bertram, and we quickly hooked into all the conveniences of home. We used the water, power *and* a phone. We called our parents and all of our friends. And before long, our cruising acquaintances from the *Aves* (and eventually nearly every cruiser in the anchorage) made their way to *Manta Raya* to use the phone. Folks from around the world wandered in and out of our cockpit day and night. Our tiny boat began to feel like the Chicago O'Hare airport; and our bill, I think, came to several million dollars. But it was worth it. We got to meet a lot of nice folks, and we ended up getting the quickest introduction to Bonaire's liveaboard scene that any cruising sailor could hope to get. Bonaire, we learned, was a cruiser's paradise.

When we pulled out of the marina, our new friends arranged a perfect mooring for us - not too close to the town dock, where there was much noise and traffic, but between the dock and the marina. This was a coveted mooring, and, had we not extended ourselves to our fellow liveaboards, it would have taken several weeks and several rounds of "musical chairs" to get it. We were moored just ten yards off pleasant, white cottages, where fishermen brought in their catch and where we could stow our bikes for jaunts ashore. We had all of the pleasures of home, and beneath our hull we had a veritable aquarium.

When we opened the hatch on the sole (floor) of *Manta Raya's* main salon, we stood over and stared into crystal clear water teaming with colorful fishes. If I were to clean out an oatmeal pan, turquoise angelfish, yellow striped grunts (yes, they do grunt), silver porgies, rainbow parrotfish, and black and white banded butterflyfish would swirl in the water just beneath our dining table. As the girls stared in amazement, I would dip the pan and scoop up the smaller fish. Unlike anywhere we had been in the Caribbean (except for the furthest out atolls, like those we had just visited), Bonaire's fish were entirely unafraid of humans. In the sixties the Bonairians had decided to protect their entire seashore and off lying waters. They had made their home a land and sea park. Where we were moored, just off Bonaire's largest city and beneath the hulls of dozens of cruising boats, the waters were a pristine paradise.

And the paradise extended inland. I recall one particular evening, sitting at the end of a point and staring out at the coming sunset, when, just as the sun was touching the water, a flock of pink flamingoes flew toward us and landed on one of Bonaire's many salt ponds. The ultraviolet pink birds flapped their great wings, settled themselves and began to stroll across the pond. As the sun sizzled into the sea, they looked as if they were waltzing the Blue Danube.

Bonaire was just the right combination of Nature and first world delights. In the quaint town of *Kralendijk*, we could ride our bikes to anything we needed. The town's Dutch Market was a tasty, first world treasure. We bought fresh produce and eggs and carried warm loaves of French bread under our arms. European delicacies like Havarti cheese with dill, smoked salmon, Dutch beers and chocolates had us blessing the Dutch colonial movement.

During one of our grocery visits, the girls ran up to me breathless and bouncing. They held baskets of a special prize over their heads. American and European tourists attracted by the commotion turned and stared. "Look, Papa! Look!" they shrieked. They were holding bright red, shining strawberries, so startling after our months at sea, that I too felt I was seeing them for the first time.

The first-world patrons of that grocery must have thought I was one hell of a parent. Obviously I had been depriving my girls of simple pleasures. But the truth was something better, and we sampled its sweetness with our meals for a week. We arranged the succulent berries on the sides of our plates and saved them until the end of our meals. When we bit into their tart flesh, the tiny seeds crunched between our teeth and released rapturous sweet and sour bursts of flavor, and we laughed and winked at each other like deranged school kids.

Island Christmas

AT ANCHOR BEFORE CHRISTMAS
(A NAUTICAL VISIT FROM ST. NICHOLAS)
by The Crew of Manta Raya with respects to Clement Clarke Moore

'Twas the night before Christmas, when all through the boat
Not a creature was stirring, not even a roach;
The stockings were lashed to the bulkhead with care,
In hopes that ST. NICHOLAS soon would be there;
The children were nestled all snug in their berths,
Dreaming of angelfish to the pound of the surf;
Mamma in her bikini; I *au naturelle*,
Were snoring our heads off in time with the swell,
When off to leeward there arose such a clatter,
I rolled off the bunk and fell down the ladder.
Up the companionway, I flew like a flash,
Tore off the netting and threw open the hatch.
The moon on the crest of the waves off our bow
Gave the lustre of mid-day to the coral below,
When, what should appear to my eyes all a wonder,
But a red and green surfboard pulled by eight giant flounder,
With a little old skipper, so lively and quick,
I knew in a moment it must be ST. NICK.

More rapid than 'cudas his coursers they came,
And he whistled, and shouted, and called them by name;
"Now, SPLASHER! WAVE DANCER! BEACH PRANCER and
PANCAKE!
On, KEELHAUL! on BILGEBREATH! on, LOWTIDE and
CLAMBAKE!
To the top of the dune! O'er the seawall!
Now swim away! swim away! swim away all!"
As French boats that before the wild hurricane fly,
When their anchors give way and they go banging by,
So up to the bridgedeck the coursers they swam,
No fender or rubrail, torpedoes be damned.
And then, in a twinkling, I felt them on deck
We listed so greatly, I thought we would wreck.
As I drew in my head and was turning around,
Through the deck hatch St. Nicholas came with a bound.
He was dressed all in neoprene, from his head to his foot,
His wet suit was dripping with seaweed and gook;
A bundle of toys he had flung on his back,
And he looked like a merman who'd had a few snacks.
His nose like a port light! His eyes -- like stars twinkled!
His dimples like blow holes with skin that was wrinkled!
His droll little mouth he wiped with his hand,
The wet beard on his chin was covered with sand;
The end of a snorkel he held tight in his teeth,
And the bubbles encircled his head like a wreath;
He had a broad beam, a prodigious belly,
That shook, when he laughed like a great fish of jelly.
He was chubby and plump, a right jolly old puffer
And I laughed when I saw the cut of the luffer;
A wink of his eye and a twist of his head,
Soon gave me to know I had nothing to dread;
He spoke not a word, but went straight to his work,
And provisioned the stockings; then turned with a jerk.
Standing on the transom by the light of the cove
He did a full gainer and in the water he dove;
He swam to his surfboard, his flounders hove in sight,
And away they all swam like dolphins in the night.
But I heard him exclaim, ere he surfed out of sight,
"HAPPY CHRISTMAS TO ALL, AND TO ALL A
GOOD-NIGHT."

There were many simple pleasures on Bonaire, like our Christmas tree. We made the thing out of a broomstick with faux evergreen boughs we fashioned from wire and strips of green construction paper. We decorated the tree with handmade clay ornaments and fishing lures. And then we bought colored lights from the hardware store, and strung them over the tree and about the cockpit. Oh, what a sight! The Spirit of Christmas was upon us. When we had our mail forwarded from the United States (thanks mom and dad), we placed the Christmas presents beneath our little tree and turned to the letters – months of messages from dear friends. We held the letters lovingly and opened them one-at-a-time. We read them aloud, repeatedly.

I am tempted to go into a long sermon about the value of these simple pleasures, but I will keep it brief. (Ahem.) On the scale of satisfaction, the simple pleasures on our boat – little treasures like fresh fruit, colored pencils and even paper towels - outstripped all of the excesses of our 21st century, commodity crazed culture. We learned to appreciate the basic blessings. Consequently, I believe my girls have a perspective I never had at their age. I know they are enticed by malls, mega movie theaters and burger joints. But I am hoping that behind all of this hype, their appreciation for the simple pleasures has kept them grounded. Today, even though we are back on terra firma, I still find myself amazed by the hot water that comes out of the shower with a mere twist of the knob. And when strawberries are in season, we cannot help but think of Bonaire. We still smile and wink as we eat the little prizes, one at a time.

Small Village

Maybe you have read It Takes a Village by Jane Cowen-Fletcher. Ms. Cowen-Fletcher served in the Peace Corps in Benin, West Africa, and in her book she retells a Benin proverb, "It takes a village to raise a child." Her book is a children's book, and like many children's books, it carries more weight per page than heftier adult tomes. In her story, a mother goes to market with her daughter and son. She tells her daughter to watch over and take care of her little brother Kokou. But Kokou gets lost. In a panic, the sister rushes through the market searching, but there are many caring eyes on Kokou. Adults throughout the market take care of the boy until his sister finds him. Though those of us from big cities might find the story farfetched, there is something dear and hopeful about the compassionate prospect and possibility that a small village offers.

On Bonaire, in the little town of *Kralendijk* in a tiny doctor's office, Diane watched a little island in action. Around fifty islanders were crowded into the waiting room, and the place was crawling with children. As she had found elsewhere on the island, everyone knew everyone. In the doctor's waiting room, folks were visiting with their friends. And while they chatted, their kids, for the most part, were running amuck. But as Diane watched, she noticed that the adults, equipped with their special parental tools of peripheral vision and adult radar, were keeping tabs on not only their own but also each other's children.

A toy car zooming across the floor would run between someone's legs, and, smiling, that someone would look up and send the car directly back to the child who had lost it. If a child fell and cried out, the nearest adult would bend over, pick him up, and then cluck, coo and caress the child's head until he was once again smiling and ready to play. An affectionate pat on the bottom would send the child on his way.

At the crowded doctor's office, Diane got excellent care – blood tests and an effective formulation for seasickness not sold in the United States. She paid surprisingly little for her lab tests, medicine and visit; and she was surprisingly pleased with the socialized medical system. But the healthiest part of Bonaire was the attitude that the small, caring place engendered. And part of this attitude may have come from the way Bonaire ignored the "real" world.

Airport CNN

On December 18th, 1998, one week before Christmas, I grabbed a flashlight and motored across *Kralendijk* Harbor toward the airport. I was on my way to pick up friends from Italy, and as I tied off the dinghy and walked along the white, clamshell road toward the airport, I steeled myself, for after so many months on a little boat, I was preparing for the press of humanity. But at the open-air terminal, less than forty folks lolled about, drinking beer, eating snacks and watching the daily news on the overhead television screens. I settled in and waited for my friends, and the television screens, such novelties after six months on a boat, grabbed my attention. They were tuned to CNN.

The image was an odd, pale green, and I was trying to make out just what it was I was watching, when a bright flash and a caption appeared. It read: "Third Day of Bombing in Iraq." Before I could digest that we were once again at war in the Middle East, the television image changed. It was a live debate in the U.S. Congress. What were the senators talking about? President Clinton? They wanted to impeach him?

I got up, walked over to the gift shop and searched through the racks for a paper in English. The gift shop attendant, a smiling lady, was chewing gum and running her fingers over the colorful beads in her hair.

"The United States is bombing Iraq and thinking about impeaching President Clinton?" I asked.

"Uh Huh," said the girl, still smiling and playing with her hair.

"Why?"

The lady's fingers stopped, and her brow furrowed. She shrugged her shoulders. "I don't know."

And there you have it: The real world concerns of Bonairians.

That same week as Christmas neared, we were to watch the play of politics and real world concerns again – this time with our own United States Coast Guard.

Coast Guard

In Beaufort, NC in 1987 a Norther (a large, cold front storm) had whipped itself into a blow of wet and grey. Diane and I were grimly making our way through the serpentine twist of the Intercoastal Waterway. In the mist we strained to see the outlines of large tugs before they burst from the gloom and skidded wide around the turns. They pushed small mountains of ore before them in what I saw as marginally controlled landslides.

We were a bit tense.

Accordingly, when we finally found a pullout and anchorage, a small bay dotted with lucky boats that were already secured and bobbing comfortably in the storm, we focused not on the three-dimensional conundrum of tide, current and water depths, but on the surface world before us, a watery parking lot filled with boats. In short order, we rode straight up on a submerged, uncharted mound of mud and came to a sickeningly dead stop.

Diane, the quicker to assess and act in such disasters, referred to the tide table and found that we were facing an eight foot ebb tide, i.e., we would soon be sitting six feet in the air - foolish kings of the mud hill. Fellow boaters, quick to rally and help out in maritime emergencies, radioed us with advice or dinghied over in the drizzle to comment on our mishap. Then, in the grey drizzle, as the water began to pull away from our hull, the Coast Guard showed up.

I was on the bow wiping the rain off my brow and considering using a kedge anchor to pull us off the emerging mound of gray slime (a solution about as likely as ripping up a great oak with a dog leash), when I heard one of the concerned boaters hail the Coast Guard by radio. He directed the sentinels of our shores, our US patron saints of rescue, toward our dilemma. And in response, a youthful voice on the Coast Guard vessel acknowledged he had seen us. As he spoke, the Coast Guard vessel advanced toward us. Our spirits rose; the cavalry was on the way. But when the helpful boater asked whether the Coast Guard intended to pull us off our emerging predicament, the official voice politely declined. "Sorry, we can't do that."

In all fairness to the United States Coast Guard, this was 1987, just a few years after several bereaved fishermen's families had sued the government for broadcasting a marine weather forecast which, the families claimed, had encouraged their fishing fathers and sons to venture out into a storm. The fishermen had capsized and drowned. At the weather station, prosecuting, settlement-sniffing attorneys had discovered an anemometer out of calibration - proof of the government's negligence, and the families were awarded $15M. Consequently the Coast Guard was taking a fresh and wary look at its civil service roles. Weathermen watered down their forecasts into generic statements that sounded as if they had been issued by political candidates. Yes, a storm might be approaching. It might arrive in a day or two. How big would it be? It could be anywhere from mild to sort of big, to really scary. Another change: the Coast Guard could no longer tell lost vessels their positions, because the Coast Guard did not want to be liable for misinformation. Hence, "savvy" boaters who found themselves in sight of a Coast Guard ship no longer asked the question "Where am I?" Instead, they asked, "Where are you?" But in our predicament, the young Coastie explained, there would be no fancy finagling. He would be happy to call for a towboat, but he could not get involved in our problem.

Before Diane, who was the acting radio officer, could respond, the helpful boater came back on the radio with a more heartfelt plaint. "Aw, c'mon!" he said, "Those poor bastards will be high, dry and on their sides before a towboat can get here!"

There was a pause. The radio was silent. We imagined a discussion on the Coast Guard boat. Perhaps we, or I should say, the insistently helpful boater had made a small chink in the boilerplate armor of the United States Coast Guard. But when the radioed response came, it was curt and official: "Sorry, we can only intervene in situations of life and death."

Diane closed her eyes, pursed her lips and shook her head. Even the rabidly helpful boater seemed flummoxed and was silent. The radio merely crackled and hissed. The rain fell, and the water continued to recede from the growing hill beneath our hull. But I had an idea, and I grabbed the mike from Diane.

"Coast Guard vessel, this is the captain of the grounded vessel."

"Go ahead, captain."

" We *are* facing a life and death situation. If you don't get me off this shoal, my wife is going to kill me."

There was another silence, more rain and then a final answer from the Coast Guard. "Captain, prepare to receive our line.

* * *

In Bonaire, eleven years later and about 1,200 nautical miles to the south, we again met with the Coast Guard. But this time our family was snorkeling and splashing in the warm water off a white sand beach, and we sat waist deep in the water and stared for a long time before we figured out what we were seeing.

"Is it a big, white tanker?" asked Diane.

"No," I said, "look at the huge cranes (these turned out to be guns). It must be a huge, floating, fish processing plant."

When the ship drew close enough for us to make out its red stripe, we were at once awed, proud and embarrassed. Here in the laid back Dutch Caribbean, a great United States ship, a behemoth of first world power had appeared. But for us it was also a geopolitically displaced oddity that seemed to boast: "Behold! Here too the United States rules the seas!"

Our reaction was nothing compared to the rising emotions of the cruisers back in town. The cruisers hailed from countries throughout Europe and Latin America, but they shared a common goal: to strike out from their own countries and their own politics to be sailors of the world. The Coast Guard ship, when it arrived in the harbor, consumed *Kralendijk's* pier. It dwarfed the cruise boats, and its great guns hung over and pointed directly at the tiny cruising fleet. Intentionally or not, the great ship seemed to say, "Hands up, you are all under arrest."

That evening we were invited to dinner on a boat owned by a French family, a delightful family of four who were willing to navigate the treacherous waters of the English language in order to nurture a growing friendship between our children. We dinghied over to their steel-hulled boat and tied off just under the stenciled name on their transom: "Froggie." The family did not suffer from a lack of humor or an excess of ethnocentric conceit.

The tall, athletic father flashed us a smile and hauled us aboard with his handshake. The children disappeared below to explore cherished treasures – the toys that had survived the tough selection process from a land-based home on another continent. We adults settled into the cockpit with some paté, some camembert cheese and some fried onion sticks - the sorts of hors d'oeurves that the French serve so readily, while we culinary clunks from the States pour out salted peanuts.

As we chatted, it was impossible to avoid the topic of the Coast Guard ship; in gleaming red and white, the spectacle hung over us like a giant boulder. And the boulder had been dropped into the family living room, as it were, so that it was difficult to converse around it. After years of cruising through Europe and the Caribbean, the French couple did not lack an international political perspective. It was the smiling wife who finally scrunched up her brow and asked us what the "frightful ship" was doing there.

We did not know.

Our hosts' quizzical frowns told us that they were surprised we were not informed about our country's foreign policy in the Caribbean and that our blithe ignorance did not reassure them. In fact, their concern became more animated. The father's palms exploded skyward. "Look," he said, "it is not as if *we* feel threatened, but can you imagine how it is to be us here, with our children, on our boat? She is our home, no? We think, how do you say, of a Hollywood cowboy. And we think to ourselves, "What if this Hollywood cowboy comes home to his big ship, and he has had too much to drink of beer? He carries a box of the Heineken, and he is stumbling around the boat in the dark trying to find the *interrupteur*... the switch, for the light, only he flips the wrong switch, and, *Boom!*, he has blown a hole through our homes!"

We laughed, sort of. But the French father had raised a question of etiquette and manners - a practical question of national ethics made more real by the solidity of a huge, armed ship. I made up my mind to pay the Coast Guard a visit on the following day.

But in the light of day, walking up to the great ship with my daughters, I wondered just how a US citizen might get audience on a military ship. Perhaps, I thought, we should knock on the hull and yell, "Hey up there! It's me, Joe Taxpayer! I've got a few things I need to get straight with you!" But my visit was made surprisingly easy. The captain of the ship, a Mr. Kowalski, had already opened his doors to the public. It seemed our military, perhaps sensing its dual roles as pugilists and diplomats, was holding an open house. The "neighbors" had been invited aboard for a visit - a cozy little chat on the steel deck of a radar controlled gun ship. My girls and I climbed the long gangway until we were high over the blue Caribbean. We were greeted by junior officers who led us on a tour of the inflatable chase boats, the bridge deck control room and the gunnery room, where I noticed, thank goodness, there were no controls that looked even remotely like light switches.

Back on deck, we met two polite pilots from the Midwest - young men who took to my girls like uncles, perhaps because they were missing their own children back home in Ohio. Riley climbed into one of the helicopters and sat beside one of the pilots. She tried on his huge helmet, and it covered her eyes, nearly falling to her chin. Sawyer stood back and held my hand. The ship had an intimidating scale for anyone used to floating about on a boat the size of a bread truck, and Sawyer was awed by the commotion of so many people. Then Captain Kowalski appeared.

He came on deck in dress whites - a thin, smiling young man with bright eyes already surrounded with creases of responsibility. I introduced myself. We talked pleasantries, hometowns and families. He asked me why we had decided to live on a boat, and I told him that the parking lots back home had gotten too crowded. He laughed and seemed sympathetic, so I warmed up to my real question. "Captain Kowalski," I asked, "Do you mind telling me what you're doing here?"

The captain paused, blinked and considered me anew, but he answered. "For the most part, drug interdiction. But we're also here to serve as a rescue ship."

I nodded, commended him and backed up by explaining the concerns of the international cruising fleet anchored just below his guns. The captain listened and nodded his head. And I wondered out loud if it were not one of the captain's jobs to simply "display a presence." After all, Venezuela, a member of OPEC that held one of the largest reserves of oil on the world, had just elected a radical, left wing president – a president rumored to be a sympathizer with and confidant of Fidel Castro. Was Captain Kowalski there to show force?

The captain appeared surprised by my question. He said he vaguely recalled reading about a Venezuelan election, but his orders on this particular tour had nothing to do with "showing force." And as far as the cruising fleet was concerned, during his trip to Bonaire he had rescued a German cruising family. In rough seas off Colombia the family's diesel engine had quit, and they had taken on water. Captain Kowalski had the family brought aboard, where he had given them a warm meal. He sent his mechanics to repair their engine. In this regard, the captain was helping distressed boaters from around the world. He did, however, also detain foreign vessels, board them and search for drugs. These were his orders. The United States had an agreement with most nations allowing such drug interdiction, and if the boats owners refused to be boarded (as many of my foreign cruising friends claimed they would), a call to their embassy generally set things straight. In the end, said Captain Kowalski, the Coast Guard always got its way.

Bonaire versus Aruba

In a few days, Captain Kowalski swung the bow of his great American ship out to sea. He un-holstered his guns and continued on whatever mission his nation, my nation, had sent him. Captain Kowalski's parking space was needed by another grand ship, a cruise ship of the Dutch America Line, the *Masdaam*.

There had been quite a buildup for the *Masdaam's* visit. Her arrival had been arranged and excitedly anticipated by Bonaire's tourist board and Chamber of Commerce. Unlike the popular Saints and sister Dutch Islands Curacao and Aruba, Bonaire had never been a major cruise ship destination; and the *Masdaam* was a major cruise ship - 1,200 passengers, two swimming pools, workout gym, running deck and movie theater. She was a premier ship and cruising extravaganza, and in anticipation of her arrival, flyers had been sent around, meetings had been held and gushing articles had appeared in the newspaper. The quiet town of *Kralendijk*, it appeared, was about to grow up and enter the tourist age.

Up to this point Bonaire had plied the tourist trade, but it had been a particular subset of the trade defined by Bonaire's unique national park. All of the seashore and surrounding waters were protected, and this sort of tourist bounty, when most Caribbean beaches were overshadowed by high-rise hotels and most coral reefs were fished clean or killed, was fairly unique within the Caribbean. Bonaire's islanders were proud of their unique bounty. The tourists - divers, windsurfers, hikers and beach bums - tended to be a peaceable lot who fit the island's laid-back lifestyle. And the visitors and the islanders appeared to be enjoying a tolerable if not symbiotic relationship. But now, drawn to the same bounty and yet propelled by the Tourist Board's 21st Century vision, a new kid of visitor would be disembarking from a cruise ship. The *Masdaam* was about to disgorge a tourist stampede – visitors with travelers' checks in their shopping bags instead of coins in their swim trunks.

On the scheduled date, a Sunday, the great hull of the *Masdaam*, even larger than the Coast Guard ship, appeared at the dock. Once again the cruising fleet was dwarfed by the jut of a great, steel bow - this time, in contrast to Coast Guard's white, the *Masdaam* was painted black, which some of the cruisers described as "Darth Vader black." Spirits sank. This, the cruisers groused, was the beginning of the end. We could forget wandering by the local cafe to read the daily rag over a beignet and coffee, while dogs stopped to lick themselves in the dusty street and the only traffic noise was the occasional shriek of kids on bicycles. *Kralendijk* would be swamped with microbuses ferrying tourists to Indian ruins and snorkeling beaches. The town would be filled with handbag toting, sunburned yahoos frantically shopping for tropical doodads, lowbrow trophies that would collect dust back home, talismans against a grey existence in snowy suburbs. The beaches would become packed with Jimmy Buffet wannabees covered in oil. Surely the fish would also be disgusted. Bonaire, like all the St. *Whatevers* before it, would become a lost paradise. For us cruisers, it looked like it was time to pull up anchor and move on in search of the next hidden paradise - further away, harder to reach, and, as yet, unmolested by cruise ships.

As much as I did not want to, I felt compelled to go ashore and see what 1,200 tourists would do to a two-block town. I was drawn to the spectacle like a bystander at a traffic accident. But imagine my surprise when I saw not hundreds of little old ladies dragging shopping bags from store to store like frenetic bees collecting pollen, but a handful of grey-haired folks looking lost and dispirited, gazing forlornly at shop doors, which all displayed the same sign: –CLOSED.– Not one shop, not even the café, was open. It was, after all, Sunday, the day of rest for the islanders of Bonaire. On this one day the island had always been, and appeared determined to remain, at peace. Most of the cruise boat shoppers had already become discouraged and returned to the ship for their champagne fountains and liver pate swan sculptures. The Tourist Board was furious. But their scorching articles in the newspaper that week were ignored. The islanders had voted with their slippers and their hammocks. There would be no tourist evolution on that particular Sunday nor the next Sundays to come. For the present, Bonaire was safe.

* * *

We were sad to sail away from Bonaire. The customs officer wished us a safe trip, and he invited us to join him for dinner at his home whenever we returned. We thought of the friends we had made, the beautiful sunset climbs over desert hills, the flamingos in fluorescent formation and the tasty European foods. But mostly we thought of the attitude and peace of the place. It was an easy paradise. But the catch in our throats could not hold us at anchor. We were bound for Aruba.

Aruba was also a Dutch island. Its size and population were similar to Bonaire's. Both islands spoke Papiamento - a spin of Dutch, Spanish, English and Antillean. Everything about the two islands was similar except for one thing - and this was the result of choices. Like choosing whether or not to welcome Sunday cruise ships, the Aruba islanders had made choices that had changed everything along the way.

We saw the first differences from sea. While Bonaire's welcoming landmarks had been bluffs, green hills and windmills, Aruba's landmarks were high-rise hotels and all of the cruise ships that had bypassed Bonaire. We docked under one of these towering marvels - a discount version of the *Masdaam* - with besotted passengers who stumbled up the gangplank after having lost several rounds with fruity rum drinks. The customs agents who arrived to clear us in were just as friendly as the Bonairian officials, but they took hours to arrive and were harried, of course, after clearing out all the drunken cruise ship passengers.

In the early 1900's, another difference, another choice, had shaped Aruba - an oil refinery. The Dutch, always skilled at getting between a valued commodity and its customer, had arranged to transport crude oil from the mainland, distill and then carry it on to Europe and the United States. This was a good, tight business until WWII interrupted the scheme. German submarines watched the tankers as they were filled with oil then torpedoed them as they left port. Overnight they turned the Dutch enterprise into flame and billowing black smoke on the water.

The islanders tell a story about those days, which is too incredible and yet too human to not be true. The island was under blackout rules; all streetlights, shops, and, of course, the movie marquee were dark and lifeless. But as a boost to island moral, movies still showed at the theatre. Payment was on the honor system, and patrons deposited their money in a cigar box outside the theatre. One morning when the movie house owner went to collect the previous night's receipts, he was surprised to find odd coins. They were German Marks. Apparently the German U-boat sailors had also needed a break, so they had taken shore leave with a night at the movies.

After the war, the refinery closed down. The blackened chimneys stopped belching smoke, and the stench of rude gases no longer wafted over the island. But along with the smoke and the smell, jobs also disappeared. The islanders, who had grown accustomed to an easy income, wondered what to do. Then someone, like the Tourist Board on Bonaire, pointed to the monies being made by other Caribbean islands. Aruba would build a cruise ship port and eventually a big jet runway. The hotels sprang up along with the casinos.

In a scream of great whistles and a shower of confetti, the first cruise ships arrived. Big jets swooped into the airport and deposited piles of tourists on the tarmac, before flying off to devour and return with yet more fodder. Hotels sprouted along the shore until the skyline mimicked Miami Beach. But few Arubans worked in these hotels. They found the pay low and the tourists intolerable. So staff was brought in from Venezuela, Colombia and from the far away but always tolerant and friendly Philippine Islands. The casinos brought in big money, but to the surprise of many (though perhaps not all), they also brought in drug money. The casinos thrived as laundromats for the mainland drug cartels; and particular characters, characters with scary attitudes, added themselves to the new stew of Aruban personalities.

Riding with an Aruban taxicab driver, I asked about all of these changes, the new Aruba, and how he liked it.

"Oh!" began the driver with enthusiasm, "you just look about you. We got nice houses, lots of shops. Anything you want to find, you find it here." Then, casting his head about as if in search of a particular example, he pointed suddenly (and simultaneously spun his steering wheel to miss a pickup loaded with rebar and to swerve into a space just in front of a honking minibus – all vehicles sounding their horns viscously in tinny Japanese indignation) and said, "Look, we got the Pizza Hut!"

"Yep," I said, "nice... Have you ever been to Bonaire?"

"Sure, I got relatives there. Now my sister just gone to Bonaire."

"Oh yeah? How come?"

"Well," and here the man hesitated, "She has a 16 yr old boy, my nephew Kalib, and she want that boy to settle down some."

I waited.

"He been getting in trouble with the wrong kids, you know some drug stuff. She lookin' for a change."

Our girls liked Aruba. But Diane and I felt uncomfortable there. There was a sort of suffocation, a low level of panic, about the place. The wind never stopped blowing from the moment we arrived. And though we tried to shield ourselves in the mangrove lagoons on the east end of the island, Aruban drug enforcement police arrived in full U.S. donated combat regalia - snub machine guns, bullet proof black vests and lexan visored helmets - to tell us we would have to move on. Our swamp was under surveillance as a drug drop.

So we sailed around to the west end of the island and pulled up in front of a high-rise hotel that provided at least a partial windbreak. We were in a bay filled with jet skis, paraglide jet boats and screaming kids on giant water weenies. Every day, as the wind rose to its usual trade wind shriek, we found ourselves in the midst of a galloping fleet of windsurfers - some as skilled as jet fighter pilots, tearing by our transom, others just beginners and wrestling their wobbly crafts, as if they were strangling a goose. These novices fell often, sometimes tangling themselves in our anchor line.

The girls liked Aruba because it offered, on the surface, what no place we had yet visited offered - a modern sensual extravaganza, a tropical Disneyland for adults and children. At the hotels they slid down the water slides and chased the iguanas that lounged poolside with the tourists. They ate at restaurants (where they did not have to do dishes), and they walked the beach, where they could stop and run freshwater footbaths. As opposed to the metered life onboard our boat, they reveled in the guilt free, flush of tourist mecca water.

We made a few friends on Bonaire. Perhaps it was our fault that we never had that pleasure on Aruba. But it was a bit difficult to get folks' attention on Aruba. Bonaire's islanders had walked, ridden bikes and laughed or waved as we passed them on sandy roads. Aruba's islanders were on the move, eyes forward and intent behind the wheels of their cars. Their faces wore the first world, hypnotic trance of busy people in a busy place. Though, like the islanders of Bonaire, they lived in the lassitude of the tropics, we could not help but feel that there was a certain panic and bewilderment hanging over their lives. It seemed to play in the strained look of their eyes, as if they were struggling to harness a runaway thought or might suddenly blurt out, "Where am I?"

At our mooring back on Bonaire, we once watched a sailboat race, though if it were truly to be called a race, it lacked some of a race's defining sense of tension and competition. The locals – fathers, sons, daughters and friends - crewed on everything from small Sunfish sailboats to open, three-man sloops. There was no gun to mark the start of the race and no handicapping to sort out the boat classes. There were only folks wearing sensible, floppy sun hats in moderately seaworthy sailboats, which they steered somewhat in the same direction - east into the rising sun. Instead of the ratcheting spin of winches and shout of sharp orders, we heard only the splash of hull against waves and the occasional call of laughter between boats. Buckets of bilge water were thrown back and forth between contestants to cool down any sense of keen competition. Sometimes the racers themselves were not visible, only parts of them - a foot sticking up lazily with a toe placed on a tiller, the torso hidden in the swaying shade of a flapping sail. Together the boats disappeared around the point, but they returned over the course of hours, one at a time, until the last boat straggled in after dark. The captain, a bottle of rum having found its way into his hold, was singing a beautiful song, a song about the sea and romance.

Keeping Ourselves Entertained

When work is over, when the phone stops ringing, when there are no friends calling us to play - when there are no chores, no yard work or dripping faucets to fix - when there are no movies, televisions, plays, dancing girls or cartoons to divert our minds, we are left with a particular silence - a silence that tells us more about ourselves than any busywork ever will. "Trial by fire" is also supposed to tell us much about our character; and Mother Ocean certainly offers big wind, big wave and hairy-chested challenges. But anyone, wooly-chested or baby bottom smooth, can test his or her mettle in a raging storm where the impetus to act is clear and directed. It is when absolutely nothing is happening that true mettle is tested. When we look about us and realize that we are left with only ourselves, this is the real challenge - the empty time only we can fill. Our true character comes out not only when the poop hits the fan but when there is not a breath of wind, and the poop simply lies there on the floor waiting to see what we are going to do about it.

The "empty time" asks questions: "Can you juggle? Sing? Dance? Play the guitar? Can you recite a poem, do a card trick?" The proverbial question: "If you found yourself shipwrecked on a deserted island..." is not a far-fetched question when cruisers find themselves in a remote anchorage. Think of the Swiss family Robinson. Just how did they do it?

The issue may not be our talents (or the lack thereof), but our discomfort with the "empty time" itself. We say we need a vacation, but what would we do if our "vacation" lasted for months, a year, two years? From whence would come our entertainment, our joy of life, our feeling of accomplishment and self-worth?

Understandably cruisers may at first feel anxiety when faced with "empty time." They might find themselves missing something. Maybe they have been planning their getaway and working on their boat for years: the charting, boat chores and provisioning becoming an occupation in themselves. But one day at sea, after months away from the *real* world, they will wake one morning and realize that their "to do" list is finished. But the demanding and nagging little voice that accompanied the "to do" list and pushed them on from task to task may not be finished. It might ask, "What next?" And they will find themselves in an empty and still place, an unfamiliar and eerily quiet place, especially if they have pinned some sense of self to their "to do" list. Honestly, the silence might be a bit terrifying.

Yet the silence offers opportunity. Cruisers of character will reach into themselves and find exactly what it is they need to do. They will, in fact, finally turn toward the things they should have been doing all along. They might end up painting. They might write an honest book. Heck, they might even develop the unifying theory of Physics or cure cancer. They might even learn how to live with and enjoy their families. When these cruisers reach into their character looking for a spark of inspiration, they might not only find the spark (for it is always there), but they might also note how they found it; and then the path to it will be better lit and easier to find the next time around. And that is the gift of the silent time.

After days in a remote anchorage, our family needed some entertainment. We needed a new ray of sunshine; we needed to laugh or cry. And though it was not easy for us to rise out of the lethargy of a languid anchorage in the lower latitudes, we could sometimes rally. We would brush off our characters, shine their little scuffed shoes and set them on stage. And every once in a while, the acts we conjured up were more than mere entertainment. They were Magic.

At one end of the entertainment spectrum was "Talent Nights." Occasionally Diane and I would announce we were staging a talent night - the pronouncement generally met with groans, or if guests were aboard, an anxious look and a panicky grasp at excuses ("I can't sing or anything. Really!.. Gosh, I'll just watch if you don't mind... Wow! Will you look at the time! Gotta be going…"). But we insisted, everyone had to participate in Talent Night. The show, we said, must go on.

The idea was that on talent nights everyone would come prepared to present his or her special talents. Presentations could be as simple as recitations from a current book or as complicated as making a dollar bill float in mid-air (no strings attached). Our family and our guests recited poetry and prose from memory, or better yet, read poetry they had written. We performed plays, complete with costumes and sound effects. (It took our girls two days to act out all of the scenes from Mozart's *Magic Flute*.) And when my brother visited, he told his favorite jokes, though we had to limit the number. There were others who suddenly recalled Mark Twain quotes or lines from Lewis Carol's *The Jabberwocky*. At Christmas, the girls picked up their musical instruments, a recorder and a xylophone, and played *Silent Night* along with mom and dad, who brandished guitar and harmonica.

To further tap talents and as an adjunct to our boat schooling, we were constantly in the midst of craft projects. The girls made dolls and sock puppets complete with curly hair and handmade skirts and blouses. However, as the boat's only male crewmember, I drew the line at sewing. It took every ounce of empathy I had to say, " Oh…Honey, that embroidery stitch is… really tiny and straight." But I enjoyed painting shells with the girls and sketching or water coloring scenes on shore. To this day I am proudest of the "Gatorade Diorama" we made together. We took a giant, commercial can of Gatorade and cut out tiny fish from crepe paper and an octopus from aluminum foil. We pasted in seaweed and coral; and with dental floss, we hung paper sharks and dolphins. Using a blue filter for a skylight and peering into the diorama through a view port, we went on our own private dives into an underwater garden. Riley would stare into the thing for hours. It was better than T.V.

And how about tattoos? No, we didn't put the girls under electric needle ("Here, honey, let's put your grandma's name in that heart; it'll make her so proud!"). Visiting friends brought us henna paste, the natural dye used by East Indians, and we stayed up all night painting marvelous designs on our hands, legs and feet: snakes, dragons, roses, fantastic mosaic patterns and even a scrimshaw whale spouting water.

Of course our children, like all children, cooked up their own entertainment using "the kitchen of the mind." I worried about how bored they might be stuck on a boat with (yawn) adults, but their imaginations took them far away whenever and to wherever they wanted to go. *Manta Raya's* boom was a giant pony, which could, of course, fly. Out on the trampoline, waving flashlights at the stars, they made up fantastic stories about faeries and ships that sailed through the air. The wide-open ocean was a big canvas that evoked imaginative paintings.

And when the boat became confining, there were always excursions. Anchored off Puerto La Cruz, I remember Sawyer fixing me with a serious look and saying, "Papa, it's time to meet somebody." And we did. We dinghied around the anchorage and found a nice husband and wife on a nearby catamaran. Sawyer got to eat chocolate chip cookies with a distinguished parrot, and I got to hear the life story of an old, yet newlywed couple who had "thrown it all away" to explore the world. I think Sawyer knew the visit would do both of us good, and bless her, she was right.

Of course, some of our excursions, particularly shore excursions, were a bit hairy; and the girls grew leery of my scouting trips ashore. (Papa, they said, tended to get the family in over its head.) But heck, tropical forests are thick with foliage, and it is easy to get lost. And when you are mucking about trying to find your way, it is highly likely that anyone could encounter a six-foot tree snake dangling from a branch. Still, we had some fun: we explored colonial forts, boated across volcanic lakes and collected Key limes in abandoned groves. On the Windward Island of Baliceaux, where Diane and I made up a treasure map on burnt-edged, crinkly paper and placed an "X" marks the spot just ten paces off a Poinciana tree, the girls found "real" Doubloons (Antillean dollars), plastic pearls and Juicy Fruit gum. Even though marauding pirates (wild goats) got to the gum before we could, the treasure hunt was a success.

Yet for thrills, I believe our wildest excursion was the airport runway off Aruba. The airport hosts big intercontinental jets, and the airstrip is short, so the planes have to come in low and touch down at the very start of the runway, which happens to be at the water's edge. I am sure the airport excursion we made was forbidden. In the United States, we probably would have been booked and questioned by Child Services. But we were in the laid back Caribbean, so we dinghied over to the runway's edge and anchored just offshore between two rows of landing beacons. And we waited.

The great, silver planes veered in from the south, dropped and aimed directly at us. The girls screamed. We covered our ears. We could see the pilots in the cockpit just before the giant underbellies of their jets blotted out the sky. We did not hear but felt the big jet engines' deep-throated roar in our chests. I watched the girls, their eyes wide and their blonde hair standing straight up, as the huge planes passing over their heads, sucking up everything including a spray of water that rose around our dinghy. Momma did not accompany us on our airport excursions. The Aruba runway was a special "Papa entertainment."

A Sea Yarn

very sailor is scared of the sea. Every seaman prays that he
will skinny through a passage and not dally Out There so
long that he gets caught in the natural forces that rule our
planet. And yet, every sailor loves to tell a salty dog, hairy-chested
sea tale. And so, dear Reader, I would like to tell a scary tale which
features my first mate, Diane - a tale of cool headed strength, and
a story about surviving the crush of wind and waves. But beware:
sailors who spin salty dog tales want their audiences to stop, inhale
deeply and listen in wide-eyed anticipation to every horrible, water
soaked detail. "Brave, they were. And, by God, they lived. They spit
in the Old Man's eye, they did..."

Listen to this quote, the response new cadets at the U.S. Naval
Academy in Annapolis were instructed to memorize and recite to
upperclassmen, whenever they were asked how long they had been
sailing:

> All me bloomin' life, sir. Me mother was a mermaid and me
> natural father was King Neptune. I was born on the crest of a
> breaking wave, and rocked in the cradle of the deep. Seaweed and
> barnacles be me clothes. Every tooth in me head is a marlinspike.
> Every hair on me head is Italian hemp. Every bone in me body is
> a spar, and when I spits, I spits Stockholm tar.
> I'm hard I is; I am; I are.

But life at sea is not really like that. After almost four years and thousands of miles of ocean passages, we have had only two or three scary moments, and the first took place on our twenty-two foot daysailor on landlocked Lake Powell - not a mile from the parking lot and a marina store stacked with cheerful racks of M & M's. I have much scarier stories about American highways. Haven't we all?

The truth is that sailing is mostly boring, at least the passages from place to place are. Seas are generally flat and calm. Winds rarely blast and, just as when bicycling, they blow not from behind to ease our way, but generally in our faces, whether we are coming or going. And on long, yawning, overnight passages, the monotony is made yet duller by the slow rocking of the waves and the low hum of the diesel, which often puts us to sleep.

But that is not the dash and spray we want to read about, is it? We want some rough seafaring tales, by God, by gum. So here we go ... in the second person, "you" are about to sail through a storm:

Belize Reef Entry - First Voyage 1988

Each time a wave sweeps under you, you free-fell 10 feet. Your stomach swings up beneath your chin, and you death-grip the slippery rail, as your feet go weightless and leave the deck. You are pretending to look for coral heads as you ride the bow of a 37-foot sailboat. The coral heads threaten to crush you as you enter the narrow passage through the Belize Reef. As you look back and smile weakly at your wife riding six feet over your head at the helm, you realize you are stuck here, holding on for your life, unable to make your way back to her and the safety of the cockpit. Through the salt spray blur of your sunglasses you see the dark wall of clouds rushing up astern. A black, angry cloud rolls before a gray line of rain. You are racing a squall - a personified fist of Nature - to see which of you will clear the reef first. Given the slow crawl of your boat through the swell and the cold rush of air sliding down your back, you put your money on the squall.

How did this happen? How did you get here? Damn it, you are from Arizona! There aren't any sailors in Arizona. You and your wife left your jobs because you needed a change. You wanted to travel. There were all of those Caribbean islands, white sand beaches; and you thought you could see them in your own sweet time. You would dodge the tourists and chill out in secluded coves of paradise, just you, your wife, Jimmy Buffet, a fresh coconut, and the smell of lobster steaming in Cajun spices. You figured a big sailboat was just a Winnebago that floated, right?

But now you have arrived at this godforsaken reef entrance after 84 hours - three days and 12 hours - of brain dehydrating monotony. Working in three-hour shifts, you repeated a dreamlike pattern of steer, eat and sleep - steer, eat and sleep... Soon the sense of passing time was lost. To escape the tropical sun you wedged yourself in the cabin below deck and tried to sleep while a fan blew across your sweat-soaked body. When it was time to adjust sails, you waddled forward on deck, uncertain of your brain's ability to tell your body what to do.

During this floating dream, the sea was an empty expanse of saltwater desert. The community in this loneliness was your wife, a good friend from Colorado and the occasional skittering of flying fish or the low dance of a brown booby sashaying in and out of the wave crests. Your friend's name is Cowboy. The name exemplifies the seaworthiness of your crew. And with only seven miles left to travel you have encountered THE SQUALL. You thought the bell announcing the end of class was about to ring, but the lesson has just begun.

By holding onto the lifeline and timing your move between swells, you manage to crab your way back to your wife's side in time for the first blinding wall of rain. The world closes about you in a dark beat of wind and water. You fall on the wheel and turn to face the squall. Shielding your face from the rain you struggle to find a channel marker, a dim hope imposed on a Central American country by the over disciplined imagination of a United States cartographer. The sails catch the windblown rain, and the boat heels over, pouring buckets of water into the cockpit. The boat strains and shudders. You swing the wheel to counter the shrieking symphony of wind, and with each gust the boat dips away and then steps coyly forward to await the next blow. You are dancing with the devil, and old vices like tobacco call to you. Honestly, you are glad the boat knows more about sailing than you do.

Your wife is below deck trying to keep a fix on your position. You josh with Cowboy to relieve the tension. "Would you like a towel?" you shout above the racket of rain and wind. The rain sweeps down your brow and runs in cold rivers through your foul weather gear. "No problem," yells Cowboy, "I'm sanforized." You glance at one another, grateful for the camaraderie that lifts you above a blind, humiliating panic. You decide Cowboy should be in your will - presuming, of course, he survives you. You ask him to take the wheel so you can check with your wife (i.e., plead with her to find your position).

Peering below you are shocked by the chaos. The cabin looks like the O'Hare airport lobby tilted on its ear after a blizzard has canceled all flights. Cushions are thrown about, dishes crash against one another, gravity has gone berserk. In the small dark space, the motion you rode outside is magnified preposterously. Your wife looks up from the chart with a creased brow and wide eyes. You are put in mind of charity posters that picture starving African children. You run your hand over her wet hair and say, as steadily as you can, "Looks like rain." A light of humor ignites in her eyes.

You grip the handholds in the cabin and make your way toward the head by stepping on the settees, which are now the floor. Your mother would not be pleased. In the closet-sized space you brace your shoulders against the bulkhead and fumble about trying to find the zipper in your foul weather gear. You notice the mirror on the wall. Why not steal a glance at what must surely be the wind blown, steely-eyed visage of a salty dog? You lean forward and glimpse instead a pinched, red-faced man with bloodshot eyes as he whizzes by on his way to an encounter with the bulkhead. WHAM! You have been hit by the idiot stick.

The chaos outside fades. The sea has grown suddenly calm. On a moonlit shore, an ancient ancestor stands on solid ground. He spits into the dirt and kicks it over with his manure-covered boot. He points a bony finger out at the sea where you and your boat float between the inky water and the dark night sky. "Damn fool kid," he says; and then he turns his back and walks toward the warm glow coming from his stone farmhouse. "Hey!" you call. "Come back!" But he cannot or will not hear.

"What?"

You hear your wife's voice and shake focus back into your brain. Once again you hear the rush of water and wind. Weak-kneed, you stumble back into the main cabin. "Are you all right?" your wife asks. You nod, smile weakly, and pull yourself toward the cockpit. The seriousness of the situation has struck you broadside and right between the eyes.

You take the wheel from Cowboy to reestablish your illusion of control. He stands to shield you from the blinding rain. Holding your course in this squall after three days at sea has drained you of your last ounce of spunk. You have stopped suggesting that the storm might be "easing up." The blows delivered after such comments seem directed at your whimsy. Your clenched jaw aches, and you can no longer think of clever quips. You are exhausted.

Your wife the navigator calls up, "You might see a marker off to port soon." You check your hands, remember that you write with your starboard hand and then you look off to port. Out of the turmoil of ocean and sky in collision comes a solid black pole. You turn sharply to avoid its concrete frame. It disappears behind you as quickly as it appeared. "I think we saw it!" you call out. You feel a mixture of relief and gratitude. You are safely inside the reef and you are proud of your wife's skill under pressure. If you get through this, you promise to re-proclaim your love to her. She is already in your will.

Gradually the squall begins to lift its gray skirt. The downpour tapers off, and the wind exhales a last breath before settling down to a reasonable blow. The ocean salt in your nose is suddenly purged by the perfume of living terrestrial things. You flare your nostrils in delight. An outline of land appears, and it stirs your soul as only an absent lover can. You pry your fingers off the wheel and stretch your hands to relieve the cramp.

The sails are furled; the anchor is down. The crew gathers in the cockpit. White faces turn from the sea to look at one another for the first time. A long thin smile spreads across your face. It is a smile of relief, a smile of sympathy, a smile with a hint of lunacy.

"We're still alive," you say.

"Where's the rum?" says Cowboy

"Look!" says your wife.

Half dreading some new disaster, you follow her pointing finger off the stern of the boat. Your gaze follows the trolling line you forgot to reel in during the excitement. It cuts a lazy zigzag through the water. You see a flash of gold, a flash of blue.

"A fish!" you all shout together.

You jump for the line, but there is no need to rush. The 30-pound dolphin fish is easily towed in. The look in its eye says it would be panting, if fish panted. You turn to one another and then look back at the magnificent animal. Without a word, you give it back to the sea.

The sun is setting. How do you describe that light? There is a sudden brightening - a shift in mood. You look up for the sun, but the sun has set. The light comes from the clouds. In a final show of strength, the sun sends a bold reflected glow off the clouds to fill the sky. It warms the colors and spreads the Magic. The greens glow with life, the blue sea becomes phosphorescent, and the tans, browns and reds warm with the amber sky.

The first sip of rum goes straight to your brain - a little water thrown on red-hot neurons that have been firing uncontrollably for the last two hours. Already the talk is warming to describe each wave, each gust of wind, each heroic deed. But before you join in, you look across the bay and see, once again, the stern visage of your ancestor. As you strain your eyes, you think you detect a softening of his sharp features. But before you can be sure, he waves you off and turns to trudge up the beach. You feel the bump on your head and wince, and you smile toward the empty shore. Silently you thank the heavens for such a "painless" lesson.

Getting to San Blas – Second Voyage
1998

To get to Panama from Aruba we sailed four days, six hours and 575 nautical miles. Good friends Cazador and Carlotta joined us for the passage, and they not only helped us sail, but also cheered and stilled our dread, for they held our hands through the most troubled waters we had ever seen in the Caribbean.

Sailing to Panama meant sailing to the furthest southwest corner of the Caribbean Sea, where waves blown by the Trades and Atlantic storms gather and collide into the corner formed by the Central and South American coastlines. If, dear Reader, you open any pilot chart, you will see concentric red circles, where wind and waves grow until they climax in a bull's-eye just off the coast of Columbia. That bull's-eye was where we found ourselves on the second day of our passage. Cazador dubbed the spot the "Cartagena Triangle."

Remember bath time as a kid? Perhaps you used to assemble your floaty toys - a frog, a duck or even a plastic sailboat – and then stroke the water with your hands to make waves? By sitting at one end of the tub, you could produce waves that traveled the entire length toward your placid toys. At first the innocent floaty toys would bob about merrily and ride each wave, but as the waves reflected from the rim and joined incoming waves, they grew. Your bath would become a terrible diorama, an ocean drama, a confused and churning sea (All hands on deck!). Soon the toys leapt and tipped from side to side, and the less seaworthy crafts would, alas, swamp and sink to the bottom - Davy Jones' locker, at your feet.

That was the way it was off Cartagena. The strong winter Trade Winds were sending good-sized waves through the Caribbean, and a Georgian storm was sending an even bigger and crisscrossing swell down out of the Atlantic. In the Cartagena Triangle the wind was blowing with an intensity that the forecasters had either failed to predict or, as fellow cruisers had warned us back in Aruba, refused to acknowledge.

We were moving toward Panama very quickly; too quickly, in fact, and we had to slow our progress, so as to avoid meeting up with the solid wall of Central America in the night. We were traveling with the waves and using only a hanky of a headsail to keep us moving downwind and answering to the helm. The autopilot, squealing as its motor driven belt zipped back and forth to keep us on course, had long since abandoned its post. The four of us were taking turns at the helm. Our watches were in pairs, one person at the wheel and the other trying to come up with distracting banter or massaging the shoulders of the helmsman (or woman) in an effort to relieve muscle strain and anxiety.

On our watch together, Cazador and I spent some time looking back at the waves. As they grew into mountain peaks and then avalanched and tumbled down toward us, Cazador, who has the measured eye of a builder, estimated their average height at twelve feet. I defer to this estimate, because I tend to exaggerate natural phenomena that look as if they might kill me. In the deep Pacific, twelve-foot waves coming in regular swells are tolerable; but in the shallow waters near the rim of the Caribbean Basin, the jumping seas were confused and cresting. They were clearly the work of a nasty child at bath time. As Cazador and I looked back and the great waves rose up and rolled down toward us, our joking and frenetic banter ceased. We were silent, because we were both wondering the same thing: "Which one of these charging walls of water will be the dump truck with *Manta Raya* as its delivery address?" We turned away, faced our eyes forward and kept them there. We had reached that point when there was nothing more we could do. We were in the hands of the storm and in the hands of *Manta Raya*. And frankly, we were both too scared to look back again.

On the fourth day we neared Panama, and the winds finally calmed. The sea quit its terrible temper tantrum and adopted a civil attitude with a regular and comfortable roll. Except for occasional floating trees, which we dubbed "passage breakers" (great monsters, sixty or more feet long and sometimes ten feet in diameter - but that's my estimate), we were able to relax. We sat out on the trampoline and played Chinese Checkers and Cribbage. We even hazarded a celebratory beer or two. That same day, the startling, tortured mountains of the Central American isthmus rose out of the sea, and we smelled the wet, delicious musk of land.

We sailed through the *Hollandes* Channel, an opening in a long reef that runs like a necklace chain between the tiny islands. The pearl-like, palm covered islands stretched over the horizon all the way to Columbia, and we were sailing into a Polynesian post card.

At first we saw no one – the bounty of far-flung cruising. But eventually we were visited by our first Cuna Indians. They paddled out in *cayucos*, handsomely carved and brightly painted dugout canoes. When they came alongside *Manta Raya*, they bowed and smiled politely. Though the Cuna men dressed in shorts and t-shirts, the women were startling pictures of tradition and color: red splashes on their cheeks, tattoos down the lengths of their noses, tie-dyed, wraparound skirts and rich, multi-colored *molas* (intricately embroidered and layered cloth) blouses. The Cuna women wore nose rings and beaded strings, which when woven around their legs, formed intricate patterns in black, white, red and yellow. When the Cuna came aboard and visited with us over glasses of lemonade and cookies, we realized we had not only made a far-flung passage, we had made a passage through time.

Hiding in the southwest Caribbean, the Cuna are almost off the charts (and therefore off the radar) of the first world. Left alone in their distant corner, they have maintained their culture and their independence. Though their race is Pre-Columbian, they have legally owned and ruled the San Blas Islands since only 1933, when they won independence from Panama. They have a long history of democratic rule, and unknowingly, Thomas Jefferson may have copied some of their governmental treatises when he adopted democratic precepts from Thomas Paine, who knew and wrote about the Cuna governmental process. Meeting in thatch covered longhouses, the Cuna use a "town hall," egalitarian system to run their villages and their nation. Land entitlements to the outlying islands and mainland farms are held by the Cuna women, and I could not help but notice that a certain independent sparkle filled their unwavering, self-assured eyes.

To date the Cuna have opted to keep first world developments at arms length. Though we saw some modern conveniences in the larger towns (outboard engines, generators for electrical lights...), there was little that could be called modern in the smaller villages. When we visited one of the larger towns in search of transportation to Panama City for Cazador and Carlotta, we were directed to the "airport manager's office," which was a thatched hut home owned by little, smiling fellow called Frederico. Frederico invited us inside his "office," where dim light filtered through wood smoke and barely illuminated his children swinging in their hammocks. Frederico would help us find an airplane to the mainland, but he asked us to show up the night before the flight to remind him. He would have to paddle out in his *cayuco* and hoist the airport *bandera* (flag) to the top of the tree trunk in the lagoon off the little island to the west. There, on a mere strip of cement that stretched through the rough grass and bushes, a single engine plane would land - but only if the pilot saw the *bandeao* waving in the breeze.

On the appointed day, we waved goodbye to our dear friends and watched the little plane they were riding hop down the sidewalk-sized runway. We hoped the little airplane would find its way safely to the mainland. But *Frederico* was not worried. He came aboard *Manta Raya* to visit, and he brought his children with him. While they ate banana bread and worked on puzzles with Sawyer and Riley, *Frederico* assembled Leggos in the cockpit. Though we were in low spirits after losing the company of our dear friends, Frederico's sons and the squirt guns they found provided diversion. We retaliated with squirt bottles and buckets of saltwater until everyone was screaming and running about the deck, except for little *Wecho*, the Mestizo (mixed blood), who, because he had a cold, sat in Diane's lap - a snuffling but smiling bundle of bright blue eyes in a tangle of curly auburn hair.

Riley on the Approach to "Starfish Island," Panama

Over the next few days we meandered through the San Blas Islands until we found a picture-perfect spot we christened "Starfish Island." From the moment we cast our anchor into Starfish Island's calm waters, we became inseparably tied to the place. Sawyer and Riley splashed ashore each morning, shouting and giggling as if every day were a new landfall. In the bath-warm lagoon, they collected great, burnt orange starfish and wore them as mermaid crowns; or, holding them lightly in their hands, they waited for the tenuous extension of soft tentacles to tickle their palms. Sawyer hid precious possessions on the island: hair ties and colored rocks; and we tromped through the silver palms and mangrove bushes to follow her treasure map and find the "gems" under a fallen palm. We spent an entire day building an epic sand castle that rivaled San Simeon; and one night we threw a bonfire beach party replete with scary sea monster stories, overhead stars that pierced our brains and odd luminescent sea worms that swirled and cork-screwed in the surf. Starfish Island, hardly two hundred feet across, gave us miles of blessings, and no matter how many times we promised to visit one of the other three hundred San Blas islands, we woke each morning to find ourselves admiring the same scenery: our island, a white sand beach draped with swaying coconut palms in a pastel, coral fringed bay.

Elacio and *Humberto* found us on Starfish Island. And after their first visit, "The Boys" sailed out to visit us almost every day. Frenetic *Elacio*, smiling ear to ear, could hardly wait for the dying rattle of his outboard before delivering a bag of fruits and cakes from the mainland and a cheerful barrage of mixed Spanish and Cuna. Seeing our clueless grins, patient and kind *Humberto* would repeat *Elacio's* message, slowly and in Spanish; although sometimes he too would stumble in translation and simply shrug his shoulders and smile. There were no words for some of Elacio's otherworld gifts– *pifa* (an orange, yellow and starchy palm fruit), *cacao* (the essence of chocolate, brown seeds in a sweet and juicy white coating), cashews, brown sugar-like *sapodillos, guabas* that tasted like cotton candy and delicious coconut bread.

On visiting days with *Elacio* and *Humberto*, we would sit about the cockpit and sip rich Colombian coffee. And since we had to use what was a second language for all of us, our "talk" was, just as with our girls and Elaciao's and Humerto's children, more about sign than language. When conversation or our tolerance for translation wore thin, we would sit in silence. Though at first this taxed my first world need for punctuating dialogue, I saw that the Boys were perfectly contented with companionship in silence - another lesson from the third world.

We enjoyed visiting with and learning from the Boys, and their favorite entertainment was leafing through our picture books. In fact, the boys *loved* our picture books. The pages brought the miracles of the outside world into their laps. They would peer through our animal and plant guides or examine pictures of corals and fishes until they would suddenly grow excited, point and exclaim. They had found a fish or bird they recognized. Conversely, when they came across a picture of something they had never seen before and could not comprehend, like a polar bear, they would wrinkle their brows and ask us to explain exactly what it was, where it lived and why it looked the way it did. Their favorite book was the National Geographic Picture Atlas of Our World, and it often exhausted our abilities to translate. Try explaining why Wadaabe herdsmen of the Niger cross their eyes and wear rouge and lipstick. Better yet, describe Antarctic mountains of snow to two fellows, who for their entire lives, have lived on the equator.

One day *Humberto* and *Elacio* pulled up to our stern and asked if I wanted to go spear fishing with them. I looked down into their leaky *cayuco* and gave their smoking outboard, which *Humberto* and I were constantly fixing, a hard stare. Then I looked up into *Elacio's* earnest, smiling face, and Diane gave me a little shove from behind. *Por su puesto,* I said. Of course, I would come.

An hour later I sat alone in their *cayuco* and paddled lightly to hold my position in the water. The Boys were diving beneath me, and I was noticing just how quickly water was pouring through one of the tar-patched cracks in the *cayuco* (for there is something unsettling about leaks to liveaboards, who spend most of their lives making sure they stay on the dry side of the ocean). I rummaged through the tangle of snorkeling gear and fishing line for the bailing bucket - well, not a bailing bucket really, but a cut-off plastic juice jug - and started scooping. As I bailed, the tropical sun dried the saltwater off my back, and I felt my skin tingle and stretch under the delicious warmth. Holding the paddle - well, not a paddle really, but a board cut away with a "handle" at one end - I took in the horizon. In the sultry afternoon air, the turquoise ocean blended with a soft blue sky and suspended the islands around me in mid air. The floating lines of white beach topped with lime-green palms made me feel as if I were in Salvador Dali's dream of the South Pacific.

The boys had taken me to their favorite reef, and we had caught *cangrejo* (crab), *langosta* (lobster) and *caracol* (conch). I was exhausted from trying to match Elacio's fifty and sixty foot deep dives, and as I paddled about the warm, glassy sea with a net bag dangling over the side with our dinner, I was very relaxed. In the gently rocking *cayuco* under the warm sun, I was nearly asleep, when *Elacio* suddenly surfaced - his eyes wide. He blasted me with words that echoed unintelligibly through his snorkel. In one hand he held a snare that entwined a grand lobster, in the other hand he held a crab - one claw the size of my fist and containing enough sweet and succulent meat to spill out of a steaming crab omelet for four. I could only catch a few of *Elacio's* words...something about *arrecife* for "reef," *profundo* for "deep," and *mucho* for, I guessed, the bounty he had found below us. But floating there beside him, over 3,000 miles from home, with the canoe spinning on the equator and my brain spinning to juxtapose our two worlds, the words were easy enough to understand. They meant, "Look at us! Aren't we lucky!" And yes, we were.

Cuna Connection

I have a favorite picture of Panama. It was taken near the end of our stay in the San Blas Islands, when *Humberto* and *Elacio* led us on an expedition up the *Rio Azucar* (Sugar River) to their farm. All of us, seven little girls and four adults, had somehow stuffed ourselves into our rubber dinghy. We were spilling out over the sides and laughing together, so that we had become either a floating monument to successful linguistics or a barely buoyant Tower of Babel. Either way, we were having fun.

We had embarked from the island village of *Azucar*, where *Elacios'* wife, tattooed and bedecked with nose rings and beaded ankle bracelets, had stood waving to us from the rickety bamboo dock. From *Azucar* we had quickly entered the mouth of the river and disappeared into the jungle. And as we had motored upstream past dark green mangrove trees alive with screeching parrots, *Humberto* had pointed to parted grass chutes along the banks. Here, he had said, the crocodiles or caiman slid into the river. And he must have noticed my concern (I was making a mental count of the kids), for he had said I was not to worry. The alligators were not people eaters. Of course, from time to time they visited his village and made off with the odd chicken or dog, but that was to be expected. Still, I could not help thinking how, from water level, our merry expedition, our overstuffed, budget version of the African Queen, looked like a giant, floating corn-dog, smothered with tasty tots.

In my favorite picture, Sawyer and Riley walk through the mainland jungle with *Humberto's* daughters. All four girls are matched in age; in fact, the Cuna girls are a bit older than our daughters, yet they barely come up to our daughters' shoulders. (The Cuna are the second shortest race in the world and taller than the Pygmy by only a hair.) The girls are surrounded by the emerald green jungle. Sawyer, lit by diffused light breaking through the thick canopy of trees, her white, blonde hair and copper skin catching the light, appears to glow. Riley, always in movement, even in a still photo, is in mid stride. Moments before she had been up to her armpits in the *Rio Azucar* collecting tadpoles. Her gait, arms waving out to her sides and body swaying, is the walk of a girl relishing the breeze as it dries and cools her with its gentle touch.

Up ahead and holding Sawyer's hand, the eldest Cuna girl is talking. She has her head turned toward Sawyer, and she is pointing, for she is approaching her *finca* or farm. She is showing Sawyer the trees, fruits and wildlife along the way. She is sharing her world with Sawyer, just as for the last few weeks, Sawyer and Riley had been sharing their liveaboard lives with her. But what makes the Cuna girls speech so marvelous is that she is not speaking English; she is speaking Cuna, a language neither of our girls understands at all.

Today, explaining this linguistic phenomenon, Sawyer simply shrugs. "You know how kids talk, Papa; they just talk, and somehow it all makes sense."

And this is the way I remember the San Blas Islands of Panama. The kids are up ahead. They are still wet from collecting tadpoles in the river, and they laugh as they bite into golden mangoes that dribble sweet juice down their chins. They walk hand-in-hand with the Cuna girls up a narrow path cut through a towering stand of bamboo. Monkeys screech and jump from branch to branch in the trees overhead. We are in a rainforest three thousand miles from home, and yet, as a family exploring the world's wonders together, as close to home as we can ever get.

I'm French, I'm French

At the beginning of our trip, when we were sailing through the Windward, French islands, Riley had a little skit she liked to perform. Dressed only in her swim suit bottoms, she would bound on deck, hands raised dramatically above her head like a circus performer posing for the "ta-da," and shout, "I'm French! I'm French!" Despite this satire - most likely inspired by her father's preoccupation with quaint, French sunbathing customs - both of our girls admired the French, and in particular, French food. They savored crusty baguettes, discovered that tasty French cheeses could be more than the colored wax found in the U.S. and sighed over crème and fruit filled pastries. They even sampled French pâtés. (O.K., they gagged and called them dog food, but they tried them.) With a little practice, the girls learned their *s'il vous plaîts* and *mercies*. In Bonaire they even befriended a French brother and sister, who, struggling graciously with their own patchy English, had invited us aboard their Family's self-deprecating aluminum sloop, "Froggie."

The girls were often our first introduction to people from around the world. On a beach off Venezuela, an elderly South African couple invited the girls for tea on their Cape Town catamaran. Offering freshly baked scones with melted butter and jam, the couple taught our girls how to play a song on recorders, and Sawyer and Riley came back to our floating home wanting to buy their own recorders and to practice more songs at sea. By Christmas, while visiting friends from Italy cooked us an eight-course meal arranged around a delicacy we nicknamed "t-shirt pasta" (because of the wrap they used when boiling the main course), the girls were playing Jingle Bell… which led to more fun: the girls translating and teaching our Italian friends how to sing "Rudolph the Red Nosed Reindeer."

O.K., so why go on and on about the "international house of pancake" the girls got to savor aboard *Manta Raya*? Because one of the best parts of a liveaboard education is the big, wide world it brings to the family classroom.

When we left the San Blas Islands of Panama, we sailed north for two days and were happy to find a tiny speck of an island in the otherwise empty western Caribbean -San Andres, the unlikely possession of Columbia some 400 miles to the southeast. When we visited the island, it was a popular free port and savored as a low-key resort for Columbia's rich. And so it was understandable that on San Andres our daughters would meet two girls whose grandma was in drug prison.

After more than a month in the way out, San Blas Islands with the Cuna Indians, landing in the resort society of San Andres was an odd experience. We "Hail Mary-ed" our way through San Andres' skinny and convoluted reef entrance and then rounded up and anchored off a tidy marina and yacht club, where the chrome and plastic of glitzy, full-throated cigarette boats filled the docks. The docks led to a grassy yard beneath shading palms and the wide porch of the "Club Nautical" yacht club. The Club included a restaurant with Tiki-torch lined walkway and a deck plank door decorated with fishing nets and colored glass floats. After weeks of canned food and meals prepared over our galley "camping" stove, the restaurant looked promising, and Diane's current passage food fantasy – filet mignon – was in the offing.

We wandered down the dock, across the yard and onto the cool marble floor of the empty clubhouse. A bored but polite clerk signed us in and motioned us toward the game room and pool - yes, pool. The girls were in heaven. After rushing back to the boat for snorkeling gear and sunscreen, we jumped in and floated neck deep in the cool, fresh water – the salt and weariness of a long passage washing away in no time.

Eyes closed beneath the warm sun, I heard the laughter of little girls…but not just my girls. I opened my eyes to see two additional blonde little girls. My girls looked shyly and hopefully in their direction. Another newcomer, a dark-haired man, sat dangling his feet in the pool.

I gathered he was the father of the newcomer kids. He looked my way and smiled.

By the time Danny and I met, our children had already dissolved in a froth of water, blonde hair and laughter. Danny was vacationing, but he was also working in San Andres. He was the island's senator - the representative on the Colombian mainland. Danny came from a noted political family. His father and mother had each held important political offices. And when I asked him where his parents lived, I was surprised to get Danny's matter-of-fact answer. His father was in Bogotá, and his mother was just outside the city, in prison. She was, Danny said, "taking the rap" for a traditional Colombian fundraising scheme: accepting political contributions from the Colombian drug cartel. Danny did not seem to be upset about his mom's time in the slammer. She was, he said, in a plush condo compound, where she could play tennis and visit with her granddaughters. She was wiling away her time "behind bars" by taking French lessons and playing Bridge once a week with her best friends.

Danny's wife Sandy joined us poolside. She was from the States – the daughter of Southern parents so genteel, that when she told them she was getting married and moving to Colombia, they thought she meant South Carolina. Semi-southern belle Sandy stretched her vowels and swallowed her consonants with such sweet, southern charm, that I found myself lulled into the rhapsodic arms of my Nashville, Tennessee upbringing. But she and her husband Danny were not typical southern parents; nor, for that matter, were they typical parents from any part of the world I knew. Besides managing Danny's political career, the couple also ran two English schools – one in Cartagena and one in Bogota. When not shuttling between the schools, Danny liked visiting his San Andres constituency. On the island he could, along with the rest of Colombia's wealthy aristocracy, unwind in safety. In contrast to the mainland, visitors on San Andres felt so safe, Danny said, that many did not bother to bring along their bodyguards.

"Bodyguards?" I repeated, and I glanced over at the girls splashing in the pool. Did Danny, I asked, actually feel threatened back on the mainland?

Why yes. In fact, just that week he had had to shoot a fellow.

"Shoot?" I gawked. "You mean like 'shoot to kill?'"

"Well," said Danny, stopping to rub on some sunscreen, "I'm not sure. He came up on me with a gun while I was stopped in traffic.

I pulled out my pistol and fired two rounds, but I didn't stick around to see what happened. The light turned green, and I had to go."

Again I looked at the kids splashing and laughing in the pool. The Caribbean sun blazed through a deep blue sky, spotted with stray white clouds. I wanted to ask more questions. I wanted to ask Danny and Sandy why they would choose to live in such a place. But I didn't. This Colombian family was outside my middle class, United States ken. And I decided to leave well enough alone.

That evening Danny invited us out for pizza and a tour of his island. Everywhere we went people nodded and waved to their senator. Sometimes Danny stopped to talk, and I could not help but notice, amidst the sandals, shorts and beach wear, vigilant fellows in pressed trousers and clean sneakers. They carried briefcases and stood very alert and very ready, just to the side of their employers.

This third world sociology was all new to me. I grew up in a Beaver Cleaver household. Our house sat in line with the rest of the neighborhood houses, delineated by cement driveways. The milkman dropped off the milk each morning. My dad smoked a pipe, wore a businessman hat and carried a businessman briefcase. My mom wore an apron. My sister wore saddle shoes. My brother was an Eagle Scout. We were all-American, all safe, all comfortable and all clueless. Danny's story startled me. As a kid growing up on Wonder Bread, the vague, disturbing stories I might have read about *other* people in *other* countries were less tangible than the previous night's episode of *Twilight Zone*. But venturing through the Caribbean wearing a swimsuit instead of a tie, and carrying a fanny pack instead of briefcase, I had yanked my family out of this middle class, United States fantasy.

In Cumana, Venezuela we had been in a tough place. Riley had grown scared of the night. Sawyer had grown silent. Sometimes we were all scared, and we knew it. But maybe that spooky peek at the real world had been good for us. Maybe our girls had learned what a desperate place the world could be, and how that desperation could drive people to their worst.

But the girls had met and would continue to meet people who had very little and yet were very happy. Later in our cruise we would raise jam jars to toast a very poor family. As pigs would squeal about our feet and oil derricks would squeak overhead, we would dine at their tiny home, a shack really, where they would somehow manage to cook us a delicious, five course meal. And we had also befriended Cuna Indians, who owned so very little.

Once in the San Blas islands, after *Humberto, Elacio* and their children had played with us for the day and their cayuco was just disappearing astern, I had commented on the leaky boat and the dirt floor, grass hut home to which it was headed. Sawyer had picked up on the tone of my voice, and she had corrected me: "They aren't poor, Papa; they just don't have a lot of stuff."

After about a week on San Andres, we finished our heavy shopping. Provisions were stuffed into every crevice on *Manta Raya*. But before taking off, we wanted to repay Danny and his family for their kindness. We had also made a few more friends on the island, and so we decided to invite them all out for a farewell, afternoon sail.

Joseph, a San Andrean famous for having been shipwrecked, came with his girlfriend. Joseph had drifted about for over three days in the remains of a burned-out hull of a sport fishing boat before the Coast Guard had rescued him. Carlos, a Brazilian who had given me rides to fill my water jugs, was a wannabe cruiser interested in catamaran voyaging, and he was thrilled to be invited to go sailing on *Manta Raya*. And Craig, a fellow cruiser and an irascible ex-biker bar owner from Santa Cruz, CA, had offered to help us crew *Manta Raya*. Craig lived on a 29-foot sloop, which bore a painting of a naked lady straddling a rocket just over the printed name "Desdemona" (taken from the space-traveling heroine of a Jimmy Buffet song).

All of these folks, their significant others and Danny's family of four climbed aboard *Manta Raya* on a perfect Caribbean afternoon. They bore gifts of *Aguila* beer, hors d'oeurves and chocolate. Once we were through the reef and into the waves, Craig climbed out on the tramp to take the ocean spray in his face. We had lunch off a small island back inside the reef, and as with all days spent outside on a beautiful planet, there had been lots of good feelings and lots of laughter. The afternoon re-taught me, a jaded cruiser, just how much a day on the water means to landlubbers, and ought to always mean to us sailors. Our new friends filled our log with exclamation marked gratitude, but we were the lucky ones. We got to see our watery world through the smiling eyes of new friends from foreign countries. They translated our liveaboard life into something yet richer than it had been.

Providencia Pirates

Western Caribbean coral atolls, now anchorages for cruisers on their late spring and early winter runs through the western Caribbean, were once pirate hideouts. After San Andres, *Providencia* was our next stop on our way north, and it was to provide a solid contrast to the jet skis and resorts of San Andres. With the jagged line of *Providencia's* 1,200 ft volcanic peak serving as a steady landfall beacon, a bouncing, beam reach daysail brought us the bounty of two yellowfin tuna. Near shore, the 400 ft spire called Morgan Head Rock led us into the harbor. The rock was named for one of the most feared and cheered pirates to ever keel haul a Spanish Don.

We arrived in the quiet harbor just before sunset. As we anchored, the arena of hills that folded into the harbor glowed lime green, and the mirror flat water about our hulls reflected lavender and silver. We ate soft and tangy sushi rice and delicate slices of tuna flavored with wasabi and soy sauce.

The next morning, for our landfall breakfast, Diane made golden blintzes filled with cheese and topped with homemade blackberry jam. Under the warm glow of morning light, we listened to the crow of roosters from shore, and I yawned, stretched and decided I loved my first mate and wanted to remarry her. As we sat under the warm sun, we drank strong Dominican coffee and planned our shore excursion. In our tattered, Caribbean guidebook, we learned that the island was rife with names like "Archibald, Robinson, Newball and Taylor" - families who could trace their ancestry back to Morgan's pirates. When Henry

Morgan had taken the island from the Spanish, he had renamed it "Old Providence," and the ruins of his fortifications were still wedged in the cliffs on the northwest corner of the island. That is where we planned our exploration.

Even a century after Morgan's pirates left, English shipping continued to alter course for Old Providence to take on important cargo - crickets believed not only to help with cockroaches, but to also bless safe passages. Despite this limey legacy, Old Providence was now a Spanish speaking possession of Colombia. In one of the backroom deals of empire building nations, Her Majesty had handed the island and its crickets back to Colombia.

On shore we hiked up to Morgan's ruins. Cannons still pointed out over the harbor to protected ghost ships in a forgotten pirate fleet. As we sat in the cliffs, we imagined ourselves searching the horizon for Spanish galleons. They sailed low and slow with cargo bound for the Old World. When we sounded the alarm, our pirate mates raced to their ships. Their eyes were aloft as they looked for the wind that would fill their sails and take them to treasures that would fill their holds.

In town, we learned that though mapmakers had colored *Providencia* to match Colombia, an independent spirit still colored the English-speaking islanders. Language and heritage linked them not with Columbia but with the nearby peoples of the Caymans, Belize and Jamaica. One Islander, when pressed, growled, "Damn it, man, we mean to get our bloody independence!" And on our way back to the boat, we realized that the Pirates of the Caribbean had not all disappeared.

Real Pirates?

The fear of piracy actually keeps some sailors from cruising. But as we sailed on *Manta Raya*, just as when Diane and I had sailed in the eighties, we chose not to believe the scary "pirate" stories we heard. Just as with gossip ashore, cruising gossip, oft repeated and oft exaggerated, could magnify one harmless experience into a horrifying, daily occurrence. Boat crimes were usually petty offences more common on the bigger tourist islands and along the northern coast of South America, where outboard engines, the shiny, expensive jewels that hang off the transoms of every cruising dinghy, become "Caribbean currency." But overlooking these crime spots (and perhaps these spots should be "looked over" from a ways offshore anyway), cruising, we believed, was safe. We used common sense. We did not wear (nor did we have) flashy jewelry. We used dingy locks, boat deck lights and alarms; and we kept our cash hidden and mug money handy. Depending on whether you hail from Modesto, CA, the car jack capital of the United States, Detroit, MI the homicide capital, or Hunter, NY, where you can find the largest quilting bee, you might have a different perspective on the relative dangers of Caribbean cruising.

After nearly four years in the Caribbean, the Gulf of Mexico and the coastal Atlantic, we have been the victims of three "crimes." A kedge anchor was stolen by kids diving off a dock in Venezuela, an outboard engine was stolen by a drug addict in St. Martin (and that was before we took possession of our boat), and In Kingston, Jamaica, a fellow tried to pickpocket Diane; but she knocked the money out of his hand

and shouted, "*Boombaclod*!" as he ran away - a dialect expletive I prefer not to translate, but one which, in the crowd witnessing the thwarted crime, produced general laughter.

But we have also had some sobering encounters, and our scariest was as a family out on the Honduran reefs just after leaving *Providencia*. But before I spin that yarn, I want to tell two brief tales that might help put cruising paranoia in perspective. The first is a robbery Diane and I witnessed in Jamaica, and the second is a friend's story of piracy near the Bahamas.

Jamaica - 1988

It was April of 1988, and Diane and I were aboard an old, Nova Scotia schooner in the prettiest harbor we have ever visited. Port Antonio, Jamaica is a steep-to, deep-water port with 360° protection. For a sailor, such an anchorage is like returning to the womb. The lush, lime green hills slide into a round basin of water, and a tidy island - once owned by Errol Flynn - stretches across the entrance to blocks ocean waves. When British naval commanders first saw Port Antonio, they must have dropped their jaws and ordered tots of rum for all hands. When we arrived there, Diane stood in the cockpit, and with a slow, 360° twirl, snapped sequential pictures of the horizon - beaches fringed with coconut palms, emerald green mango trees, bananas beneath fan-sized fronds and green hills rolling up to great, cloud tipped mountains, where Blue Mountain coffee ripened in the rainforest mist. Today, stapled together, these prints form a circular panorama, that when worn around the head like a loose crown, re-conjures the magic of the place. It is the warmest hat we own in the dead of winter.

Aboard a thickly planked schooner we visited, with its creaking deck and rope rigging, the ambience of Port Antonio was complete. The owners of the sturdy vessel were a Canadian couple with two white-blonde daughters. The father was an interesting and entrepeneurial sailor. He had converted the vessel by adding a mast to an old fishing boat and had sailed his family all the way through the Panama Canal from Vancouver and back, sometimes carrying cargo like Blue Mountain coffee and mahogany to finance his voyages. His rugged vessel's prehistoric diesel engine could be started in one of two ways: either by pressure pumping (like bicycle pumping) piston cylinders and then discharging them with a great whoosh and roar of engine life, or by dropping a small grenade into the cylinder head and screwing it shut. Bombs away.

The Canadians were throwing a party, and it was a hit with the cruisers at anchor in Port Antonio. Cruising kids were chasing each other about the deck like monkeys, while their parents shared tales, laughed and watched the approaching sunset. I sat above the calm water, my legs dangling over the edge of the thick wood deck and picked every succulent piece of barbecued chicken off the bone, as an old Jamaican man sat down next to me - wizened hair, smiling white teeth - and introduced himself. He spoke of former days in Port Antonio, of Errol Flynn ("Dat mon did some funny tings wid goats, you know?") and of courtesy to tourists ("We treat you wid respect back den, mon – instead, today, deez chilren got no respect..."). I had finished my meal and was looking for a place to stow my paper plate and Styrofoam cup, when the old gentleman offered to take them for me. I was surprised and grateful. Then I watched him pile our plates together, smile and toss the whole mess overboard. Yes, the old days were more courteous, simpler too.

Late that night, when most of the kids had transitioned from their frenzies directly into comas, the family cruisers began saying their goodbyes. They rowed or motored off in their dinghies - kids asleep across the thwart seats and draped over shoulders. When we rowed back to our own boat and laid down in our berth, we drifted off to the muffled beat of reggae punctuated by the sharp splashes of the last partiers as they hit the water.

It was not the party but what happened after the party that was the buzz of the cruisers the next morning. Two of the partiers, a couple from Houston, had returned to their boat and turned into their bunks, just as we had, when they heard a noise on deck. The husband made his way quietly topside and peered into the darkness of the cockpit. He could just make out the gleam of wet skin in the starlight.

He yelled. A body dove into the water, and before he could think what he was doing, he had grabbed his flare gun, hopped into his dinghy and motored off in pursuit. He caught up with the splashing body quickly, and still not thinking, found himself pointing his shaking pistol at two, wide eyes in the water.

"What were you doing on my boat!" he yelled.

"No-ting, mon. No-ting," Hands raised and treading water, the body sputtered and choked. The cruiser noticed a glint on the body's wrist - obviously the silver band of a wristwatch.

"Take my watch off, and throw it in the dinghy."

"But..."

"Just do it!"

"O.K., mon."

Then, with no flashlight and no moon to clarify the situation, the cruiser did the only thing he could think to do at the time: "Take off your clothes," he said, "all of 'em, and throw everything in the boat!"

"What?"

"You heard me!"

Soon there was a pile of wet clothing in the bottom of the cruiser's dinghy. Warning the thief that he should never come anywhere near his boat again (even though there was no hope of knowing what the thief looked like), the cruiser ordered the body to leave.

Back on his boat, the cruiser found his flashlight and turned it on the watch and pile of wet clothing. The wristwatch was not his. There was nothing in the clothing. He had robbed the robber, naked.

The Bahamas

When we first thought of cruising, a few well meaning, NRA friends wanted us to arm ourselves. One thought we ought to carry an Oozie and offered to get us one. The other, a more practical fellow, who had fended off grizzlies while living in Alaska, thought we ought to carry two firearms: "You'll need a long distance rifle to keep folks at a distance," he said; "something that would put a good-sized hole in someone's hull. And for close range," he continued, "you'll want something that would stop a fellow in his tracks... I'm thinking a short barrel 12 gauge shotgun and a semi-auto' .308 M1A with armor piercing bullets."

Thanks, but no thanks. We did not know how to use these weapons, and before we thought about learning, we had to ask ourselves the ultimate question: "Were we prepared to use guns to defend ourselves – to shoot someone? To kill them?" Maybe we were just chicken, but we chose a gun-free philosophy, our philosophy, and we did not expect other cruisers to feel the same way. In fact, we befriended and cruised with responsible gun owners and respected them for their cruising philosophy. Still, armed cruisers do present a different aspect when sailing abroad. Customs agents in many countries are leery of boaters who carry firearms, and they demand that weapons be locked up onshore - to be returned only when the cruisers clear out. And in terms of effectiveness, I know of boat confrontations where it would appear that already tense situations were merely escalated by cruisers who brought guns into play. They did not know how to use their guns properly nor did they deploy them seriously. Sad stories. But wife Diane reminds me that cruising advice should come only from first hand experience, and even then, only when requested. Therefore, I offer you this advice as to the appropriateness of guns on boats: your call. Noble or naive, our cruising approach was gun-free. But we were betting that the robbers would be mostly unarmed kids, that the pirates would be figments of our paranoia and that, in either case, the answer to threats would be to readily relinquished our possessions, which were much less valuable than our lives.

Our cruising mentor St. Frank was solo sailing on the open ocean near the Bahamas. There was no land in site, an empty sea from horizon to horizon, and a small ship appeared in the South - nothing alarming, just a vessel to keep one's eyes on. But then the boat changed course and headed directly for St. Frank.

On the open ocean and outside the established shipping lanes (the imaginary water highways over which giant cargo ships make their way between major ports), seeing another vessel is a rare occurrence. In the vast loneliness of the ocean, spotting another boat can actually be reassuring - humanity in the empty desert ocean, two ships passing in the night. But two vessels heading toward or overtaking one another is cause for alarm. Helmsmen, hopefully of both ships, pay close attention and take every precaution to avoid one another. So a ship suddenly altering course and heading toward another boat is not only odd, but alarming. It is, though the reaction times are different, as shocking as a car suddenly swerving toward you from the oncoming lane. On the empty sea, such an encounter suggests ill intent. And, yes, farfetched ideas like "piracy" come to mind.

St. Frank, after seeing the boat turn and head toward him, muttered "oh shit" and jumped below to get *the bon voyage* present his brother had given him: a shotgun. But St. Frank's boat was lurching in the lumpy seas, and below he found himself half sick before he could get to the gun. Stumbling over the cushions that he had thrown about during the search, he tripped over his box of shogun shells. The box burst open and spat shells everywhere, which turned into ball bearings under his feet. Down went St. Frank. He cursed again, threw down the gun and climbed back topside. When he came on deck, he was just in time to see the intruding boat drawing alongside.

It was a great wreck of a boat, a wooden fishing trawler with three booms sticking up from the deck. And it was covered with passengers. They were everywhere: scattered on deck, draped over the sides, and hanging from the rigging. There were men, women, children and goats. This was no pirate ship.

"Bon Jour!" came a shout from the rigging, and St. Frank looked skyward to a figure waving from the tallest mast. "Hallo!" repeated the figure.

St. Frank returned a feeble wave.

"Escuz me," shouted the man, "but could you tell me ze way to Miami?"

The boat was filled with Haitian refugees sailing to what they hoped would be a new life in America. But with their boat overloaded and riding low in the water, St. Frank knew that any landfall would be a miracle. He reached for his chart, but before he could shout out a compass bearing, the fellow yelled again: "No, no, monsieur. No compass. Weech way?"

St. Frank blinked. Given the Gulf Stream and the variable winds between the floating disaster of a boat and Florida, even a solid compass bearing would be iffy. Still, what could he do? St. Frank made a hatchet chop wave in the general direction of Florida. He could see the man's broad smile. "Merci, monsieur!"

And off went the lumbering boat in a direction Frank hoped would put it somewhere between Cuba and Connecticut.

Vivario Cays – 1998

From Providencia, our family headed toward the *Vivario* Cays. The Cays lie about 30 nautical miles north of the dogleg of Central America, where the haunch of Honduras meets the leg of Nicaragua. Larger ships and most cruisers coming up this stretch of the Caribbean choose an offshore route and make their way toward the Greater Antilles or through the Yucatan Channel. They ride the great rush of current that flushes into the Gulf of Mexico between Mexico and Cuba. This offshore route bypasses the mud banks of the Mosquito Coast and avoids reefs like the *Quita Sueño* and *Serranilla* Banks, which poke their heads up suddenly from 6000-foot depths. But since we were on our way to the Bay Islands just north of Honduras with the prospect of Guanaja as our first landfall, we chose an inshore route over the shallows, where we might rest along the way in the *Vivario* Cays. The reefs, we knew, could be looked upon as either hull crunching hazards (with the canted hulks of sad cargo ships delineating their sharp edges) or beautiful, protected anchorages. Despite the tricky navigation, we found the promise of calm anchorages behind coral more compelling.

For me, the Mosquito Coast along which we sailed was disconcerting. It's steamy equatorial jungles felt like the original stew of creation - a long way from the dry, clear deserts of Arizona. The coastal town of Bluefields, Nicaraguan slogs through 250 inches of rain each year. Muddy rivers slither and wind through dense jungle to vomit great tree trunks and slimy brown water into the blue Caribbean.

Odd birds screech. Strange fish with humped backs and gaping, toothy jaws hide in the black water. Sloths, dazed and dreaming, their dripping backs covered with green moss, hang from trees as if hypnotized by the primordial pall of the place. Even on the warmest days, a misting rain, which might be falling down or up (one cannot be certain), recalls Joseph Conrad's <u>Heart of Darkness</u> and lends a particular chill to the tepid air.

As we sailed, the feel of the Mosquito Coast, foreboding with a hint of menace, extended offshore into the sunshine and blue water of the Caribbean. Perhaps I was too anxious as we neared the ravage of Hurricane Mitch, which had recently passed over these waters, or perhaps I was merely tense with the usual passage concerns. But my uneasy mood was the perfect setting for paranoia, and the arrival of unwanted guests fed my fears.

As we threaded our way through the shallows on our way to the *Vivario* Cays, we passed just north of *Media Luna* or Half Moon reef. Almost one year to the day later, Half Moon would be the site of an unfortunate "accident." A Dutch family of three, a mother, father and a teenaged son aboard their steel sloop *Hayat*, would be robbed by men, who boarded their cruising boat while the father and son were off snorkeling. When the father and son, who would see the boarding, would motor back to their boat, the bandits would open fire, sink the dinghy and wound the son. After a harrowing and interminable sea rescue, the son would survive, but he would lose his liver and be paralyzed from the waist down. When interviewed for the television show "20/20," the son, then confined to a wheelchair, would say he was glad the bandits had shot him instead of his parents. If his parents had died, he would have been sad for the rest of his life.

On our own passage past *Media Luna*, this prescient vision of a sad and terrifying story would have been more than we could have handled. As it was, rising winds and seas were giving us plenty to worry about. Though we got some pleasure cursing the NOAA forecaster who had predicted "moderate winds and seas," the passage was proving to be, as our log records, our "most troubling yet." Waves rebounding off the mainland had built punching seas into foaming curlers that roared down from astern. The wind shrieked through the rigging with a high-pitched whine that made us clench our teeth. The kids and I were, of course, seasick. And as such disorienting and debilitating circumstances often demanded, Diane was left in charge and had to handle all of the thinking tasks, like navigation, for only she could manage going below to check the charts. The rest of us were a grim and listless crew, but we woke up quickly when we spotted a boat coming upon us from astern.

Seeing the boat was no great worry - beyond the usual drill of calculating speed and direction to make sure there would be no collision. But like the Haitian boat that approached St. Frank, this boat changed course in order to head directly at us.

The boat was a shrimping trawler. Its outriggers swung crazily in the following sea, and its grey hull split the rolling whitecaps. Each time the boat's hull emerged from a wave trough, it grew alarmingly larger. It was bearing down on us and catching us quickly.

I thought of Joshua Slocum, the first man to sail alone around the world, and how, when beset by pirates off the coast of Madagascar, he had done some quick thinking. Joshua's privateers had also come upon him from astern, and he had hoped to outrun them. Though he was armed, he was alone, so there was no hope if they caught him. But Joshua realized that the pirates had no idea how many people were on his boat. So he thought if he could fool them into thinking he had a full compliment of sailors, he might take the heart out of their chase, or at least confuse and stall them until he could run to safety.

If the fellows on the boat behind us meant us harm, a skinny papa and three girls in bathing suits were not going to give them second thoughts. Despite our queasy stomachs, we all went below. I put on my visor cap and an orange life vest and went back on deck with my binoculars. What I saw did not make me feel better. On the foredeck of the trawler a swarthy fellow stared right back at me through his own binoculars, and another fellow by his side held what looked like a machete. I went back below. Riley asked what was happening. Both girls knew something was up. They could not help but notice Diane's drained face. Mine, I am sure, was even paler.

"Everything's fine," I said. "We're just making sure we miss a boat that's behind us."

Neither Riley nor Sawyer looked reassured. I took off the hat and life vest, threw on a blue foul weather jacket and went back on deck with the binoculars. This time there were three men on deck, and I could make out the boat's name "Alre Jr. Third," but I quickly swung the binoculars away from my face. The men, their boat and its sharp bow slicing through the waves were all too close. The binoculars added more detail to a spectacle that was already too vivid.

I went below and started changing clothes again. I was donning farmer john pants when I heard Diane's voice, loud and clear, like a summons. She too had seen the boat's name. Echoing through our cabin and, I'm sure, positively roaring over the radio waves of channel 16, she hailed the vessel: "ALRE JUNIOR THE THIRD! ALRE JUNIOR THE THIRD! THIS IS THE SAILING VESSEL MANTA RAYA!"

I was about to ask what on earth she was doing, but I stopped, for the tone in her voice put me in mind of another story - this time not a story out of a book, but a real life story about Diane riding her bike around a hilly curve in Flagstaff.

I was pedaling behind her, when a panel truck barreled past me and pulled up beside Diane. As we rounded the curve together, the truck began pushing Diane off the road. But she did not stop; she did not even slow. Gripping her handlebars with both hands and pedaling with one foot, she lifted her free foot and began stomping on the side of the truck - BOOM! BOOM! BOOM!

The truck jerked away from us, lurched ahead and then stopped a block or so down the street. As Diane pulled up alongside, the driver's door swung open, and I figured the big fellow who started climbing out was going to kill her. But Diane jammed on her brakes, skidded to halt just in front of the man, and had her index finger pressed into his sternum before he could speak.

"Do you know you could have killed me back there!" she yelled. "You nearly forced me off the road!"

Diane's dark eyes were burning black and terrible. The trucker's face flushed. His mouth began working, but no words came out. Blinking, he finally stammered, "I'm sorry. I didn't see you."

"Didn't see me? Well, next time," Diane seethed, as her accusing finger poked the man's chest and punctuated each word, "pay more attention!" And before the fellow could answer, she flipped her hair, jammed her foot down on her bike pedal, and rode off down the road. Then I too pedaled by the dazed fellow, tipped my bike helmet and offered a curt "howdy."

Off the coast of Honduras, it was that same voice, the voice that had pulled the trucker up short, which Diane now used. She spoke firmly and evenly into the microphone. She repeated her call to *Alre Junior*, and after a pause, a voice came back in Spanish, "*Si, Manta Raya.*"

"*Usted estar el capitán* (are you the captain) *de Alre Junior the Third?*" demanded Diane.

"*No.*"

"*TRAE* (GET) *EL capitán PRONTO!*"

There was another pause. We could hear the thump of the microphone, as it was laid on something hard - then the hum of the engines and shouts in Spanish. Evidently the microphone had been keyed and left on. There was shouting, some sort of argument, then another thump and finally a cracked and gruff voice.

"*Si.* [Clearing throat] *Es el... capitan de Alre Yunior... Que pasa.*"

Was the man drunk? Had he been asleep?

Diane: "Do you speak English, captain?"

"Yes."

"Captain, your boat is too close. Move...away...immediately!"

There was no response. The radio went silent. Watching with my binoculars from behind the companionway, I could make out the facial features, t-shirts, beards and mustaches of the three men on deck. One fellow was definitely carrying a machete.

Suddenly, *Alre Junior* lurched to port – so suddenly that all three men were knocked off balance. Belching white smoke, the big grey hull surged by our stern quarter. It passed on ahead of us, and, as if we had been in an empty sea all along, *Alre Junior* was suddenly gone. We saw nothing but roiled waves, humped and leaping, from horizon to horizon. Only then did Diane and I breath, look at one another and chime simultaneously, "Whoa!"

Did *Alre Junior* mean us harm or was her crew merely bored and out for a joy ride after a long night of trawling? Had Diane's call made a difference? Until Diane's hail, the boat had definitely tailed us - not more than twenty yards astern and closing. Did Diane's voice, the angry voice of a woman and mother, chill and sober the crews' Latin boy hearts? To this day we do not know. We only know that we were scared.

As I write, I ask my daughters if they remember this story: the boat that followed us on the way to Guanaja, the boat Mama had to yell at. They have no idea what I am talking about. Happiness, Arnold Schweitzer said, is health and a poor memory.

Swimming with the Sharks

Near the tale end of our wash cycle passage up the Mosquito
Coast to the *Vivario* Cays, the winds calmed, and the reef
broke the humped back of our tormentors, the bucking
waves. We anchored in twelve feet of calm water in front of three
small palms on a speck of land that had just managed to grab a
foothold on the reef to support the clump of trees. Off our starboard stern quarter, the largest island in the group, Grand Vivario
Cay, was covered with Cassurina trees. Their graceful green sweep
reminded us that we were drawing near to the Caribbean we had
visited a dozen years earlier, as well as the coastline of Florida. We
were nearing home. The *Vivarios* embraced us like a familiar friend
and blessed us with a sound night of sleep – they also gave us a
pulse-raising present.

The *Vivario* reef was a Green Peace poster child. Its coral nooks and
crannies had been picked clean of lobster and the lobsters' shy cousin,
the conch. Both are easy catches for third world fishermen. Lobster
climb willingly into one-way, labyrinth traps, lured by no more than a
strip of leather. And conch graze the shallow ocean floor at about two
feet per hour, when motivated. Honduran fishermen had made quick
and easy money off the conch and lobster in the *Vivarios*. And this story
had been repeated throughout the islands of the Caribbean. Lobster
and conch were usually the first tenants to be forcefully evicted, unless
bleach, a reef killing poison, were used for a terminal and massive
harvest of all of the fishes. With the exception of the few islands that

protected their reefs or islands that simply did not have the resources (fuel and boats) to support total despoilment, lobster and conch were disappearing throughout the Caribbean Sea.

The clue to the animals' disappearance in the *Vivarios* lay on the largest island on the reef, Grand Vivario. Concrete ruins (like a Spanish *fortina*) and broken, slat wood traps were all that remained of a lobster cartel. The island, about 50 miles off the mainland, was now silent as a ghost town, but it had once rumbled with diesel generators and a behemoth ice plant. When the weather had held, boats had landed non-stop along the tiny island's green-fringed skirts. Fishermen had set their lobster traps and dived for conch throughout the surrounding reefs. Then they had sailed back to Grand *Vivario* and offloaded brimming buckets of shiny conch guts and great baskets of wriggling lobster. After depositing their catch in the icehouse, they had gone back for yet more lobster and conch, and more, and more ...until, there was no more. All that remained were mountains of empty conch shells, bleached and crumbling in the sun. I imagine the lobster had given out first, and then the conch. The barnacled debris of broken wooden lobster traps littered the reef. And when we eventually dove the reef, we saw nary a conch; until one, lonely, moss-backed holocaust survivor tottered into view. Even Diane, the indefatigable Conch Huntress, shook her head and let the old codger be.

But the reef, like a lover awaiting the return of a lost mate, had kept herself beautiful. Corridors of blue, lavender and orange coral opened into surprising calderas and valleys and then fragmented into spurs of brown and gold Elkhorn and Staghorn coral - battlements arrayed at the edge of the reef against the great expanse of Mother Ocean. At this border, where the coral ended and the reef dropped off into dark blue depths, I got (as I always do) the willies. There is something about swimming along the dark, pelagic edge of the Caribbean, hovering there next to the drop-off and staring into the deep blue. It reminds me of crawling on my belly to peer over the edge of a cliff. It causes me pause. At the edge of the *Vivario* Reef something held me tethered, clinging to Mommy Earth's hand as it were. Perhaps it was acrophobia. Perhaps it was the humbling awe I felt at the brink of our planet's greatest surface element – the Ocean. Or perhaps it was the knowledge that alien fish, fish about my size or larger, fish who might be intrigued by my scent and flavor, lurked just beyond my eyes' ability to penetrate the water depths.

After nine months on the water, Sawyer and Riley had become good swimmers. At every anchorage they dove off the pointy bows of Manta Raya, sometimes diving so deeply that Diane and I could not help but count each interminable second until their smiling faces reappeared. After hours in the water, they would climb, wet and shivering, back on deck. And while they hugged themselves and spun before me, I would rinse them off with fresh water; and I could not help but peer behind their ears to see if they had grown gills.

Sawyer was an able and relaxed snorkeler. She paddled about with her flippers and, with a kick, disappeared into the water like a dolphin. Because little sister Riley wanted to do everything her big sister did, she also asked for a set of snorkel and fins. At a department store in Venezuela, Diane found Riley a cheap, shrink-wrapped set. The little mask, straw-like snorkel and pink fins were a bit of a joke. And we figured that once our five-year-old daughter wrestled with the clumsy equipment, she would blow a fuse and walk away. But being a dutiful and tolerant mom, Diane strapped the mask on Riley's face; and after three failed and flailing attempts (Diane reminding Riley each time that she must breathe through her mouth, not her nose, and try to avoid ripping her mask from her face), Riley gripped the bottom rung of the stern ladder, kicked her feet and managed to keep the mask on her face as she ducked into the water. On this fourth attempt, instead of jerking her head back out of the water and sputtering in frustration, she held herself rigidly in the water. Her kicking feet gradually slowed, relaxed and came to a stop. She floated, transfixed, for what to mom and dad seemed an impossibly long time. When she finally pulled her head up and showed her face, all we saw were two wide eyes framed in glass and a wide smile. "There!" she shouted. "I did it!" It was not long before Riley left the security of the stern ladder and swam off with her sister; both girls' heads swiveling this way and that, snorkels pointed skyward and echoing with shouts and laughter.

I read once about a Labrador puppy that grew up on a cruising boat. To keep the dog from jumping overboard while at sea, its owners taught it to leave the boat only by first jumping into the dinghy. The dog did its business on a carpet square, which was attached to a line and could be kicked overboard for cleaning. The dog grew up on the water. It would ride the bow, bark and go into point whenever it spotted fish or dolphins. One day when the dog's owners reached a mainland big enough to support minor mammals, the dog came upon a squirrel. It was so shocked by the furry thing that its ears shot up, and it turned tail and ran directly back to the ship. Its owners found it sitting in the dingy, patiently waiting to be taken back home to the sea.

Our girls knew nothing of roller blades, bicycles and skateboards (we are still trying to catch up on some of these land skills). But they dove, swam and snorkeled like fish. Sawyer once said of snorkeling: "I like that feeling when you don't go up, and you don't go down. It's like magic." She was describing the weightlessness of neutral buoyancy - the perfect balance in a warm sea amidst great statues of coral and surrounded by the flash of colorful fishes.

When we dove through the *Vivario* reef as a family, we held hands. I had already scouted the reef, so I knew the path to swim through the winding canyons of coral. I also knew what we were about to see. I had Riley's small hand buried in my fist, and Diane was swimming with Sawyer. We glided through a silent garden - our own, private park - no shouting people, no honking cars, no distractions of any kind. Together we took in the beauty of billowing brain coral and traced (with our eyes, not our rough hands) the intricate grooves and impossible patterns of its folds. In bold gold and blue, a pair of angelfish swam up to our masks and inspected us, calmly, face-to-face, until a burst of bubbles from our snorkels sent them flying. The kids pointed and gurgled, and we swam down together to poke a great sofa of soft orange coral and to see the waving hair-like antennae and raised red and white striped claws of a banded coral shrimp, only two inches long. We were together in a place of beauty, a place of enchantment, and there was warmth in our shared discoveries. Diane and I felt enchantment's heat in the clasp of the tiny hands we held. We felt it spread up through our arms and envelop our hearts.

Before long we came to the spot I had wanted to show my family. We rounded an overhanging cliff of coral and hovered over a sandy valley. We stopped and stared. Three nurse sharks, one over ten feet long, lay on the ocean floor. Two smaller lemon sharks swam circles over their heads. We came to the surface together, pulled the snorkels out of our mouths and all started talking at once.

Riley; "Those are sharks! Those are sharks!"

Diane: "Do you think this is safe?"

Sawyer: "They're huge! Did you see the biggest one on the ground?"

Me: "O.K. Remember gang. They're more scared of us than we are of them. We'll go together, but two at a time– let's check 'em out."

Diane was not entirely onboard with my plan, and I knew there was a danger that her doubts would infect the girls. To be fair, her worries, like the worries of all good moms, were often the caution that kept me (and all fathers) from getting our kids into deep trouble. But I did not want to go down the path of reason. I had been amongst these sharks, and despite the more tender and enticing human bait I planned to bring them now, I was sure we would be all right. Well... pretty sure. So before the nay saying could gain momentum, I turned to Riley, "We'll go down first" (I knew that Riley tended toward motion and often took the fast track to adventure). She pulled on her mask and jammed her snorkel into her mouth.

Nodding to Diane's open mouth, I turned to Riley, counted "one, two, three," and ducked into the silent deep. Down we swam together. I pulled her with me to give her the time she would need to reach the bottom, see the sights and return before running out of air. The sand sharks scattered. The nurse sharks lay together like drugged prizefighters in a sauna - long tapered tails, signature shark dorsal fins and barbels protruding from their great rounded snouts. Riley and I swam down until we were just above the biggest shark, and I stopped. I had to forcibly remind myself that objects underwater appear 25% larger than they really are. But in this case, the reminder did not help. I knew this Nurse shark was harmless. Heck, in the Bahamas I had watched a crazy kid grab Nurse sharks by their tails. But my heart raced nonetheless. There was something disquieting about facing this animal, an animal larger than I was and an animal that ate only other animals. When we rounded and faced the king shark, it did not move a muscle. I was sure it was sleeping. But when I stared into its eyes, their pupil-less, dull, and silver sheen spoke not of sleep and definitely not of fear. They reflected a cold mechanical watchfulness and a hard, emotionless and alien animation. The animal was a perfect, underwater eating machine. When we swam back up, I was glad to reach the surface, but I found myself irrationally troubled by the pedaling of our feet under water. From below did we look like wounded, struggling fish?

I took Sawyer down with me next, but we did not visit the largest shark. This time we visited the littlest fellow. Afterwards, as we swam back through the coral toward Manta Raya, I could not help but look over my shoulder and past my kicking fins to see if we were being followed. This was, after all, the sharks' watery world, not mine. But as we decompressed in the cockpit amongst our dripping fins and snorkels, the flush of excitement and the stories we told each other were filled with both a sense of accomplishment and a sense of relief. No Disneyland ride could touch this.

Guanaja

Our passage from the *Vivario* Cays to Guanaja was tough. Diane called it… well, let us just say she called it " troubling." Forty-knot gusting winds and heaping seas tossed and bumped us all the way to the island. We did not try coming into port on the windward side of the island, where we were supposed to clear in; instead, we blasted around the corner to the leeward side looking for shelter. Our log reads: "… anchor down 1030 after 155 nautical miles of second thoughts about our lifestyle choice." We guessed our way through a narrow channel entrance, while trying not to make sliced sushi out of scuba divers near the channel's entrance. Then, as we got near enough to the island to hide behind the lee of its towering mountain, the wind eased and the water settled. When our anchor touched down, we danced a little jig.

Part of the anxiety of sailing to Guanaja may have been the island itself. We had heard such terrible things about what Hurricane Mitch had done there just a few weeks before our arrival. The tough S.O.B. storm had sunk the tall ship *Fantone* with all hands and, as if diabolically aiming its fury, had roared directly over Guanaja's head.

We were in Venezuela when Mitch had struck, and we had discussed our Northwest Caribbean passage plans with a number of cruisers, including a tough old liveaboard cruiser who had sailed the region some years before. "You're headed where?" the gruff old cuss had asked, "The Bay Islands? Why would you go there? All you're gonna see is wreckage and floating bodies."

This was neither a pleasant prospect nor an appropriate comment to make before our two daughters. Never mind that the curmudgeon of a captain had not been to the Bay Islands since the hurricane and that he had not actually spoken to anyone who had. He and several other cruisers, who also felt they were "in the know," told us we were headed toward disaster.

As we looked about us at the island, there were clear signs Mitch had been there. In my post-passage delirium, I could not see the damage, at first. The island's central mountain was green, not scoured bald as I had envisioned. But then I noticed that all of the palms and hardwood trees had been sheared from the mountainside. They had been lifted like dandelion fluff and blown out to sea. At the base of the mountain, lumber, now in splinters, was all that remained of hillside homes. Every home had been flattened into matchsticks.

But the place was being rebuilt. Folks were smiling and carrying on, and the only floating bodies we saw were the happy scuba divers we had managed to miss at the channel entrance. Ten miles away on Roatan, where we sailed the next day and where we were told we would meet with yet more devastation, we did not find one frond from one graceful palm out of place. The island appeared untouched. Taxis idled under the shade of canopied hotels, while the hotel managers stood outside their resorts wringing their hands and wondering when all the tourists would come back. We ended up having the place to ourselves, and at bargain prices.

This sort of truth versus scuttlebutt had happened to us before. Jamaica, which we had been told was crime-ridden and unfriendly in the eighties (Remember the "Come back to Jamaica" ads?), had been a cruising paradise. We had loved the place. We had learned that the common wisdom was often the common delusion and that we could use this dementia to find idyllic spots other folks were avoiding. Even when we were able to speak with someone who had sailed to a proposed getaway, we had to consider the source. One man's dread might be another man's dream.

Why were we cruising anyway? Maybe we loved the ocean and her water treasures, were inspired by her far flung destinations, or took pride in using our own brain and brawn to cross her unpredictable waters. But whatever the reasons, they did not include "hanging with the crowd." Heck, if we had wanted to march to the beat of everyone else's drum, we would have used a *terra firma* vehicle and traveled the turnpike. Avoiding the common wisdom ended up being a great way to escape the crowds (See Appendix 5: Ten Ways to Get Away).

Sunken Treasure

W̲e were in the wee hours of the morning; and yes, rum was involved. *Manta Raya* was docked alongside a great stone wall that surrounded a Roatan resort. Because of the brouhaha about hurricane Mitch, the once busy resort, a great complex of tennis courts, peacocks and bougainvilleas, was now a ghost resort. It was so empty that we had tied up to its long dock for practically nothing. We were flanked by the teak and brass of massive pleasure yachts, also empty and tied off with double lines for the winter. They awaited the whimsy of their highbrow owners, who one day would come south again from their shivering cities.

But now we had the place to ourselves, and the bounty of fresh water, a laundry and a step ashore playground was making us a bit giddy. Having befriended kittens and an excited puppy with pin sharp teeth, the girls were ashore all day screaming, either in delight or pain. French-Anglo friends we had met back on the island of Providencia were anchored nearby, so we all had playmates. Fourteen-year-old Billie Jean, a smiling girl who could play the concertina, befriended our girls and provided a third pincushion for the puppy. Her parents were dive partners and "adult time" playmates for Diane and myself.

When the few tourists at the resort came back from their dive trips, they wandered by *Manta Raya*, and some became curious about the liveaboard family recently delivered to their dock. We spoke with two schoolteachers, who had traveled far from the grey winter of Kansas to live their tropical, blue dive fantasies in the Bay Islands of Honduras. Late in the afternoon, a beautiful, double-decker yacht pulled up off our stern. Its delivery crew, a barrel chested captain in baritone and his beautiful blonde wife in tenor, joined the general fray of acquaintances and upped the ante of good will until a party became the inevitable conclusion. Someone donated tuna steaks. We fired up our grill. Salads and appetizers appeared, and our cockpit patio once again filled with laughter. It was a long party that lasted until the resort's twinkling lights tag teamed the tangerine sunset, and the crickets and tree frogs sang the dusk into night.

Late into the night, when the excitement of the party began to drift away with the hugs of departing guests, the barrel chested captain and his promise of aged Honduran rum carried me over to the double-deck yacht. The night had created its own magic, and I was not ready for bed. Somehow I knew that the best flourishes were yet to come. I found myself seated in a wood paneled salon with the Captain and his wife. We sat amidst satin pillows around a glass coffee table on which rested the tongue loosening rum. And we began to speak of things.

Perhaps ethanol makes braggarts of men and prompts their fictions. And perhaps it pulls forth facts, even Truths, which might otherwise lie hidden beneath a blanket of self-conscious propriety. Regardless, our tongues were loosened that night, and we were enjoying one another's company as we prattled on earnestly about the loves, adventures and misadventures that had brought us together on a starry night in the Bay Islands.

The Captain had studied mechanical engineering. But finding himself too serious and overworked at his first engineering job, he had one day asked himself, as all cruisers do, if his office job were really the way he wanted to live out the rest of his life. So he traded his job for a captain's license and headed to sea. He found himself running a boat for an owner in San Diego, whom he described, without rancor, as "a pure asshole." It was this fellow (AH) who led the Captain to sunken treasure.

As we sat about the luxury salon, the Captain revealed only the hint of his treasure story, and it took much more coaxing and several pours of Honduran elixir to convince him to tell more: "Look, I'm no psychic or some sort of heebie jeebie man," he said, waggling his fingers in the air, eyes wide and lips pursed. "I'm an engineer. Fortunetellers, séances and sunken treasure are not something I go around yakking about. Hell, I didn't believe what was happening when it happened... I have trouble believing it now."

I waited, and the Captain continued.

He had worked for AH for two years. AH had a son, a teenager the Captain liked, who developed a chronic and debilitating nerve disorder. Professing to be looking for a cure outside traditional medicine, AH had contacted a mystic in Los Angeles. He had asked the Captain to accompany him, but the Captain had begged off, until he heard the visit was "for the boy." The mystic lived in Hollywood.

"Great," the Captain had groused, "fortune teller of the stars." But in the course of their first visit to the lady's home, a strange shift of plot took place. Foregoing any polite introductions or conversational niceties, AH had immediately tested the woman. "Tell me why we're here?" he had demanded.

The Lady paused, considered AH for a moment and said, "I see gems and coins in water." AH's face had brightened.

Over the course of the next few months and many more visits, the Captain had learned that his boss and the Lady were somehow in cahoots. Both were intent on finding an 18th century ship that had sunken somewhere off the coast of Madagascar. Apparently the ship contained treasure. Besides the Lady and AH, other players were brought into the drama: the Captain met more mystics and a scientist from NASA. All of these people, he was informed, would be part of a treasure hunting expedition on which he was to be the captain. The Lady with her prescient cohorts would "direct" the operation from California. The scientist would sail with the Captain and bring along equipment that could measure the signal sent by the mystics - a psychic "homing beacon."

"Oh boy," thought Captain, "a long cruise with an asshole and a frizzy haired, sci-fi scientist from the planet wacko." The planned voyage was a plot straight out of a B movie, but it sailed to a warm spot with pretty water, so the Captain found himself agreeing to skipper the voyage. Besides, he had begun to suspend his disbelief. There was something about the Lady - something decent and helpful. She did seem to be able to tell folks things about themselves and their futures. But still, the Captain did not want his own fortune read. At one point, the Lady had pulled the Captain aside and asked him why. Did he not like or trust her?

No, the Captain had answered, he had actually grown to like and trust her, but he was leery of the whole fortune telling "thing." He liked the course his life had taken so far. Despite the dips and turns, he was enjoying the trip; and he did not want to know where the road led. Knowing, he felt, would somehow spoil the fun.

The Lady had taken his hand and smiled. "You are a good man," she had said, "and smart."

As we sat on the Captain's boat at the marina, he eyed the nearly empty bottle of rum. "To make a long story short," he continued, "we found ourselves in a few hundred feet of water off the coast of Madagascar. AH was in the pilothouse in radio contact with the séance folks. The scientist, whom I had actually come to like during the course of our trip, was up with me on the bow. He had an entire collection of odd instruments, but he was concentrating on a handheld gizmo with meters, dials and an antenna-like thing that sprouted out the front. It beeped from time to time. I was wearing a headset connected to the bridge, and I had my handheld GPS. We were sailing a grid pattern over the area we had been told to search, and the two of us, the scientist and I, were staring into the blue water off the bow. It was a calm day, warm, pretty, and I reminded myself that no matter what happened, I couldn't complain about the working conditions. That's when the scientist's gizmo started beeping. He pointed at the thing and showed me the pegged meters. Through my headset I heard AH ask if anything was happening. The Hollywood mystics had told him we had to be close. I told him we had a reading and punched the locator button on my GPS." With the position marked, the scientist's readings recorded and the mystics celebrating back in tinsel town, the Captain turned the boat back toward Cape Town, where more wonders were to occur.

With the treasure supposedly located, the Captain was charged with hiring a salvage team. And just as the Lady had told him he would, the Captain found a Greek salvage company - the owner sitting on a pile of nets at the end of a cobblestone wharf in Cape Town, smoking a cigarette. It was exactly the scene the Lady had predicted he would see, and by now the Captain had given up being surprised by such predictions.

"My crew," said the Greek, "will have be paid in advance. They have families, kids to feed. But me, I will take a percentage. If we find nothing, I get nothing." The Captain agreed as he shook the Greek man's hand.

The first step was the mapping of the site. That same week they sailed back to the site, this time aboard the Greek's salvage ship. With AH, the Scientist, the Captain and the Greek all standing and staring at a sonar screen, they watched the pinging lines form an image - sweeping curves coming to a point - the bow and the undeniable outline of a hull. The boys on the bridge nodded to one another and smiled.

But before salvage could begin, the expedition had to return to the United States. There was money to be raised - the salvage operation, AH predicted, would cost millions. AH traveled across the country telling his tale to private, moneyed audiences. He showed slides and produced copies of historical paperwork that described a ship lost off Madagascar - a ship loaded with gold coin and jewels. In the excitement, even the Captain contributed to the venture. When AH mentioned in passing that a temporary shortage of bandwagon travel funds was curbing his fundraising, the Captain willingly fronted him $7,000. Now he too was invested.

One night as the Captain waited for the next phase of the salvage expedition to begin, he happened to catch a National Geographic special. It was about sunken treasure, and it raised the question of who owned the rights to ancient shipwrecks. Treasure hunters argued that they did the work and therefore should own whatever was discovered. Diplomats argued that the wrecks belonged to the country with offshore rights or the country of the ship's origin. But the archeologists argued that antiquities belonged to all mankind – that the real value of the treasures was in the stories they told us about our past. The documentary caused the Captain pause. But after all, he was only the Captain; AH was the boss.

The next day the Captain got word that AH was gone. After raising his millions, he had skipped town and apparently the country. And so ended the treasure hunt, the Captain's employment, his dreams of treasure and any hopes he had of ever recovering the $7,000 he had fronted Mr. Asshole.

Back in the luxury salon of the Captain's boat, I was not ready for the story to end this way. I stammered, "But you *know* where the treasure is!"

The Captain gazed into the empty bottle of rum and smiled. "Sure, I've got the coordinates."

"You could go after the treasure yourself!" I said. "Hell, I'd help! It's not that deep. You said so yourself. It's in shallow water..."

I was caught up in the excitement. In fact, I was already riding high on a pile of jewels and gold coin. Surely, had there been a mirror in the salon, I would have seen the wild-eyed reflection of Humphrey Bogart in "The Treasure of the Sierra Madre."

The Captain looked across the salon at his wife. They shared a private and indulgent smile. "You know," he said, "we might go back one day, but only with the Lady's blessing... I saw her not long after AH skipped with the money, and she wasn't surprised by what he'd done (of course). She told me an odd story. She said the whole thing had been AH's karma. She said that when it came to fortune telling and fortunetellers, it was a white and black magic gig. She was one of the white mystics. She was there to help. She told me that her visions were like gifts - that they were given to her to facilitate a critical event in someone's life. Her visions went forward and backward, and they only came to her occasionally. After all, if fortunetellers could see everything, the stock market and the lottery would be ransacked."

"When AH had first visited her," the Captain continued, "she had seen who he was and who he had been. He was a conniving cheat and had been a cheat in a former life. He had been the slaver on the ship we'd been sent to salvage."

I am sure my mouth hung open. The Captain waited and let me digest this part of his story before moving on.

"The ship's voyage had been dark from the very beginning. It was a classic story of greed. The boat had been overloaded with slaves and stolen treasure. In the storm, its own weight had turned it over and brought it down. Our treasure hunt, it seemed, had been AH's chance to make up for this greed - the deaths and the tragedy. I think something good could have been done with the salvaged treasure. Instead, my boss had blown it, again."

I knew now why the Captain had been hesitant to tell me his story. The Captain's story rang true, but it called for a particular twist of logic and a wide suspension of disbelief. Sitting about the table in the Captain's salon, we stared into our glasses and smiled. We rehashed the story a bit, but the hour was late and the Magic was waning. So I said my thanks and took my leave. But as I stepped out into the warm moist air, I reiterated my offer – only this time with more care.

"If you ever do decide to go back for that ship," I said, "I'd like to help; but only for the adventure – nothing else."

"Thanks," said the Captain with a smile. "I understand."

And like the drunken sailor I was, I swaggered down the dock toward my boat and my home. But despite the swagger, my mind was as sober and clear as the full moon riding in a cloudless sky high over my head.

On to Guatemala

Before leaving for the Bay Islands, we had packed up whatever medical supplies and extra provisions we could scrounge back in Venezuela and San Andres. Our idea had been that once we got to the Bay Islands, we might be able to help with the aftermath of hurricane Mitch. But with Guanaja under repair and Roatan lacking nothing but the return of its tourists, we sailed toward Central America with our "red cross" supplies still stowed. Our next stop was a beautiful little cluster of islands called the *Cayos Cochinos* or pig islands, where the supplies would find a home.

The *Cayos Cochinos*, *Grande* and *Pequeño* (big and little), were steep-to, volcanic and covered with lush vegetation. Broom Palms bent to strong afternoon breezes, and smooth, red barked hardwoods with white and red flowers dotted the hillsides. A beautiful little home was literally carved out of the rocky hillside just off the southern shore of *Cochino Grande*. A registered nurse from Texas used the home as a clinic during the summer. In 1998 she saw over 2,000 patients, some traveling over 100 miles in leaky *cayucos* to get her help. Her clinic was free, so we gathered up our old prescription medicines, soap, toothpastes, band-aids and leftover Honduran currency, and dinghied up to her wharf. We were met by her caretaker, his wife and a *loco* dog, who were all grateful recipients of our gifts – the dog leaping and performing enthusiastic flips when we landed. In a room decorated with swordfish bills, leopard skins and shark jaws, we laid out our donations on a thick plank table. We added our gifts to what was already a large pile of supplies waiting for the nurse's return. As usual, cruisers, who sail with little on the open ocean, had given whatever they could when compassion called.

The next day we anchored off *Cochino Pequeño* - "the big pig's little brother." We found a clean reef for diving and a deserted beach tucked into a cliff-lined cove. Under the coconut palms, the girls played in pools that had been formed in the volcanic rock. As they collected snails, Sawyer met with the wrong end of a cantankerous Hermit Crab. And during a hot hike inshore, Sawyer also spotted a pale brown snake as big as a python dangling from a tree branch. This was Sawyer's day to mingle with Nature. After our hike, we swam back out to *Manta Raya*, where light, cooling winds blessed the perfect day.

But the next morning the Honduran Navy showed up. Polite and officious, they told us to move on. We were, they said, anchored near a protected *aricefe* (reef). In Honduras, as in the United States, the military owned much of the prime real estate. But unlike the military in North America, here they ran the show. We motored on in a light wind that barely filled our headsail but pushed us on toward our next destination: Guatemala.

Livingston Port Captain

We arrived at the Central American mainland at the "hip joint" where Guatemala meets Honduras, and we were excited because our landfall was about to give us a break from Mother Ocean. We hoped to sneak away from Her waves, winds and saltwater by motoring up the *Rio Dulce* River into the Guatemalan jungle. It was time for a safari. But first we would have to deal with the usual permissions, and that meant once again meeting with the military in Latin America. In the ramshackle town of Livingston at the mouth of the Rio, we motored ashore to speak with the Port Captain.

William Faulkner once said that the reason he wrote such seemingly endless, complicated and run-on sentences was that he was trying to illustrate, in literary form, the complicated, intertwined and almost infinite ancestral motivations of the characters in his stories. He felt that the convoluted archetypical inheritances, both conscious and unconscious, were what made his character and, as reflections of humanity, all people behave the way they did. Then again, maybe Mr. Faulkner just liked to write long sentences.

As we traveled the Caribbean, each village, island and country, like Mr. Faulkner's characters, had its own personality; and one of my passions was unraveling the history that might have shaped each destination. There were stereotypical islands like the former British possessions, which, no matter how poor, still maintained Britain's orderly systems. Post offices with faded prints of the Queen on peeling paint walls were still run by polite and officious postal workers - each transaction logged, letters and cards sorted and the satisfactory thump of a rubber stamp concluding business. On the roadsides, laughing schoolchildren carried their books in satchels as they walked home wearing their crisp blue and white uniforms. On the French islands, there was a lower order of discipline, which ebbed and flowed depending on the circumstances, the time of day and the approximation to a repast, like a long lunch of warm bread, intoxicating soup and a meditative cabernet. The former Spanish colonies operated in a character diametrically opposed to the British. Though offices and uniforms abounded, the officials themselves were driven not by a system of order but by a system of title, privilege and what might be thought of in the United States as greed.

I have a friend from Madrid who once enlightened me about Spanish colonial history. She told me that though we Americans think of the early crusading Spanish as silver breasted, standard carrying conquistadores; the 17th century Spaniards knew them for what they really were: criminals. Spain's colonizing armies were gathered from prisons, heaped into boats, armed and then unleashed on the Americas. Once there, they reaped whatever profit they could, first for king, and then for themselves. Never mind the complicated and mixed motive religious angle that accompanied these conquests. In the colonial era of profit and sense, the king was out for the money. He underpaid his officers knowing they would skim the rest of their income off the river of wealth flowing back to Europe. He expected this, and he expected the same of his titled landholders. But the skimming had to be within reason; otherwise, there would be reprisals.

In Spanish hierarchy, as important to the Spanish sense of self as breath itself, there were the landed and titled, the officials, and then everyone else: peasants, workers, slaves, Indians, *piones* (peons). Today, though royal titles have disappeared, the system of entitlement has not. Station and office are still the currency of Latin America. Though the attitude of entitlement, which in societal hegemony reveals itself as political pick pocketing, occurs in all cultures, in the Latin American system, inherited entitlement is both expected and respected. In its extreme it is known as *La Mordida* or "The Bite." Our visit to the Port Captain's office in Livingston, Guatemala was a prime example.

Sawyer and I walked through the hot dusty streets to collect rubber stamps from the immigration officer (all paperwork in triplicate, please), the town doctor (no sign of plague aboard, you may lower the yellow quarantine flag ... remember not to drink the river water), the customs officer (did you bring any alcohol into the country? I'm afraid I must confiscate it), and our final stop and last rubber stamp at the office of the Port Captain.

As we approached the office, we noticed that it was not like the ramshackle offices we had just visited - dangling light bulbs, chipped plaster walls, flea bitten dogs lounging on the stoops. The Port Captain resided in a compound, a brocaded, wrought iron fenced, shrub-trimmed mini-palace, before which stood a rifle toting guard in uniform and polished shoes. As we approached, the guard jumped up from his siesta stool and strode toward the iron gate, which though rusted and off its hinges, provided a symbolic sense of boundary. The guard considered me sternly, then gazed down at Sawyer and failed to hide the softening of his features. In Spanish he asked me the nature of my business (knowing full well that any gringo wearing shorts and sandals and carrying a passel of passports had come to beg for the Port Captain's clearance). He then escorted us to the Port Captain's office but still could not help smiling at my blonde daughter, who, hand in mine, smiled back. The guard knocked on a solid teak door. There was a murmur within, and the guard, in subdued and subservient tones, announced our visit and opened the great door.

The Port Captain had been caught off guard - yet another *siesta interruptus*. He rose from his swivel chair and hurriedly threw on his uniform shirt of epaulets and colorful ribbons. The uniform had been recently pressed. Though caught napping, the man was not flustered, he was smiling, a big Cheshire cat smile beneath a drooping black mustache. He was tall and handsome and had the heavily lashed, brown eyes of a Latin lover. The window air conditioner, the only air conditioner I had seen in town, blew a tepid, tropical blast over his desk, which was covered not with official paperwork but scattered newspapers and magazines.

"*Adelante, senor!*" he said, grasping my hand as he continued buttoning his shirt. "*Por favor, sientese.*" I smiled, shook his proffered hand and took the offered seat - the only chair before the desk, a naugahyde affair, split and oozing foam. The Port Captain glanced down at Sawyer, and his 200-watt smile dimmed a bit before resuming its brilliance. "*Su hija?*" he asked. "*Si,*" I say, "my daughter. Do you speak English?"

The Port Captain smiled humbly and shrugged, "Only a little." But I suspected from these few words and the way he had spoken them, that he spoke and understood English quite well. Still, this was his kingdom, so we continued speaking his language - one of the ground rules of the impending match.

There was polite chat. How old was my daughter (the answer to which I asked Sawyer to give in Spanish). Where were we from? (With the "Estados Unidas" answer, the quick flicker of a raised eyebrow.) How long would we be visiting? To what purpose? And finally to business: Had I seen the other officials in town?

Yes. I handed him the documents gathered thus far. He flipped through each paper and studied it as if he had never seen such paperwork before; and then furrowed his brow, intimating that something was wrong. And here, finally, came the important questions:

How much, might he ask, did I pay the immigration officer?

I told him, and I detected a fleeting look of disappointment, for we had paid the stated fee and no more thus far on our paper chase through Livingston.

The tall Port Captain leaned back in his creaking chair, and his mustache rose as he filled his nostrils with air. Had I been told that the town of Livingston was instituting a new fee, a donation of sorts, to support the "park" along the Rio Dulce River?

No, I was not aware there was a park.

Oh yes, a grand park to help the animals and preserve the valuable trees and flowers.

Hmmm. But did the Port Captain mind if I asked him a question? No? How long had he been the Port Captain in Livingston?

The officer blinked at this non sequitur: *mordida interruptus*.

From a cold start, but warning to the conversation over the next half hour, the officer told us how he had come to the town of Livingston. In mid discourse, frustrated by the stumbling pace of my Spanish, he switched to flawless English and rambled on enthusiastically. He was the son of a wealthy government official (son of son of a son of a son of a conquistador), had attended the University of Miami, trained as an officer in the Guatemalan navy and received his first assignment to the shabby port town of Livingston. Soon he would be moving on, a position in Guatemala City for sure, and perhaps foreign relations and travel; this last prospect lighting some sweet sadness in his eyes.

It was then, as if on cue, that Sawyer asked the question that time and again had helped us through Latin American red tape boondogglery: "Papa, are we done yet?" And then she looked up with her clear blue, darling eyes at the Port Captain and asked him, "Can we go now?"

I believe the only time one my daughters, my port clearing partner Riley, uttered an interrogative more direct was when she walked up to a customs official and pointedly asked, "Why do we have to do this?" The question brought flustered but immediate results.

In the Port Captain's office, the mouth of babes facilitation may not have been necessary, but it ended the interview nonetheless. The Port Captain, pleased with our chat and foregoing his usual *mordida* mission, opened his desk drawer and offered me a parting cigar. In return, I pulled a five-dollar bill from my wallet and pressed it into his hand.

"For the park," I said. And we both smiled.

Back aboard Manta Raya, we unloaded the provisions we had gathered - freshly baked breads, pastries and *Gallo* (rooster – cock-a-doodle-doo) beer. We hurried through our preparations for our river trip, because the tide was changin. "Any problems clearing in?" shouted Diane, as she raised the anchor. I glanced at Sawyer, raised my eyebrows and answered, "No, not really."

Within a few minutes we were steaming into the Rio's entrance, where, just inside the river's mouth, we were swept into a different world. At a sharp bend around the base of a steep cliff, the ocean disappeared behind us and jungle surrounded us. The Rio's steep banks were covered with dripping ferns and colorful flowers. Vines hung down from a thick canopy of trees and dipped into the chocolate brown water. Overhead, swallows darted through our rigging, and high on the cliff top above us, I saw something big and brown move through the foliage. Was it a monkey? The girls rushed up onto the trampoline with their binoculars. For the rest of the day, until we anchored in a languid lagoon just off the main river channel, we were not aboard *Manta Raya*; we were cruising on the *African Queen*.

Occasionally we came upon palm-thatched huts. Mayan Indians snorkeled the shoreline towing their dugout canoes behind them as they checked their crab traps. All waved as we passed. White herons, black cormorants and pelicans filled the dark green trees about us. When we anchored that evening, there was no wind, no waves, just the slow moving river beneath us.

The next morning I woke disoriented. What was wrong? The usual motion of Mother Ocean was gone and something was making berserk chicken sounds? Twitters, quacks, peeps, whistles, hoots, buzzes, you name it; the place was alive with sounds. Then I heard the "hootie-hoo!"

of our girls – their morning call to one another out the transom hatches of their berths and across the stern of our boat to see if one another were awake. "Hootie-hoo!" came the reply, and I was smiling – thrilled to be on a real jungle adventure with my girls.

Tarzan Finds a Daughter

I am a bit embarrassed to admit that one of my wife's and my inspirations for family cruising came from a 1939 movie entitled "Tarzan Finds a Son." If you recall, or, if you were deprived of seeing the 1939 Johnny Weissmuller/Maureen O'Hara classic, a plane crashes into the African jungle, and Tarzan and Jane find the sole survivor: a baby. They become the sudden and surprised parents of generically named "Boy." After all, dear Reader, what mom or dad, no matter how eager or prepared for parenthood, has not felt as if their gurgling bundle of dirty diapers, drool and smiles fell out of the sky and into their arms? In the movie, as Jane coos and cradles Boy, Tarzan wrinkles his brow and asks: "Jane want?"

But as with any father, who has even the smallest crack in his heart, Tarzan succumbs to the baby's charms. He adjusts his daily schedule of jungle romping and takes time to harvest ostrich feathers for a cradle and get milk from a deer. Soon Boy and Tarzan are swinging through the treetops and playing hide and seek with hippos. They dive together into deep pools and come up laughing. And at the end of the day, as the wild birds squawk and lions roar into the sunset, they return to their family tree house, where a simple "Ungowa" lifts them in an elephant driven elevator to Jane's dinner of ostrich egg omelets.

For Diane and me, the whole Tarzan and Jane thing – free and swinging through the jungle or swimming side by side in a tepid, gator infested pool - was the subliminal seed that grew into a lush and vibrant jungle of our minds. It bloomed into our dream of sailing the Caribbean. "Tarzan Finds a Son" made us believe that a Caribbean jungle adventure could also include kids. As soon as both Sawyer and Riley could swim fifty meters and stay ahead of the gators, we packed up and sailed away to the rainforest. "Aayeeeaah!"

Road Warrior Child Rearing

I once had the good fortune to work with a guidance counselor from one of our local high schools in Flagstaff, Arizona. I liked this fellow, and his students liked him too. They smiled at him when he walked down the hall; and they brightened when he called them by name. He was one of *those* members of the school staff, who by some miraculous stroke of fortune, are both respected and liked by their students. So when I sat with this counselor to talk about the problems in his school, I paid attention.

Over the nearly 30 years he had spent in the public school system, certain problems, problems that could destroy kids, had gotten worse. Drugs were taking hold of too many kids, and the one-sided burden placed on ill-equipped and unprepared young women, pregnancy, was on the rise. More kids than ever were quitting school.

I could not resist. I had to ask the counselor *the* question – the one I figured was impossible to answer. I asked him whether there were an overriding reason, a root cause, for the problems. And he hesitated only briefly before answering.

"There are no studies," he said. "And I can't prove what I think, but I think the problems start when school ends."

"Do you remember coming home after school?" he asked. "Maybe it was a good day; maybe it was a bad day; maybe you liked your parents, or maybe you wished they would evaporate. But when you came home, you threw open the door, flopped onto the couch, and no matter how rough your day had been, no matter how unsteady your world felt, you were home, and you were safe. You had reached the castle, and you were behind the moat. And at the sound of your homecoming, one of your parents would yell, "Welcome home, honey!"

"Today kids get home from school and nobody is there. Both parents are working, and chances are they're divorced. I'm not saying this explains everything, but it's somewhere near the heart of the problem."

Not long after this conversation, Diane and I caught a tag line for the television nightly news. Our little TV, whose volume buttons had been held in place by stringy blobs from a glue gun, did not usually receive a signal. It worked for Holy Grail events like the World Series, but only if we prayed to the one-eyed monster of television and pointed it's bunny ears just so. Still, the spotty reception was a good thing. It was good discipline for a family in training for the liveaboard life. But when our T.V., which rarely worked anymore, suddenly sputtered to life to present a promo for the news, it was a bit of a miracle. For the moment, we were captivated.

Two news anchors were hooking an upcoming story. They turned to the camera, and with eyebrows arched, asked the parents in their audience just how many meals they shared with their children. That and more questions about 21st century parenting would be coming up on the hour.

Then our faithful TV, after bursting to life to deliver this provocative question, resumed its usual programming: it went blank. However, the newscasters and their question played on in our minds. Just how many meals was the average American family sharing these days? Two? One? None? Or, as a mother later suggested to me, perhaps the question should have been phrased: "How many meals do parents share with their children each week, or worse, each month?" This mother and her husband had recently eaten dinner with their teenaged daughters, and the father had asked one of the daughters to pass the butter. The daughter had burst into tears and run from the table. The mother paused, turned to her husband and said, "It appears we have an issue."

Since meals can indeed be that convention over which surprising and important topics arise, I had hoped families still sat together over my favorite meal: breakfast. That is when I get to lord the fact that I am awake over the rest of my family, which is not. I give them inane advice and race through a thousand coffee induced jags before they are able to defend themselves. But more importantly, breakfast is when I have a chance to possibly help set the tone for the day - upbeat, if there is an option.

American families still lunched, I supposed, *in abstentia*, just as I did when I was in school. Lunch was when I took advantage of the fact that my parents were *not* around to see how long I could get the cafeteria mashed potatoes to stick to the lunchroom ceiling. But dinner...surely families still ate dinner together. Didn't they?

A fellow I admired, a fellow who had studied under Frank Lloyd Wright and worked with Walt Disney, once told me this: "When it comes to your kids, it's not the quality time that counts; it's the quantity time."

I was stunned. "Excuse me? What did you say? We parents, already overworked with two jobs are *also* supposed to hop out of bed, drag our kids into their clothes, and, while they yawn in front of their cereal bowls, throw a cheese cracker in their lunch boxes, sign their permission for "whatever" slips, and then push them out the door toward the bus stop, so we can drive through bumper-to-bumper traffic to work and drive back home at the end of the day in time to get our kids to soccer, ballet, 4H or whatever sport or club is in season, magically produce dinner, pay the bills, fix the broken faucet, kick the dog, and after all of this is done, spend a little "quantity time?" I think not.

Working Daddies

I attended my first corporate meeting in the early eighties. There was a small group of employees who met with the founder of the company and his wife at their modest home. We ate simple dinners on T.V. trays, which we balanced on our laps. Talk was not only of work but also of family. And we ended our gathering quickly so that we could get on with the other parts of our lives.

Then things changed. By the end of the nineties, we were flying on corporate jets and spending whole weeks at corporate "retreats." Ballroom presentations and heated break out sessions preceded banquet style cafeteria food beneath candelabras bigger than small planets. When the day finally came to a close, when the last dinner speaker had spoken and we had clapped our hands numb, most employees retired to the bar, where they might dilute and rinse off a bit of the day's dirt.

If you, dear Reader, could have listened to the conversations at the elbow bending fests that followed such meetings, you would have heard what many fathers said, as they rolled into the bar at the end of a long day. They would throw themselves down into leather chairs, sip at their beers, and then sooner or later the first father would kick off the conversation:

"Third weekend in a row I've been away from home." (Long sigh)

"Yep," another father would agree. "This weekend I'm missing a father-son scouting trip."

Yet another father would cough. "This'll be the second year in a row I've missed my daughter's birthday. And she's turning sixteen."

Heads would nod at this trump. The waitress would be asked to bring another round of beers. But someone would buy a drink for the last father, the father who had won the greatest honor amongst the wounded work heroes. This father had given the most blood for his company. He had won the red badge of idiocy.

I not only sat at these honor ceremonies, I was a contender. The girls were growing up. Sawyer was learning to write, and Riley was speaking some of her first words. Diane was saving Sawyer's papers and recording Riley on tape so I could catch up when I got home. But I was missing "quantity" times. I did not know then, but I know now, how Riley liked her eggs and which shoes were Sawyer's favorites. Worse, when I arrived home after a long business trip, I felt odd, like a stranger. Even with *mi Vida* Diane, whose life was filling with diapers and school time, I was beginning to feel out of touch.

But still, the little voice inside of me, the one that will not be silenced without consequences, knew something had to be changed.

And so, we sailed. We went up a slow river in a steamy Guatemalan jungle filled with mahogany and bamboo, with the girls, just waking and shouting to one another over the steamy water. "Hootie hoo!" they yelled. And I figured I would make breakfast… maybe an ostrich egg omelet.

Belize – Coming Full Circle

Our trip up Guatemala's *Rio Dulce* was a steamy adventure. We beat the heat by taking a wild little bus (called a *litegua* – which translates, I believe, "abandon all hope") up the mountains through Guatemala City to the earthquake destroyed colonial town of Antigua. We met beautifully dressed Mayan Indians, strolled the ruined colonnades and churches, dined on mangoes, pineapples, French toast and *café con leche* at a converted abbey, and returned to our beloved *Manta Raya* with colorfully woven hammocks and jade earrings. Back in the sweltering heat of the tepid river, we could not believe that just one day before we had been shivering on the shore of an alpine lake.

It was time to head back to the breezes of Mother Ocean. With friends who were arriving by (shudder) *litegua*, we would retrace our jungle cruise back to the sea. And then? Then we would rendezvous with another friend, a dear old friend we made a point of visiting once every decade: Belize.

The white sand, the warm water swishing about our ankles, Diane's hand in mine - these were our memories of Belize. We envisioned ourselves on the white sand surrounding the little town of Placencia in southern Belize. I had shed tears on that beach. But that had been on our first visit to Placencia, and this would be our fourth. We were, in a way, once again coming home. Now, unlike the rest of our cruise over the past year, we would be sailing to "charted" waters.

We had first visited Belize in 1984 with four other friends aboard a charter sailboat, *Cinco Tejanos* - a big, clumsy 40-foot Irwin with a swing keel pinned up permanently so that charterers would plow through less coral. Before sailing the monstrous Irwin, we had sailed only our little 22-foot O'Day sailboat on Lake Powell. The Irwin felt huge, but even with all sails billowing and the engine whining at maximum RPM, it sailed more slowly than our tiny O'Day. Still, we did not care. In 1984 we were making, even if it was aboard a worn out behemoth, our first cruise through the Caribbean.

But we had responsibilities. We felt responsible for the unfamiliar boat and all of our friends who were sailing with us. We hoped to keep them safe and show them a good time (the curse of any captain and first mate with visiting crew). But even with decent charts and constant use of our new, book-learned skill, dead reckoning, we lost our way among Belize's infinite islands. (These were the days before Satnav or GPS.) We were steering along the smooth waters inside Belize's barrier reef; and at one point, Diane, even then the navigator, motioned for me to join her below. Our friends were on deck sunbathing and swizzling rum drinks. When Diane and I met at the navigation station and had only each other to frighten, we turned to one another in panic. In unison we hissed, "Do you know where we are?" Then, after frantically searching the charts and realizing we were, without a doubt, lost, we strolled back on deck, smiled and asked if anyone was ready for another Belikin beer and some hors d'oeuvres.

But the "fools and sailors" maxim worked in Belize. We found our way to the next anchorage, and Belizean fishermen told us where to anchor so that we were shielded from a blasting Norther that night. And the next day Fate helped us off a sandy shoal. We ran aground with all sails flying, and only a mighty blast from the dilapidated diesel engine got us off. As if we had depth charged a submarine, we left a broad oil slick behind us. Terrible stuff. When we finally docked in Placencia, I somehow snuggled up to the zigzagging dock without ramming it. I jumped off the boat and walked the beach with Diane. I was working the ache out of my clenched jaw, when the reality of where we were and what we had done hit me. We were in the Caribbean. We had sailed a boat, poorly, but sailed it just the same, and navigated it to a tropical paradise. Graceful green palms leaned over white sand, and a scarlet sunset sea broke on frothing waves. The air was warm and delicious, and my eyes grew watery. We had arrived, and something about sailing and the cruising lifestyle began to make sense. We had started a dream, and Belize was a nice place to start dreaming.

In the Caribbean, Belize is an anomaly. It murmurs lazy English, while its neighbors in surrounding countries like Guatemala speak rapid fire, staccato Spanish. At 8,867 square miles, Belize is smaller than New Hampshire, and only 170,000 folks live there (a quarter of them live in Belize City). Nearby El Salvador has over five million people packed into the same area.

Belize's small population has allowed it to keep its bounty – beautiful islands with white sand beaches and tropical rainforests, largely unchanged since the days when the Mayan Indians were the only folks about in the region. For visiting sailors, Belize is still a Bali Hai. The longest barrier reef (and a World Heritage Site) in the Western Hemisphere runs down the country's entire length. The reef provides, on one side, baby wave, protected sailing, and on the other side, turquoise blue Angelfish, giant grey whale sharks and some of the prettiest corals in the world. There are 450 islands or cays to explore off Belize. And on the mainland, sandy beaches give way to mangrove swamps, which in turn give way to open grasslands, pine woodlands and mountain rain forests. Although endangered elsewhere, Belize has healthy populations of the morelet's crocodile, iguana, tapir and manatee. Unlike almost all the lands we visited in the Caribbean, Belize is not begging for an environmental second chance, it is still living out its first. And one lady is making sure Belize doesn't blow this chance. Her name is Sharon Matola.

We met Sharon on our second visit to Belize in 1988. She was standing by the road bouncing a scuffed and dented motorcycle helmet off her hip. She was tall, attractive, had frosty brown hair and was wearing a t-shirt and mud splattered jeans. We talked with her only briefly before she invited us to visit the Belize Zoo. In essence, she had invited us to her home or, better yet, her art studio, for the Belize Zoo was Sharon's masterpiece.

From the day she arrived in Belize in the early eighties to the day she found herself baby sitting a movie cast of tropical animals, Sharon never imagined she would create one of the foremost zoo and tropical conservation centers in Central America: "If someone would have tapped me on the shoulder while I was feeding the peccaries (wild pigs) and said, 'This is the beginning of something important, even royalty will be dropping by to support this zoo,' I would have told them they were suffering delusions of grandeur."

It all started when Sharon left the United States bound for Mexico. She had a biology degree under her belt and plans for a graduate degree studying mycology in her head. Her idea was to visit markets all across Mexico and collect regional mushrooms, but she was not sure how she would finance and manage her travels. Her answer and her transportation came from a Mexican circus. She applied for and got the job as lion trainer.

Traveling with the show in southern Mexico, Sharon met a British movie director who was shooting a documentary about animals of the rain forest. He hired Sharon to manage twenty "actors" recruited from the Belizean countryside. Dazzling parrots lived in wooden cages next to spider monkeys, and a toothless crocodile swam in a small pond where the director often took his afternoon bath. When the film was finished and the director left for Borneo, the movie company announced it could no longer support the cast. The company told Sharon to "get rid of them."

Sharon knew the tame animals could not be released back into the wild. But she had trouble considering the alternative. "I was there all alone," she said. "But then I started to think...the odd person drifts down the road now and again and wants to see the animals."

She visited J.B.'s Bar, a favorite hangout for British jungle troops training in Belize and the only watering hole on a long stretch of the Belizean Highway. She told J.B. her plan. He liked the idea and agreed to direct the occasional, thirsty and adventure seeking tourist to Sharon's outpost. And so the Belize Zoo was born.

But the early days were not easy. "It was such a day-to-day struggle," Sharon said. "I never left, except to bring in supplies...for years." Sharon started a chicken farm to support her animals, but it was not enough. Afraid they would recognize her, she had to sneak by the banks in town. Nor were the "Powers that Be," the great, United States zoo foundations, sympathetic. The director of one such organization, which Sharon describes as "a very political, old boys' club," told Sharon that if she were in the United States, he would have had her shut down.

But Sharon thought about her growing collection of animals and decided the director could not see beyond his own million dollar exhibits. She wrote a newsletter she knew he would see entitled "Give Us a Break." An excerpt: "...Certain zoo officials haven't found the Belize Zoo up to their standards. Perhaps it's because we haven't any camel rides or golf carts…' As she recalled her letter, Sharon smiled, "I got into some trouble, but I didn't care."

Sharon was finding out that her real supporters, even if they could not finance her zoo, were closer to home. The people of Belize were coming to the zoo. Just by word of mouth, they came to see the animals. They did not care if her morelets crocodile was in a muddy pond or that her king vulture was behind chicken wire. They were amazed and thrilled to learn that anteaters were slow, shy creatures, which, contrary to Belizean mythology, would not suck the brains out of a dog. They found out that white hawks, like Sharon's hawk with a farmer's bullet through its wing, actually killed the farmers' worst enemy: snakes. With these lessons Sharon began to see the purpose emerging behind her work.

"It became evident that though I had been working in the film industry trying to inform people in the United States and the United Kingdom about the importance of preserving wildlife, the people who needed to get in touch with the animals were being ignored." Sharon renamed the Zoo "The Belize Zoo and Tropical Education Center." Its primary goal: education about conservation and endangered species within Belize.

She started traveling to schools and adult community centers. She brought along some of her animals, like snakes. They were witnesses for lessons on ecology, pesticide use, deforestation and predator extinction. She took her show all the way from mountainous San Ignacio to coastal Dangriga. And her simple lessons sometimes brought simple solutions. Learning that river deforestation caused erosion and habitat destruction, Belizean farmers started preserving bands of trees along the water. Other lessons were not as simple, but they started important discussions: "What do we do," Sharon asked, "when a jaguar comes into our fields and tries to kill one of our pigs?"

Not long after meeting Sharon, we started noticing Belizeans walking around in t-shirts that read: "Belize – The Land of the Free and Endangered." Sharon's programs had caught on. And when she realized she had gotten the country's attention, she turned the programs over to Belizean educators. "The kids were so excited to see slides, to see a snake," she said. "But after you got past the introductory part, you had to carry on. You had to start saying, 'Let's talk about holes in the ozone layer.' For that you needed to get the local people involved. That was the only way to go."

When we visited the Belize Zoo with our girls, Sharon's opus was coming of age. It was looking like a real zoo with an education center and several habitat areas. Shady paths wound between the exhibits. But despite the uptown splendor, there were still no golf carts. Sharon's animals remained her fist love. And our family was there to celebrate one of her first romances. It was April the Tapir's birthday.

The tapir, an animal that looks a bit like a hog with a short elephant's trunk, is Belize's national animal. Its bulk and bucolic, nearsighted visage have earned it the affectionate nickname "mountain cow." April had come to Sharon in the arms of one of her early Belizean visitors. The baby tapir was dying from a maggot infestation called screwworm. Sharon had cleaned the baby up and begun feeding her high vitamin, banana milk shakes. Since tapirs are nocturnal, Sharon's sick bed vigils went late into the night. "She lived with me in my room," she said. "We stayed up and listened to music - the Rolling Stones and Cat Stevens."

At April the Tapir's birthday party, along with a gaggle of Belizean school children, we watched as April munched contentedly through a three tier, banana, carrot and papaya cake. Backstage a wildlife biologist from Florida was hiding April's biggest present: a handsome male tapir. Romance tingled in the air.

The Belize Zoo had become a Central American showpiece. The Rhode Island Zoo was donating medicine and veterinary supplies, and the World Wildlife Fund was sponsoring an iguana-breeding program. Wildlife Preservation Trust International was funding new facilities, and there was more money coming in for education. Celebrities like Harrison Ford, Jimmy Buffet and Princess Anne were lending their support. But Sharon, despite her growing notoriety and her new duties as an international fundraiser, politician and, yes, ecology and wildlife expert, had not changed. She still wore a t-shirt and muddy jeans, and just that morning before the Zoo opened, she had unlocked one of the animal cages and stepped inside. Inca the puma had rumbled a deep-throated greeting and flicked her tail in recognition. In the quiet of the early dawn, the mountain cougar and the lady who had raised her had greeted the dawn together.

* * *

Sailing back to Belize as a family was a good "homecoming." Besides visiting the Belize Zoo, we swam with spotted eagle rays out on Gladden Reef. In the jungle, we pounded our chests with howler monkeys. And in Placencia, as we walked the beach on our way to double dips of homemade ice cream, we had, as we always did in that off-beat town, an odd encounter. We heard high-pitched cries of "Help, help! Let us out!" And when we investigated, we found two practical jokers, laughing. "Ha, ha, ha!" The pranksters were hopping about in their cage – two scarlet macaws.

But perhaps our oddest animal encounter occurred when we were anchored off Ambergris Cay further north in Belize. The girls had been swimming off *Manta Raya's* stern platforms, and somehow Riley had gotten her ankle stuck under the swim ladder. She could not get her head up for air, and she was literally screaming underwater. I heard the noise and was making my way aft, when Sawyer, who was also in the water but further astern, was suddenly surrounded by a pod of dolphins. They swam past her and gathered around Riley. As I leaned over and lifted the ladder to release her foot, Riley came up spouting saltwater and gasping for air; and one dolphin, a youngster, stuck its head out of the water and eyed her, then me, as I pulled Riley onto the transom.

Riley was O.K. Sawyer was still in the water, and the dolphins were swimming about her. But when I stepped down the ladder, the dolphins disappeared – all except the young dolphin, who was eventually herded away by, I'm guessing, its mother. Intrigued by the dolphins, Riley recovered quickly, and she and Sawyer discovered that as long as they stayed in the water, the dolphins swam around them, but at a distance. Occasionally the young dolphin would try to swim up to the girls, but an adult would cut it off and bring it back to the rest of the pod. Every time I tried to enter the water, the dolphins swam away. Were the dolphins trying to protect the girls? Had they heard and felt Riley's panic? Whatever the reason, they felt safer with kids than with adults, and we felt blessed by their visit.

In Belize we were also blessed by the visit of a friend who flew down to join us from the States. In his company, the routine of our liveaboard life shifted and gained new focus. And this new perspective was illuminating. The following log entry, which I have named "Jigsaw Puzzle," was written by our friend:

Jigsaw Puzzle

"...when I first stepped aboard Manta Raya, the yacht was empty - nobody home. The yacht seemed small. Surely the four Scantleburys couldn't live aboard this little place <u>all</u> the time!? Then, once we were all stuffed into *Manta Raya*, it was like one of those puzzles where you have to re-arrange all the pieces, except that you only get to move one piece at a time. Todd moves to the main cabin. Riley moves into her room. Diane slides out onto the deck. Sawyer doesn't move at all because she's already in her room racing through her new book. And finally I get to go to the bathroom.

At first this process was awkward, mechanical, jerky. But as the days passed we all began to predict, accommodate and enable each other's movements. It was never slick, but it served the purpose, and, well,

MANTA RAYA BECAME BIGGER."

As exciting and beautiful as Belize was, and as comfortable and at home as we felt there, the seasons were changing, and the named storm season, the spur in our britches since the start of our cruise, was again prodding us from behind. The idylls of Belize had held us for a long time, but we had to make a choice. Was it time to sail back to the States? Was it time to head to the barn? As you will see, dear Reader, in some ways, though we had talked about sailing home many times and had come close at times to "abandoning" our trip, coming home to the land we knew and loved so well was the hardest and most disorienting part of our cruise. But in Belize we had not predicted this "landfall fallout." We filled our tanks with diesel fuel and water, assembled our abandon ship emergency bag, strapped on our safety harnesses and battened the hatches. It was time to sail home.

You Can Go Home Again
(But It's Weird)

L andfall was early morning, Wednesday, June 2 beneath the Loggerhead Key Lighthouse, which guided us in with a strong, steady flash every twenty seconds. We loved that beckoning light. In the night, in the midst of freighters and tugs towing barges at the end of long steel cables, the lighthouse light was the only light that did not scare us - the only light we could trust. After four days at sea, we had grown more than a bit "bread dain." It had become increasingly difficult to hold a course, let alone a thought. A Gulf Stream counter current had held us on the last day of our passage. It stole two knots from our 8.5 knot speed through the water. We slogged on, banging into waves and rising wind and not understanding until we arrived near shore why the ride had become so horrific. We found that garbage bags had clogged the forward scuppers and trapped a few hundred pounds of water in each of the bow compartments. Poor *Manta Raya* had been trying to run with cinder blocks tied around her ankles.

When my mother learned we arrived back in the States, she wept. At the Loggerhead Key landfall, I believe we too may have cried, though we were probably too tired. I know Diane and I hugged beneath the lighthouse beacon. Darkness, light, darkness, light... The kids were fast asleep and safe. And yet, our homecoming trials were not over.

The next morning as we sat together over a celebratory pancake breakfast, Ranger Rick from the Fort Jefferson National Monument motored alongside in an official, green-striped powerboat. Ranger Rick was pleasant. He welcomed us back to the States, but he told us we would have to move. All boats, he said, had to anchor within a mile of Fort Jefferson, the park headquarters. The area was protected, and we were out of bounds.

At the fort, the protected inner basin anchorage was stuffed with weekend boaters, so we anchored out with the stragglers. The irony of this outside anchorage was that it was in the midst of coral … so much for protecting our fragile reefs.

Then, just as we secured our anchor, a seaplane (the first of many tourist toting buzz planes) flew directly over our mast, turned and touched down on the water. It roared across the anchorage spouting spray, then turned, aimed right at us and looked as if it intended to plow directly between our hulls. This, I took it, was the pilot's way of informing us we had anchored too close to his runway. We re-re-anchored, doing our best to kill as little coral as possible.

We were back home in the U.S. of A., our home. And the sights that greeted us brought along a full bag of emotions - awe, pride, relief and confusion in one bundle. The red brick walls of mid nineteenth century Fort Jefferson filled Garden Key. Through its massive gun ports, past its cannons and their black-eyed threat of doom, we could see green, manicured lawns and shade trees swaying in the breeze - a bit of a metaphor for the promise and hurdles of a home-landfall. A perfect dock (no third world rollercoaster with sways and missing planks) led up to the fort's entrance. Tourists wearing colorful tropical outfits and expensive sunglasses disembarked from the seaplanes and strolled down the sturdy dock. They were reading brochures, pasting on sunscreen and eating ice cream…Yes! Ice cream. The imposing fort, the manicured lawn within, the ice cream… It all felt surreal. We were back in the mighty, inviting and tidy U.S. of A.

Yet we felt out of place amidst the shiny weekender yachts and sailboats. They had no laundry hanging from their lifelines or diesel jugs lashed to their coamings. Ashore, the gift shop overwhelmed us. It was filled with shiny ornaments – miniature license plates, mechanical birds and tiny stuffed porpoises. Next door a theatre showed an historical video ("This is Fort Jefferson"). We watched the screen with our mouths wide open. We were third world hicks gawking at the first world United States.

That night we planned to take the "ghost tour" – a spooky walk through the aged fort, where we would see the cells of prisoners like the Civil War's rebel president Jefferson Davis and Lincoln assassination co-conspirator Dr. Samuel Mudd, who had treated John Wilkes Booth's broken leg. Laughing nervously in anticipation of the spooky 8pm show, we dinghied in to the dock but found we had arrived a bit late. It was midnight. We had not reset our ship's clock to the U.S. time zone. In fact, we had adjusted very little in preparation for our landfall.

Our homecoming reward, cheeseburgers in Key West, was still sixty miles away. So after a day or so stumbling about the fort, we weighed anchor and headed up the Keys, sailing past the Marquesas and arriving at Key West Harbor mid-afternoon. As we sailed, we were dreaming of city delights and phone calls to friends and family, and the only distraction from our beautiful, flat-water sail was a long line of squalls traveling with us out on the Gulf Stream. As we approached the ship channel into Key West, the squalls decided to hook a left and visit the city with us.

A cold breeze swept the deck, and rain burst from the dark sky. We hopped about our deck performing our usual storm drill, sails reefed, girls in their life vests, Diane hunkered down at the navigation station and watching the GPS, and me squinting into the rain trying to catch a glimpse of anything. But the rain had closed like a shower curtain just beyond the foredeck. Cold drops whipped the water, and the ocean leapt up to meet them.

Diane was feeding me directions, giving me a countdown for a turn I could not see but she had calculated using her GPS screen, when I heard one of the strangest things I had ever heard on a boat. A voice, as if out of the heavens, called to me.

"Captain!" it said.

I looked up into the rain.

"Captain!" said the voice again. "Over here!"

I turned to starboard, and not ten yards off our beam, our old friend, the Coast Guard, was motoring alongside. In the cockpit of the orange striped boat stood three men wearing foul weather gear and life vests. One held a megaphone and waved to me.

I yelled for Diane to turn on the radio. We were soon hailed, and Diane responded. But I could not hear the ensuing conversation. I held my course in the downpour, and I wondered just what the hell was happening.

Finally Diane stuck her head out the companionway. "They want us to leave the channel."

"What?" I yelled.

"They're trying to start a race – jet boats. Apparently we are in the way."

"In the way?" I yelled. "They're running a race through the main channel to Key West… in this squall?"

"You wanna talk to them?" Diane offered, holding out the radio mike.

"Hell!" I spat, as the water guttered off my foul weather hood. "Ask them where they expect us to go. We don't have charts for anything except the main channel."

Diane disappeared again. There was more radio talk, but I still could not make it out, though I *could* hear the edge in Diane's patient but insistent "mommy" voice. The Coast Guard Boat continued to pace us on our starboard side, and I held my course through the grey sheet of rain. Diane re-emerged. Our chart, now crumpled and wet, was under her arm, and there were furrows in her forehead.

"They *think*" she said, we can carry five feet through to Wisteria Island, if we turn East now and bear up.

I looked to port where I guessed the turn was supposed to take place, and I saw no markers, no buoys and no island - nothing but grey sheets of rain.

"Oh hell," I said, repeating myself, disgust temporarily overwhelming my ability to improvise. "This is a fine 'homecoming'. We get shooed away by our own Coast Guard to founder in one of the most notorious shipwreck graveyards on the East Coast so some armchair, Bud Lite, motor heads can stare at their boob tubes and watch water borne penis extensions guzzle enough gas to buy an Arab sheik a new harem of BMWs."

Diane gave me her "nice-tirade-but-what-are-ya-gonna-do" eyebrow raise, and I asked her whether the Coasties were willing to escort us to the anchorage.

"I tried that," she said. "They have to stay here and monitor the race."

"Oh hell," I said.

We turned to port, and Diane stayed on deck with her soggy chart, but we never glanced at it. We spent all of our energy trying to construct imaginary landmarks in the downpour, as we glanced nervously toward our depth finder, which immediately skinnied to four feet.

Our blind groping took forever. At one point we had inches under our keels, and a serious pain began to radiate from my stomach. I motored dead slow, ground my teeth and found I was shivering. We were wet, and we were, for the first time in a long time, cold. Finally we spotted a grey outline - Cassurina trees. Wisteria Island.

As we neared the shore, boat hulls began to take shape. It was Sunday, and the anchorage was packed, probably for the powerboat race, so I pulled around to the channel side of the island, knowing there would be fewer boats in the current and figuring we could anchor there temporarily until the squall blew over and the crowd thinned out. When the anchor went down and we had tested our holding, I went below. I was still shivering, so I stripped off my wet gear. Diane, bless her, kissed me and pressed a mug of hot tea into my hands. I was taking my first sip, when Riley spoke.

"Papa, there's another boat out there, and it's awfully close." She was staring out the forward porthole, where there had been nothing but open water moments before, and now the rear end of a large power yacht filled the view. Riley was right. We were seeing the boat's backside entirely too clearly. It was too close, backing down and about to ram us with its stern.

Diane and I jumped on deck; we ran forward and shouted as we ran. High above us on the flying bridge of the yacht, two ladies stared down at us. As we danced and shouted, they looked down as if from a tall tower, and they looked bored.

"Can you get your boat in gear!" I yelled. "You are about to ram us!"

One of the ladies folded her arms. The other shrugged and tugged on her cigarette.

"Where's the captain!" Diane pleaded.

Cigarette Lady motioned forward with her cigarette, where we could just make out a figure squatting on the foredeck - a man with his back to us. He was looking out over the water. But it was too late to involve this fellow. The current was carrying the yacht swiftly and directly toward a solid impact between our hulls, straight into our aluminum forebeam - the structure that braced our floats and held our hulls and our home together. There was no time to release our anchor chain and back out of the way. We prepared for impact.

Without talking, Diane and I each reacted the same way. Right before the boat slammed into us, we threw our shoulders into it, as if we were fending off a piling. We tried desperately to protect our poor *Manta Raya*, our home in over a hundred anchorages, the boat we had worried about through storms and had babied through third world boatyards. Over the past eighteen months, she had taken such good care of us, and we of her, Now, just within sight of the barn, she was about to be molested.

We did little good pitching our puny bodies against the bulk of the power yacht. It struck, there was a walloping thud and a sharp crack of fiberglass. Like a vibrating gong, our mast wobbled crazily over us. With my shoulder still jammed against the cold plastic of the power yacht's transom, I looked up and saw the captain staring down at me. His eyes were wide; his mouth was open. And before I could say anything, he jumped to his steering station and threw his yacht into gear.

I tried to yell, Noooooo....! But it was too late. His prop thrashed the water, and we felt the thuds as it wound our anchor chain and harness into its maw with a deep throated "THUNK, THUNK, THUNK." Our bow began to pull down into the water in heart breaking, gut wrenching jerks. Then, thank goodness, his engine died.

"Oh my goodness! Oh my goodness!" came the captain's voice over the transom. I squinted up at his pinched face, then down at our anchor line and then over to the shore to gauge whether we were dragging. Now our anchor held not only us but also the captain and his plastic yacht. Much depended on that anchor. And when I had made sure that it would hold, I walked away.

Diane followed me. "What are we going to do?"

I was too upset to talk. I sat down in the cockpit and started yanking on my diving boots. I was shaking again, but this time not from the cold.

Back on the foredeck I looked up at the Plastic Captain. "Do NOT," I said, "under any circumstances, start your engine! Do you understand?" The little man nodded, and I dove into the water. In the murk, I found the tangle of prop and chain and put my foot against the power yachts hull. The chain and harness were wrapped around the propeller shaft in tight coils. They held the entire shaft in tension between its propeller and the cutlass bearing. I yanked, and there was a great thud and jerk as each wrap came undone. The prop slammed back toward the hull with every turn. Surfacing for air repeatedly, I unwrapped our chain one ripping turn at a time and was mindful not to get my fingers clamped in the tangle. The thought of me pinched to that mess in an underwater death grip was sobering: "Giant, Fiberglass Clam Drowns Tarzan."

Back on deck, Diane and I shoved the plastic yacht free. Our harness was shredded. We fastened two dock lines to the anchor chain. Meantime, as the Plastic Captain should have done in the first place, he anchored off our stern. By radio I told him to stand by. I would be visiting him shortly.

After drying off, I went below. Still, I could not speak. I made some more tea, and Diane, the kids and I sat around the table in silence. We were a grave cast of pale faces. I took my time. I was waiting for my blood pressure to drop. Then we talked.

There were many things we discussed. Would we dance the "liability insurance fandango" and sing the popular American tune: "My lawyer can kick your lawyer's butt?" Should we go for the throat? After all, the Plastic Captain's homeport was Palm Beach. His boat might as well have had "Deep Pockets"written on the transom. But these nasty thoughts were only fleeting thoughts. Thoughts made in anger.

Instead, we assessed the damage. We were alive, and we were not sinking. *Manta Raya* seemed all right - except for her shredded anchor tackle. We took out our marine catalog and itemized the parts we would have to replace. We did not consider charging for our time or adding a penalty for emotional damages; we just listed the parts it would take to splice the rigging back together. When we were finished, I got up and lowered the dinghy.

"What are you going to tell him?" Diane asked.

"I'm going to tell him," I said, "that he has no business being on the water in anything bigger than an inner tube."

On the Plastic Captain's boat, the apologies began before I could tie off the dinghy. And they continued as I took a seat on the white, marinized leather couch, which curved around the gleaming glass table. The Plastic Captain was sorry. He had no idea. He had been trying to secure his anchor up on the bow (a tiny toy anchor— a mere fishing hook against his plastic yacht's bulk). He had not realized he was drifting backward with the current. He had had a terrible day. In fact, it was his first day on his shiny, new plastic yacht; and he had already run aground once that morning. He had had to hire a tow. Now his wife and his sister-in-law (the noncommittal crew) would not speak to him.

As the Plastic Captain went on and on, I thought, "Fine, apologize, but when you are finished, I am going to tell you a thing or two about boat ownership. And you are going to hear what it feels like to have an irresponsible idiot plow into your family home."

But just as the Plastic Captain was winding down and I began winding up for my tirade, he started to cry. The man stopped, hung his head and wept. The tears ran off his cheeks and splashed down onto his gold necklaces. His little shoulders shook. And suddenly my harangue lost all of its thunder.

The Plastic Captain cried a long time, and when I could not stand it any longer, I patted him on the shoulder. "Look," I said, "nobody got hurt. There was some damage, but we can take care of that without involving the insurance companies."

The Plastic Captain stopped crying, and I handed him my itemized repair list. The little man sniffed and then sat up straight. He may have been lost at sea, he may have been an inadequate and terrified captain, but he understood the world of buying and billing. And my bill, for him, was trifling. He pulled out his wallet and began peeling off hundred dollar bills.

"But you need to get this boat into a dock," I said, recalling one topic in my proposed harangue. "And if you don't feel comfortable maneuvering it, you should call the marina for a water taxi and hire a captain to take it in for you." The little man nodded and smiled. "And take some boating lessons, damn it. Get some experience before you take the wheel again. Boats (and I looked astern out the sliding glass door to reassure myself that I was indeed on a boat) are wonderful things, but you must learn how to handle them."

The little man beamed. And as I tried to leave, he kept thanking me, patting me on the shoulder and pumping my hand.

The next day when we motored in to the Key West Marina, we saw his shiny plastic yacht tied to the very first dock near the marina entrance. The Plastic Captain and his reluctant crew were nowhere to be found. On the side of the boat, a sign read, "FOR SALE."

Like a good slap to the face, the collision put an end to our homecoming troubles, and our spoonful of forgiveness seemed to turn the tide. We were anxious about what lay ahead in our voyage: where we might hole up for the hurricane season, whether or not we should continue cruising in the Fall or whether we should "get real," get a job and return to a land-based home. But these decisions could wait. For now we were back in the U.S. of A., and it was time to celebrate.

We got our cheeseburgers. We took long walks through Old Key West and visited its quiet cemetery. There along clamshell paths, where Live Oaks draped with spanish moss shaded the graves, one tombstone really did read: "I told you I was sick." Diane visited a Nursery, cooed over the plants and brought home an armful of orchids. Sawyer found a used bookstore and carried back a pile of books so tall that only her smile was visible above the stack. We called our families and friends, and our voices cracked with emotion. When we handed the phone to Riley, she stared at the thing, furrowed her brow and tried speaking into the listening end of the handset. In "kid years," we had been away for quite some time.

For every disappointing incident or person we encountered (like the Plastic Captain or the bored customs agent, who yawned when I told him we were returning from a fantastic family voyage), there was a caring person to lift our spirits. When we tied up at the Key West marina, the dockmaster, who was from Colorado, helped us into our slip. He shook our hands and welcomed us back to the United States. Later he returned with maps and advice about how to get around town. We festooned *Manta Raya* with the flags from all the islands and countries we had visited. The liveaboard next to us brought his parrot, Captain Cook, over to admire the display. We had been told this particular liveaboard was a rough fellow, a nightclub owner and roustabout; and he did look a bit rough with his tattoos and bushy black beard. But he too welcomed us home and then went back to his boat to bring the girls a present.

"I bet you girls haven't seen fresh fruit in a while," he said, and he dangled a bunch of bananas before their eyes.

The girls, who had just finished trying to eat forty pounds of bananas a Belizean customs agent had given us, had hoped to never see a banana again (we ate the things with every meal, sautéed them, made banana bread with them and eventually raced them against one another across the ocean). I watched nervously as Riley and Sawyer stared at the bundle. They hesitated only slightly before saying, "Wow! Bananas! Thanks!"

And so we came home, to the North American lagniappe of both clueless and kind strangers, to both disinterested and caring officials, and to both dangerous and helpful boaters. We had returned as a family, so I knew we had accomplished at least two of the goals we had envisioned for our adventure. We were closer as a family; and, if nothing else, we certainly had great tans.

Sailing to Music City

S till, our return to the U. S. of A. had been a bit disorienting –
an odd and out of place feeling that was at times maddening,
since I knew we should simply be feeling relieved and grateful
for having returned "home" safely. Yet we felt confused, and we felt
overwhelmed. Worst of all, we felt "misplaced." (And if we were all
to be honest, dear Reader, we would have to admit that this happens
to all long-distance cruisers – it had happened to Diane and me in
the eighties – and it happens to all travelers who wander far away
from their homes, where they gain a new perspective of the world.
In the extreme, Mr. Gulliver comes to mind.) At the time of our
Key West landfall, I was rereading Kurt Vonnegut's Hocus Pocus,
which was perhaps a poor choice given our circumstances. For the
past year we had been sailing the slow-paced, out islands of third
world countries - no prime time news, no stoplights or fast food
drive-throughs… just lots of stars, clear water and empty horizons.
The U.S. of A. had not changed since we had left it. But we had.
Folks were still racing after the almighty but ephemeral U.S. dollar.
But now the manic pace caught us off guard, and the extra hyper
pace of southern Florida only intensified our confusion.

So we set our sites on what we thought might be better and more
inviting waters to the North. Somewhere in the backwaters of Georgia
or the Carolinas, we hoped we might decompress in a pseudo, third
world hideout, wait out the hurricane season and decide what to do
next as a family.

Honestly, as we sailed up the Intercoastal Waterway of Florida, we were trying to decide not only what to do with our boat but what to do with our lives. Returning home had reminded me that I was *supposed* to be a father with a job, that my kids were *supposed* to be in a good school aimed at an even better college, and that all of us were *supposed* to be living in a house with a two car garage and a trash compactor. Yet I was not sure I wanted to return to all the things I was *supposed* to do. But trash compactor or not, I did not have a clue where or how we might settle ourselves to reestablish a landlocked life. I had cruised the Caribbean with my family just as I had dreamed we would; but like a kid sitting in a pile of shredded wrapping paper after Christmas, the unwrapping of this present left me feeling lost, as I realized with some panic that I had no plan for what we were to do next.

Cruising was still an option. If we budgeted ourselves the cruising kitty might hold out for another year or so. But as I looked back over our past year, I grew leery. I remembered the storms we had weathered, our purgatory in the Venezuelan boatyard and our long, seasick passages over vast Mother ocean. It had been a lovely cruise, but I was ready to quit my job as captain, or as one of my sailing friends once joked, ready to walk inland with an anchor over my shoulder and not stop until someone asked, 'Hey, what's that?'"

Diane and I held late night parent conferences and agreed that at the very least we should change our setting. Perhaps we would find a quiet, inland marina in Georgia, where we could hide from the crowds and the season's named storms. Or perhaps we would find a boatyard in South Carolina, where we could haul Manta Raya and live ashore in a small community. Maybe there would be a nice cottage nearby where we could finish up the girls' home schooling, ride our bikes and do some inland exploring.

But all of these "maybe" conjectures were about to be muted by a very real limitation. *Manta Raya*, so small and agile at sea, so versatile in her ability to anchor in skinny waters throughout the Caribbean, was, in the U.S. of A., an ungainly and towering oaf, whose size would determine our next move.

When we telephoned marinas and boatyards in Georgia and South Carolina, almost none could handle Manta Raya's girth. Those that could were in major cities near industrial ports. We shuddered with the Cumana, Venezuela *déjà vu*. Then one day, trying to make our way north in the Intercoastal Waterway near Vero Beach, Florida, we faced the first, real obstacle to our northbound plans: a fixed bridge. At dawn (a sleepless night having insured our early morning departure) we approached the Vero Beach Bridge at low tide. Its tidal marker showed a height of 64 feet above waterline. The night before, by running a tape measure along the mainsail halyard and adding what I guessed might be the mast step height above waterline, I had guessed at our mast height. My best estimate, depending on how much the halyard had stretched and how optimistic I was about my other measurements, was somewhere between 63 and 65 feet. The bridge was going to be a tight fit.

We backed (yes, backed) toward the metal span with the tide pushing us away rather than toward its very solid, iron deck. I was using the "Braille system" to test our height, and I was backing toward the bridge because most of *Manta Raya's* expensive rigging components were forward. Diane had her binoculars trained on the mast top; and the girls, with hands over their brows, were standing beside her staring up at the bridge. "Screeech!" went the mast antenna. It bent and scraped beneath the bridge bottom. Then "clank!" went the mast, as it caught on a beam and shuddered. I reversed engines and quickly retreated. Another day, another tide and perhaps with a full cargo to sink us deeper in the water, we might (with all of us sucking our guts in and scrunching our shoulders) have made it under, just. But with dozens of fixed bridges in our Intercoastal Waterway future, I could not handle the pressure. I foresaw a growing bridge ulcer. And simultaneously I decided I had had it with our floating home. The needy rig (for boats never tire of our attention) had become an extension of our homecoming worries. Still, I tried to hold it together, because captains who abandon ship do not inspire their crews; and berzerk fathers do not inspire their families.

We turned south, but before we sailed back into the fray of Southern Florida, we caught our breath and anchored off a quiet preserve and science center: the Harbor Branch Oceanographic Institute. Along a bend in the ICW, the Institute had bought and preserved a broad expanse of coastal property. Here Florida's population thinned and green mangroves lined a shore filled with herons, cranes and pelicans. We set our anchor. I looked north toward the bridge that had just blocked us. And I looked south toward the crowded cities we had left behind. I looked east and thought of the open ocean and the undisciplined forces of Nature I no longer wished to face there. And I imploded.

Suddenly everything, even simple decisions like what we should eat for lunch, became overwhelming. I panicked. I came apart at the seams, and frankly, my disorientation bordered on insanity. (And perhaps you too, dear Reader, have known times like these, desperate times, when the world looks quite bleak.) I gave up. I quit thinking about Georgia and the Carolinas, and I quit thinking that I *ought* to know what to do next. And this, the giving up, turned out to be the first step toward finding the next step. I took a breath. I let go of my plans, and I called upon an old friend: my faith. (Fear not, dear Reader, this will not turn into a plug for a new denomination, nor will I ask you for a donation after handing out my literature.) When giving up, I believe we are left with only two choices: either the infinity of despair or the tiny seeds of hope. I prefer the seeds (little but potent fellows that, for me, were harvested from my Christian grandmother, my readings about Buddhism (which I found to be much like my grandmother's Christianity -minus the German heritage) and my appreciation for the awesome forces of Nature. Let us call these seeds Buddheo-Christo-Pantheistic seeds and think of Christ smiling and perhaps even telling a joke, as He reassures his fellow sailors that they will indeed step ashore again to smell the roses after crossing stormy waters.

Sensing my implosion, Diane, not prone to such reflective machinations of spiritual bend, but sensing my quandary none the less, suggested we take a break – no more fruitless worrying and bridge bashing for a spell. She suggested we dinghy in to visit the Institute and its nature preserve. So we loaded into our rubber boat and idled through the lush mangrove inlet that opened to modern buildings arranged in grassy fields along quiet, wooded trails. We visited a museum and marveled at the odd, horned and scowling deep-sea fish behind glass. And we watched a submarine being commissioned for an underwater scientific exploration. We ate lunch beneath the outstretched and shading arms of a live oak. And there, a new thought occurred to me: "What if we had already arrived and were already doing exactly what we ought to be doing?" (Within three months we would be taking aquaculture courses at the Harbor Branch Institute and soon after learning hydroponics, our next life phase, but that is another story.)

On our way back to our dinghy, we happened upon a nice fellow – the mechanic for the Institute's small fleet of boats. I asked him if he happened to know of a boatyard that might be able to handle *Manta Raya*, and he named a yard not far away and in a quiet inlet. He offered us his phone and dialed the number. Within minutes I had scheduled our haulout. And once again, we were on our way.

The next day, at the lowest possible tide, we braved the only fixed bridge between us and our new destination. Again our antenna bent and scraped beneath the underside of the span's metalwork, but this time it "sproinged" free on the other side. We had literally scraped by the bridge, and suddenly a loudspeaker blared behind us: "Good'n, boy!" It was the Florida Maritime Police. "We's watchin' you, and we hain't seen anyone come that close afore!" We waved, cheered and danced a little jig, as our antenna swayed crazily above us.

Within a few days we were tied up alongside a quiet marina in Port Salerno. And a few days later, after I had retrieved our minivan from my parents' home in Tennessee, we celebrated with a delightful Father's Day dinner at a waterside restaurant - Cuban sandwiches, oysters, clams, shrimp, crab legs, chocolate cake and strawberry cheesecake (two cakes for two delightful daughters). The girls were thrilled. They came home with swizzle sticks shaped like mermaids. And with their recorders, they played me a duet of "Hot Crossed Buns." Could life have been any better? Could any father have asked for more?

I woke early the next morning. The full moon was setting out the aft companionway, and it backlit the Stars and Stripes atop a tall pole in the boatyard. It was "D-Day," dry dock day, and *Manta Raya*, our home for the last year and a half, was to be pulled from the water and safely (I hoped) "put in storage" for the next few months. We would pack up our clothes and toothbrushes and once again head north toward Georgia and South Carolina; only this time we would be traveling over and not under the Waterway bridges. After Georgia, we would visit Nashville and stay through the hurricane season in my childhood home, with my parents. And after that? I was not sure, but I no longer cared.

As the dawn light lifted and the Stars and Stripes flapped in the growing breeze, I thought through the coming day's activities – the infinite list of de-commissioning tasks – but most of all, I thought about a baby cardinal. The baby bird had appeared at my parents' birdfeeder, when I was visiting to pick up our minivan. With its beak wide open, it had begged for food, and a weary but obliging, bright red parent had stuffed its beak full of seeds.

"Wasn't I getting a bit old," I pondered, "to be freeloading off my parents?"

It is with no little trepidation that a man, a 42-year-old father, along with his wife and children, returns home to live with his parents. His hold on his identity becomes a bit tenuous. He is, in some odd way, returning to his childhood, so is he the father or is he the son? And as for his parents, their son is returning with a family they did not foster. And there are reasons birds kick their young from the nest.

I worried that my father would try to father me by, for example, criticizing my grammar (and he did), or that my mother would try to mother me by, for example, telling me to wash my hands after using the bathroom (and she did). I was concerned that my parents would try to press conservative political views upon me and my liberal wife by asking us to listen to rabidly conservative talk show hosts (and they did). But most of all, I worried that my children, bouncing balls of uninhibited energy just recently released from an eight by ten floating "pen," might drive my aging parents to distraction (and they did). And yet my family needed a safe port for the next few months, and flying above my worries was a number of winged hopes.

I wanted to show Riley and Sawyer my middle Tennessee childhood treasures, like densely treed hilltops, where they could hike beside Civil War walls. I wanted them to hunt for ocean fossils with me along the road where I used to walk to grade school. And I wanted to take them to a science museum, where they might lean back in soft chairs and see the planets play across a dark, domed sky. I also wanted to canoe with my parents, Diane and the girls on green, Tennessee rivers, where we might float with the snapping turtles beneath shaggy barked hickory trees. And whether I realized it or not, I hoped that a bit of Magic might pass between my children and my parents. Because whatever tangled emotions wove the knots of my parental ties, I loved my parents and admired them for who they were. I hoped that the best part of them - their humor, their charity and their intelligence – would be gifts they could also show my girls (and they did).

Our extended reunion worked. And there was certainly an initial, manic celebratory feeling to the homecoming. We were on the ground, and the worries, decisions and vagaries of being a vagabond family floating on the sea were behind us. We were in a real home with a real yard and beautiful woods. And every time we got into the car to get groceries, pick up a piece of hardware or, luxury of luxuries, eat dinner out, we felt as if we had won the lottery. We were riding the high of our sailing adventure, and we shared pictures and stories with my parents, their friends and my high school friends. We were treated like explorers returning from the hinterlands – Mark Twain and his family on their lecture tour.

In the beginning, we let this euphoria carry us. We let my parents cook for us, and we allowed our friends to fawn over us. But then, just as the "vacation" atmosphere had eventually dissolved after we had first moved aboard *Manta Raya*, the "visiting royalty" distinction also wore off, and we settled down to function as an extended family. Here, again, our training on *Manta Raya* paid off.

We started working. We mowed the yard, planted gardens and fixed electrical appliances. We made meals, and the girls did dishes. We woke up each day and saw it as a new adventure. We picnicked in the park, paddled down rivers, visited museums and hiked Civil War trails. And when our new home grew a bit too "confining," just as *Manta Raya* proved confining at sea, we freed up space by heading out on our own extended adventures, i.e., we got out of each other's hair. The girls went to day camp, where they raised money for Habitat for Humanity. And my father and I worked on a Habitat for Humanity home. Diane even accompanied my mom to an entrenched and staid, Old Southern, women's society meeting, where a writer discussed her books, and the ladies sat about with finger food arranged on silver trays atop their laps. A difficult motion was raised and discussed at length: whether the club should allow members to wear pants to the meetings. The previous year, open-toed shoes without stockings had created a similar stir.

In the end, we did *whatever* we needed to do to mix up our reunion with my parents. And when all else failed, we road tripped. We visited the mountains of North Carolina and picked grapes and apples. We went to New York City and stared open-mouthed at the Blue Whale suspended within the Museum of Natural History. We found our dear friends, Cazador and Carlotta, who had bought their own boat and were sailing down the Hudson from Lake Placid. Sipping tea with them in a little Thai food restaurant in New Jersey, I offered to help with their first offshore passage from Cape May to the Delaware Bay (a big step for a captain who had nearly jumped ship and sworn off Mother Ocean just a couple of months earlier). And after a few *Singha* beers, we made more sailing plans: We would meet up and cruise together in Florida.

And all of these travel adventures were made possible by our first decision – the decision to go cruising as a family. As scary as that decision had been, as scary as it still was, the original decision, the adventure and its rewards continued to unfold.

Before we knew it, the hurricane season had passed, and it was time to return to *Manta Raya*. The freeloading I had worried about with my parents had proved fiction. Something much more wonderful had happened. We stood in my parents' driveway and hugged one another goodbye. Families we knew had so little time together – children, now adults, had scattered across the United States. These families had ceased trying to untangle the knots of their family relations, and their reunions were short holiday affairs. But we had gotten to know one another in a much deeper way over the last few months, as adults.

With tears in his eyes, my dad bent down and hugged both of the girls. He would, he said, miss the way they had placed dolls, tiny beds and furniture in every corner of every room in his home. He would even miss finding stuffed animals in his underwear drawer. And this, I believe, was proof our visit had succeeded. It was also the ultimate confession of love.

New Keys and Another Millennium in the Islands

When we had left *Manta Raya* in Florida, I had said good-bye - convinced I would not be coming back to sail her. But our time away from her had put our cruising in new perspective. As Diane and I reasoned with one another late at night, we figured we still owned a boat, and we might never get a chance to sail as a family again. Our girls were still at the age when family was sufficient society. Besides, we were in the cruising "groove." We knew how to sail *Manta Raya* without banging into too many hard-ships; and, as Diane pointed out, we knew how to ask for and buy sterilized milk in at least four different languages.

For round two, we planned a new approach. We would take our time - no more running from island to island, chasing after destinations and being chased by the hurricane season. We would choose one cruising ground, a nearby destination; and see it in detail, at our leisure and during the best weather season. We would take some of the heat off the confining cauldron of family cruising by encouraging friends to visit. Better: we would cruise *with* friends. Cazador and Carlotta would sail beside us. Together we would sail to the Jewel of the Caribbean, a "forbidden" destination.

But first we would have to get *Manta Raya* back in the water. And in keeping with our new cruising philosophy of taking our time and enjoying it, rather than living aboard while we re-commissioned, we booked a nearby hotel. With complimentary breakfast, lots of room for home schooling and a Jacuzzi for washing away boatyard aches and fiberglass shards, the hotel helped take the edge off our preparations. We also enjoyed another luxury (actually a necessity for the far-flung shopping destinations of the United States): wheels. Right or wrong, outside of the major cites, the United States demands a car. There was no more calling for taxis, squinting at bus schedules or walking miles across busy highways with our girls as we tried to find hardware and provisions. We drove our land bound tender, our minivan.

Our re-commissioning went smoothly. Before Christmas we were afloat and underway, or as Diane wrote in our log, we were "un-velcroed" from the dock. The feeling was delicious. Our shakedown passage to Palm Beach brought back memories of the previous year, but we were prepared. The girls wore seasickness patches for the rough passage, which, as Diane also wrote in the log, was like "breaking a bronc' inside a washing machine – top loader, double rinse."

We were once again into the rhythms of cruising. And this time, instead of resenting the congestion of southern Florida, we embraced it. We dinghied into posh marinas and docked our cracked and patched dinghy next to the teak and chrome luxury yachts. And we walked the plush grounds as if we were guests staying in high dollar suites. We roller bladed down palm lined sidewalks next to marble fountains in front of Boca Raton mansions. We ate croissants on shady benches beneath fig and banyon trees, and we scooped up jamocha almond fudge with silver spoons.

Only once did Diane let the congestion and attitude of southern Florida get the better of her. In a basin in Ft. Lauderdale, as she drank her morning coffee and prepared the day's boat schooling lessons for the girls, she looked up just as a Florida Maritime Police boat roared alongside. The uniformed officer, without so much as a "good morning," demanded to know how long we were planning on staying."

"I have a feeling," said Diane, "that you are about to tell me."

"These people," said the man, scowling and waving his arms around the basin to indicate the decadent homes along its banks, "have paid a lot of money to live here, and they don't care to stare at a bunch of transients on boats."

"This is not a boat," said Diane. "This is our home, a cruising yacht, for which we also paid a lot of money. We "transients" happen to be a family, and we are raising two girls in our floating home. They are nice kids on a beautiful boat, and I should think we improve the view considerably, wherever we choose to anchor."

At this point I stepped on deck, thanked the red-faced officer for his warning and promised to move along within the next 24 hours. Southern Floridians were certainly getting testy about liveaboards. But I did not blame them. As I had learned in Biology 101, rats, when overpopulated and confined, often attacked and ate one other. Besides, we were headed further south to greener pastures. The houses and highways were about to give way to the Keys.

For boaters, the Florida Keys, though also facing development pressures, have managed to hold onto much of their laid back appeal. Flagler's railroad and the highway that followed it connected the string of islands and brought people to the Keys. But the distance from Miami and tropical hurricanes, Nature's great cleanser, had maintained some balance. In the watery world between the Florida Keys, boating still prevailed. At the boating Mecca of Boot Key we saw more types of boats than we had seen anywhere in the Caribbean. There was even a boat that looked like a giant Clorox® Bottle. I am not too sure what it was for, but it looked quite clean.

Just shy of Key West and one day before Christmas, we found a delightful island run by a National Park ranger and his wife. They had children, and in between collecting Key Limes in an abandoned grove and visiting a grassy park where we played paddleball, the kids got together to play. At one point there were eight little girls jumping on Manta Raya's trampoline. They dove into the water about her floats and swung from her rigging. Several families, friends of the rangers, were also visiting the island. We were on the cusp of the second millennium, and the families had gathered in part to celebrate the start of the new year and in part to avoid mainland anxiety over Y2K. There were no roads or land bridges connecting the island to the mainland. Peace would reign. Here too, boats ruled the day.

Our last Christmas present arrived on New Year's Eve. Cazador and Carlotta steamed into our little anchorage just in time to celebrate. The rangers and their friends, momentarily suspending Federal regulations, quaffed champagne and shot bottle rockets across the water. On board *Manta Raya*, we staged a New Year's performance. Diane, the girls and I hefted our flute, xylophone, harmonica and guitar to play "Silent Night." Then we sang the song in three languages – English, German and Spanish. Cazador, quite touched by our performance, made up a new verse on the spot, in yet another language - white-trasheze:

"Shut up y'all. Git me a beer. Some chick got pregnant, and I don't care..."

Indeed, the year 2000 was off to a good, if irreverent, start. After a long round of charades with the kids, we sent them off to bed yawning; and then we talked late into the night about our cruising plans for the forbidden destination - Cuba. We still had some hurdles ahead of us. Key West was about to become a trying limbo we would have to endure before we could sail; and Cuba herself would become an even more troublesome destination than she had been in 1999, all because of a little boy, lost and afloat on a raft in the Gulf Stream.

In Miami, the Elian story was building to a showdown. The little boy had rafted from Cuba to the United States with his mother, but his mother had drowned along the way. And now the boy's estranged father, still in Cuba, was asking for his son's return. Castro was pounding his fist, and sweet little Miami Cuban grandmothers were clutching their purses to their chests and lying down in front of public buses. Things did not look good. We tried to separate our Cuba passage plans from the political tension and media hype, but they played a shrill and uneasy tune, as we plotted courses and read Lonely Planet guidebooks. Meanwhile, a succession of horrific Northers played a very real and very shrill tune through our rigging.

As rain swept across our anchorage in Key West, cold wind buffeted the boats about us. At one point Cazador and I had to rescue a Vancouver woman on her 45-foot sloop. Her husband had anchored and immediately left for town, but the rising wind had drug his boat across the soft anchorage. On the radio his wife's pleas for help grew nearly hysterical. Shivering in the rain, we got her safely re-anchored (with two anchors), after raising her single anchor and finding a beer can speared on its point. In the end, we were more than ready to leave Key West behind and take the leap to Cuba.

But we had more than the usual pre-departure items on our checklist. We pulled on our foul weather gear and made daily trips through the rain for laundry, bank account balances, insurance and bills, propane, water and diesel fills and last calls and letters to friends and family. We also had to wait for parts to replace Cazador's and Carlotta's transmission, which had given them fits all the way down the east coast. Finally, we had to perform a legal duty we had never had to perform before: a Coast Guard notification. By law we were required to submit our plans for visiting Cuba. At first we thought about ignoring this bit of bureaucracy, but in the end we decided that if this red tape boondoggle were to get us into trouble, so be it. Surprisingly, the Coast Guard simply acknowledged our passage plans with no questions asked, and one day we found ourselves ready to sail.

On a Thursday evening in the winter of 2000, with Cazador and Carlotta just ahead of us, we motored out of Key West harbor, took a deep breath of the warm, clear salt air, and sailed south across a calm sea toward Cuba.

Cuba

There is an itinerary on the back of my grandfather's 1932 marriage license. It is a travelogue of his honeymoon. Ralph Scantlebury wed Mabel Entweiss. Their marriage license is a complete diary of their honeymoon trip to Cuba – except for one part of the trip, noticeable by its absence.

Ralph was an engineer, a talented and precise man from Ohio, whose father was a Methodist minister. The diary of his honeymoon is handwritten in precise and even script. Every detail of the vacation - the departure date of the train from Cleveland, the hotels in Valdosta, St. Pete and Miami - is itemized, until Ralph and his new bride boarded a Clyde Line ship bound for Cuba. Then the record goes blank. Like a romantic movie fade or the pulling of a curtain to hide the passion of two lovers, the details of the newlyweds' stay in Havana are obscured. One can only guess what happened when Ralph and Mabel stepped off the ship in Havana. The last entry on the back of the marriage certificate is this: "… arrived Perle de Habana."

Correspondent J.J. Van Raalte writing in the early 1900s called Cuba the "paradise of cocktails," the "ideal country of personal liberty." He wrote: "When we come here again next year we should bring with us the Statue of Liberty, to place in the port of Havana, where it properly belongs." Only ninety miles from the extended Key West toe of the United States, Cuba offered not only respite from long, cold North American winters but also escape from its frigid morality. Under the umbrellas on Cuba's sandy beaches by day and in Havana's brightly lit hotels, cabarets and casinos by night, many things guilt-ridden and at times illegal were not only accessible but encouraged. During Prohibition, nearly 7,000 bars opened in Havana. The Cuba *Cervecera* Company purchased the entire factory of the US Brewing Company of Chicago and bottled five million liters of beer each day. In the fifties, Havana's monthly gambling income exceeded $500,000; and *Life* correspondent Ernest Havemann wrote, "This is going to be another Las Vegas, only like Las Vegas never imagined." Even fastidious publications like *House and Garden* remarked on the lusty attractions of Havana: "A certain amount of sin, naturally, is to be expected in a city as whole-heartedly devoted to love and romance as Havana... this Latin temperament and the beauty of Cuban girls who are well aware of their enticements, having the tendency to unsettle susceptible Americans and induce erratic behavior."1

Nearly 33,000 tourists visited Cuba in 1914. 90,000 visited in 1928, and by 1957, my birth date, the year Sputnik was launched and just a few years before Kennedy would begin turning off the Cuban spigot of tropical passion, 356,000 people visited the island. Hollywood movies gilded the lily of Cuba's romance. The mambo became a national dance craze, and each week more than 50 million TV viewers watched Ricky Ricardo on *I Love Lucy* electrify his orchestra with splashy rumbas at the *Club Babalú*.

Where passions flourished, dollars flowed and organized crime grew, especially when the U.S. legislature began weeding out underworld crime in the United States. By the 1950s, organized crime had control of most of Cuba's major hotels and casinos. The estimated number of prostitutes in Havana increased from 4,000 in 1912 to more than 11,500 in the late 1950s. Cubans grew weary of the corruption, particularly in their own government; and a series of revolutions, each designed to wash the government clean, culminated with Fidel Castro's coup in 1959. Then when Castro went to Washington to see if he could keep some of the US money spigot flowing, he got the cold shoulder from a young vice president by the name of Richard Nixon, so he turned to the Soviets. And in the early 60s, all trade and travel between Cuba and the United States was cut off. The United States lost its passionate

---

1   "Image of Identity" from *On Becoming Cuban: Identity, Nationality and Culture* by Louis A. Perez Jr. © 1999 by the Universtiy of Carolina Press. Also taken from *Inside Cuba, The History Culture, and Politics of an Outlaw Nation,* © 2003 John Miller and Aaron Kenedi, Marlowe and Co., New York ISBN 1-56924-484-7

playground, and though the finger of blame could have been pointed in many directions, clearly the United States had sullied its own sandbox. We had loved Cuba to death.

In 1988 when the island was off limits to all non-communist countries, a Canadian family we met in Port Antonio told us about spending a month in Cuba. They had been blown there by a storm, and when they came ashore, they had been held as "prisoners" near a small town on the southern coast. Their detention amounted to being "guarded" by town officials, who wandered down to the beach each day to visit them on their boat. At first only government officials called, but eventually these officials brought along their wives, kids and friends. The Cubans also brought fresh fruits and vegetables, and while the adults sat about trading stories and laughing like neighbors at a block party, the kids played beneath a nearby waterfall. When word arrived from Havana that the family should be released, there was general disappointment. But the town recovered by hosting a huge farewell party - bonfires and barbecue on the beach. There were teary goodbyes and hugs.

Out of supplies and in need of repairs, the family sailed directly to Miami. By radio they forwarded a report of their Cuban visit, and at the Miami docks they were met by a long row of black sedans. As they tied off to the pilings, men wearing black suits and dark sunglasses stepped out of their black cars. They *requested* permission to come aboard.

The Canadian father told me this story as we stood on the deck of his converted fishing boat. It was a balmy night, and we were surrounded by the laughter and warm conversation of our fellow cruisers - sailors from the Americas and Europe, who had gathered on the antique yacht for spicy jerk chicken, mangoes and rum. "Those fellows asked us a lot of questions," said the father. "They wanted to know exactly what we had seen; how the Cuban people had looked. Were they hungry, happy, disgruntled? Had we taken any pictures? They asked if they could have something from our boat. Can you guess what it was? Our garbage. They took every scrap of it. It was a cruising sailor's dream come true. When the fellows in the black suits left, they left carrying our black bags of garbage. Vroom! And they were gone."

When we finally got the opportunity to sail to Cuba as a family, we knew the way. In the spring of 1988 on our way from the Bahamas to Jamaica, Diane and I had sailed around Cuba's west end. We had been sailing for thirty-one hours, trading four-hour shifts at the wheel.

Cuba's startling escarpments and lush green mountains appeared out of misty clouds. We were stunned, and we made a pact that one day we would visit the "Jewel of the Caribbean." Back when we had been in diapers, too small to care and too young to do anything about it, old men, politicians, had taken the place from us. And in a world of enticements, nothing was more desirable than a Jewel within reach but denied.

In the year 2000 we still knew the way to Cuba, but I was not sure we still had the will. We had heard tales of the Cuban government confiscating U.S. boats. We had heard that a beautiful Hatteras fishing yacht had been blown into Cuban waters and had been taken by the Cuban Coast Guard (the *Guardia Costa*). Before long Castro had been spotted on the yacht, smoking his cigars and fishing. And now the misplaced Cuban boy, Elian, was upping the ante of political tension.

So we sailed toward Cuba with many things on our minds: the weather, the set of the Gulf Stream, the timing for a daylight landfall - the usual survey of sails, engine and bilge; but most of all we thought of this: how we were headed toward the oldest and greatest Jewel in the Caribbean, but a forbidden land and a dark mystery that had been locked up and hidden away since 1961. As Venus rose to herald the sun and we steered toward the glow of Cardenas beneath the Southern Cross, we wondered just what we would find and what sort of reception we might get. After all, by some strange twist of Fate, we were no longer just a cruising family, friendly tourists afloat; somehow we had become "the enemy."

So this is what happened: The coming dawn painted a pink and blue sky with sparse white clouds over a sweeping, green landscape. The dark blue of the Gulf Stream gave way to startlingly turquoise water so clean and clear that we felt we had come not the 90 miles from Key West but thousands of miles to a new world (or 50 years back to an old one). To port we saw a line of white sand dotted with, wonder of wonders, palatial resorts. Just ahead we could make out the *Paso Malo* entrance to the *Marina Darsena*, where we hoped to clear into the country. We smiled as we watched a black, 1957 Buick Special glide over a palm-lined highway.

Diane gripped the radio mike and pressed her night rusted vocal chords into service. In faltering Spanish she located who she guessed was the port captain, who in turn asked the usual litany of arrival questions: boat name, crew size, last port... until he came to the question we had all been dreading: "¿*Que bandera?*" (What flag do you fly? Where are you from?)

"*Los Estados Unidos,*" said Diane, and we waited.

But without pause and in sudden ringing English, the voice on the radio came back, "Welcome, my friends, to Cuba!"

And so the romance began, a romance that took our family to empty beaches, cobble stoned colonial streets, protected green lagoons, dripping mountain rainforests and pristine coral gardens. All the while we would be courted by the warmest, politest and most hospitable people we had met anywhere in the Caribbean. We would visit Hemingway's ghost, sample world class rum and outstanding cigars, knock lobster unconscious with our anchor, say prayers in a voodoo church, meet doctors so poor they had to hitchhike and eat a gourmet dinner in an oil field. All of this, every bit of it, would turn our romantic notions of Cuba into a full-blown love affair. The end result would be that Cuba would teach us, change us and even now call us back to visit again.

Our first lesson in Cuba was learning what could happen in a highly regulated country lacking the wherewithal to pillage its own resources:

"Aha!" I heard Diane yell, "Here's some!"

I trudged through the white sand following her tracks and made the only other set of footprints I could see across the broad expanse of beach bordering *Cayo Santa Maria.* The day was so clear, the sun so warm and the water so perfect, that I had no control over the silly grin that kept spreading across my face. We had anchored off the protected curve of shore on Cuba's north coast just a week after clearing in, and in the hour we had been ashore, we had collected a couple dozen clams in the lagoon behind the beach. The kids had a kite "Aunt" Carlotta had given them. With the thing in tow they were bouncing about as if they had just gotten new batteries. Where had we ever found such a perfect beach and not a single sunburned tourist, park service sign or boat (besides our own) in sight? But Diane's shout meant she had finally found the article we had been hunting for: garbage.

We had been looking for the omnipresent choker of turtles and clutterer of beaches from Rock Hall, Maryland to Los Roques, Venezuela: a plastic bag. We needed the bag to hold our treasures of clams, pink fighting conch shells and sand dollars.

When I reached Diane, I wrapped my arm around her waist and stared down at the sand to see what she had found. We were ankle deep in sparkling water, and she reached out with her toe to nudge what looked like a black fold of polypropylene. But the joke was on both of us. Our "bag" turned out to be a blackened tree root.

With a few industrial city exceptions, we found the same clean and sound environment everywhere we traveled along the coast of Cuba. Up ahead near *Cayo Guillermo,* with the Bahama Banks only twenty miles to port, we glided through transparent waters so clear we felt as if we were suspended in mid-air, twenty-five feet off the ground. We saw rays fly from their nests and leave clouds of sand. In the narrow channel between Cuba and the Bahamas, the waters dropped into the Gulf Stream. Here Hemingway had conjured his stories for Islands in the Stream, and golden Sargasso Seaweed hatched the Great Fish, the Dorado. These muscular fish live only five years and grow to thirty pounds quickly by chasing after squid and flying fish. They swim at a blazing 50 knots, and we caught one that stretched our finger thick shock cord and 200-pound test hand line to near their breaking points. After twenty tiring minutes, the magnificent animal was still streaking sideways in splashes of blue and gold that set our line humming. When we finally got the startled fish in the cockpit, it stood up on its stomach and tail slapped me four times, knocking me out of the cockpit and through the companionway. Pow! Round two. I came back waving my *lignum vitae* bopping stick; and in that moment felt Hemingway's presence. I could imagine his delighted smile. I believe I even heard him laugh.

Cuba's unspoiled Nature was always beneath our hull. On No Name Key east of *Caiman Grande* with its limestone overhangs and blowholes, I took the girls snorkeling into shallow caves where our air bubbles collected into pockets along the cave roof and ran like quicksilver. Off the north tip of *Cayo Blanco* near *Cayo Cruz del Padre,* we dove Staghorn, Elkhorn and Brain corals along the pelagic fringe where Bonito swam with Jack and ever watchful Mr. 'Cuda hovered nearby. Hawksbill and Green Turtles stuck their heads in the coral on the pretense that if they could not see us, we could not see them. And octopi as big as my head ghosted over the rocks, turning red with alarm and disappearing in holes smaller than quarters.

And the harvest ... If stone crab omelets and lime soaked Grouper fish fingers were not enough, there was always "Larry" the lobster, everywhere. O.K., we did not actually knock Larry unconscious with our anchor, but we did find him every time we went looking, and often right around our anchor line. In the modern day Caribbean, that was a miracle.

Our second lesson was about the Cuban people themselves, *Cubanaos*. Anchored in the *Canal de Los Barcos* just a day's sail from the *Marina Darsena*, we watched two fishermen row toward us. They rowed past iridescent green mangroves so lush they appeared to be growing before our eyes. The fishermen were in a small, battered wooden boat, and they were alternately and earnestly bailing as they pulled against the stiff current. We were looking forward to meeting them. Earlier in the day they had pulled their rusted and wheezing fishing trawler alongside to ask us if we would like to follow them through the convoluted *Pasa de la Manuy* and east over the *Bahia de Santa Clara*. All day we had watched their reassuring belch of smoke off to port and followed their waving lead through the winding and shallow channels. Given the brown water that had churned up behind them, I believe they may have dredged us a channel. The fellows had been helpful guides, and I was looking forward to thanking them. But just the same, given some of our experiences in the Caribbean, I wondered what they would expect in return. Shame on me, as you will see.

The curly haired and burly shouldered captain smiled shyly as he and his friend *Gilberto* climbed aboard. We shook hands all around: "*Mucho gusto* (pleased to meet you)." "*El gusto es mio* (the pleasure is mine)." We sat around the cockpit. Would they like something to eat, to drink? No, they had only come to visit.

Two hours later as the sun began to set and rich colors began to light the lagoon, we were still visiting and having a grand time of it. The kids were transfixed as *Gilberto*, a diver, told them about wild dogs and sharks. He showed them long white scars on his leg. Both girls gasped. *Gilberto* smiled, shrugged and confessed, "I fell off my bike." When the sky darkened, our friends left for their ship, and we waved good-bye, but our visit was not finished.

The next morning the ancient trawler pulled up alongside us again. Again the captain and *Gilberto* rowed to our transom. They poured a bushel of stone crabs, oranges and potatoes into our cockpit. The crabs raced sideways and brandished their claws as they searched for cover, and Sawyer and Riley danced about and screamed. We offered the fishermen gifts of canned food and milk, but they declined. These Cubans, who could certainly use our gifts and help, were a people whose kindness and generosity we would have trouble outdoing, as we were to learn further on *Caiman Grande*.

Caiman Grande was just a short sail from the wide, beautiful beach at *Cayo Santa Maria*. But when we rounded the protected corner of the beach, we sailed straight into 20 knots of wind and pounding waves. By staying inside the skinny reef to avoid the bigger waves outside, we made our way to protection under the cliffs and candy striped lighthouse on *Caiman Grande*. And by the end of the day we understood how Columbus had discovered the New World. He did not have a choice. He was blown there by the Trade Winds. Going the other direction was madness.

After our leisure days in the sun flying kites, eating clams and generally enjoying the white beach of Santa Maria Island, we had stuck our noses into the Trades to re-learn this lesson in prevailing winds. To top off the lesson, our arthritic knee, the port engine, had decided to develop a leak around the prop seal. Seawater had mixed with gear oil to make "mayonnaise." This was not good.

But tucked beneath a white, limestone cliff and a towering red-striped lighthouse, Grand Caiman, Cuba was a beautiful anchorage in turquoise water. The place was romantic, and I did not have much trouble putting the consequences of a deteriorating port engine out of my mind. Even the walls of the *Guarda Costa* station, which bore the fading motto *Socialismo o Muerto* (Socialism or Death), could not detract form the romance of the place.

We shared the anchorage with a wooden fishing trawler owned by the Cuban fishermen's co-op. Cazador, believing local knowledge might provide relief from the Trade Wind licking we had been taking, decided to pay the fishermen a visit. He dove into the warm water and swam over to the helpful hands of the fishermen, who pulled him aboard.

There were six men - strong, smiling and clear-eyed. Their boat's simple, wood bench interior served as workplace and home for month long fishing stints offshore. After polite introductions, Cazador asked and learned about protected anchorages that had not appeared in our guidebook. He was reminded that light Northers provided breaks in the Trade Wind and allowed helpful offshore and following west winds. Then, when the conversation turned to broader issues, like fishing and navigation, Cazador found himself translating nautical maxims like "give way to tonnage," all the while apologizing for his Spanish by saying that he "*hablo español el mismo de una vaca inferma* (spoke Spanish like a sick cow)." Cazador liked these good men. They listened attentively and laughed easily. And despite the hurdles of language, culture and politics that could have gotten in his way, he swam home with the gifts of new friendships.

Then after sunset, more gifts arrived. In the darkness a leaky rowboat pulled alongside *Manta Raya*. The lone *Guarda Costa* soldier shipped his oars and hissed, "*Cazador.*" Soldiers were not supposed to fraternize with "gringos," and in Cuba, this fellow was risking much. He had just visited with our fishermen friends, he said, and they had sent him to us. From the bottom of his wooden boat, he hefted a huge tuna filet and a dozen lobster tails. We were amazed. "*Mil gracias!*" we whispered gratefully, asking him to please thank the fishermen. The soldier's smile shone up from the darkness, "*De nada*" (it was nothing), and he was off.

That night, in a cabin decorated by our girls with red crepe paper, we gathered for a feast. Carlotta, who cooks in this world using talents stolen from Heaven, served us steaming lobster *etouffé* followed by moist coconut cake topped with cherries. There was no way to top this evening, unless you counted the sweet embrace from Diane, *mi vida,* my life, as the four-armed sweep of the lighthouse reached out into the darkness over our heads.

The Shirts

Cuba's coast and topography provided just about every setting and anchorage we had seen in the Caribbean: Bahamian blue water with flat, white sand keys, Caribbean islets dotted with palms, towering mountains whose shoulders sagged into cliff lined bays, and drying mangrove flats with pink flamingos. In short, we saw everything we might want to see with almost no one but ourselves to see it. Cuba had more coastline than Georgia, Florida and a good part of the Gulf states combined. We had spent late nights with *Cazador* and *Carlotta* marking our charts, reading Nigel Calder's guidebook and planning a full circumnavigation of the island. We had it all planned out.

But our old Achilles' heel, *Manta Raya*'s port engine, had a different plan in mind. Our hearts were in the trip, but *Manta Raya*'s mechanical realities were not. I thought about swearing. I thought about arranging a haul out and somehow finagling replacement parts through Cuba's customs wall and the United State's daunting embargo, but the writing was on the wall, and this time I read and understood it.

We held a cockpit conference, where rum was the bipartisan negotiator. We would sail as far as *Guillermo* and then turn back to the *Marina Darsena* in *Varadero*. For me, giving up was hard, but not nearly as hard as it had been when we had started cruising. Perhaps I was beginning to learn my lesson.

Cazador and *Carlotta*, the most can-do and enterprising couple we know, spring boarded from this disappointment. The next morning, Carlotta dinghied over with her *Lonely Planet* guide to Cuba. She had already selected her favorite pages to show us. We had a lot to see, and we could still see it all by car or train. Land touring, she said, would be easy and safe - there was little chance we would capsize or drag anchor. But first we would learn another lesson about Cuba

In a country with a sizable military guarding its shore and a large, centralized government riding herd over its people, we expected fairly stiff regulations. Looking back, we had been "disinsected" in Grand Cayman, boarded by gun toting DEA agents in the Bahamas, and we had paid "extra" fees to the grinning port captain in Guatemala. I once had a German cruiser tell me that the United States was the most regulated country he ever visited. I disagreed. How could a German, given Germany's anal retentive attention to order, iron clad social morays and preoccupation with on-time everything, think of the Untied States as regulated? But the German cruiser explained: everywhere in the United States, he said, there were signs and regulations: keep out, private property, stay off the grass. He had never been in a more regulated place. And as I thought the matter over and considered, for example, small lakes in Germany, where nudists swam as couples smoked marijuana on park benches, I realized he might be right.

Cuban officials, who boarded our boat upon entry and again at every port listed on our cruising itinerary or *despacho,* came *en masse* but unarmed to enforce simple rules. Because of their various uniforms, badges and striped epaulets, we called them the "Shirts."

We heard horror stories from fellow cruisers who had just visited Havana (enough stories that we opted to leave our boat docked in *Varadero* and drive to the capital city instead). Purportedly equipment like handheld VHFs, GPS and satellite telephones had been sealed and confiscated. Odd payments, fines and "donations" had been requested. Some cruisers claimed to be missing belongings after boat inspections. Cruising gossip? We did not know. But we did not have these experiences. We do know that whatever the regulation, when tempted to question or enter into a "discussion" with the Shirts, it was helpful to remember the adage: "Don't try to teach a pig to sing. It doesn't work, and it only annoys the pig."

For us, episodes with the Shirts were harmless. There was always the same entourage: customs, immigration, port captain/*Guardia* officer, agricultural inspector, veterinarian, doctor, and a young, idealistic but silent observer from the *Ministerio del Interior,* i.e. the communist party. We had to remember that this poor, socialized country guaranteed jobs for everyone, so not a few of them had to pass the time by cramming into our boat.

The gathering of Shirts at every port might sound overwhelming (and it could get tedious), but look again: Other countries like Mexico, Jamaica and Venezuela required clearances at all ports along a cruising itinerary. In Cuba, we chose the ports on our permit where inspections were to take place. The Shirts came to our boat; we did not have to traipse all over some sweltering or frightening third world seaport to find them. And the Cuban officials were as polite as grandmas at a Sunday tea. They removed their shoes so as not to scuff our boat. *Guardia* officers patted our kids on the head and tended to be more interested in toys than stowaways. I remember one fellow, smiling, who held one of Riley's baby dolls in one hand and a bright orange slinky in the other. My wife traded gardening tips with an agricultural inspector who simultaneously admired and turned a blind eye to her potted oregano. There was general laughter when a veterinarian asked if we had any animals aboard, and I answered "*solamente las niñas* (only the kids)."

We had a choice. We could see the Shirts as an invasion of our privacy or an awkward social call, in which the shy but inquisitive Cubans were as interested in us as we were in them. Our experiences were that the Shirts, though starched, were friendly. No biggie for a ticket to paradise.

In *Guillermo*, Cazador and I had just finished our rounds with the Shirts, and we were visiting with the marina manager *Angel*. He had stayed behind after the entourage of officials had left. *Angel* was an ex-heavyweight boxer who had trained for the Olympics in Russia. Listening to this big, Cuban man speak Russian and hearing about his battles in the ring, as well as his battles with Moscow snow drifts, had more than captured our attention; it had redefined our definition of the odd directions life can take (Just how does a kid from the Tropics end up in Leningrad?). We were enthralled and hoped *Angel's* tales would never end. That was why we were especially pleased and honored when he invited us for a beer at the marina café. After all, it was not often that a Cuban could afford to treat visiting yachtsmen to a drink.

Several rounds of boxing and beer later, we found ourselves joined by the port captain, the port captain's assistant and a growing number of marina employees: lots of folks with little to do and now lots of free beer with which to do it. Another round of *Mayabe* beer was ordered, more fellows trickled in. We were riding the camaraderie. After all, in any language, we were guys in a bar talking about sports. That was when Cazador decided to bring up one of his favorite topics: the impending United States invasion.

Did the Cubans realize, Cazador asked the small crowd, that eight million U.S. tourists visited the Bahamas each year? *Thoughtful nodding.* Could they imagine how many tourists would descend on Cuba? *Polite silence.* Could their beaches, their culture, and their people handle the pressure? Were they ready for this onslaught?

A few more beers, many handshakes and backslaps, and Cazador and I realized we had said goodbye to the last of our new friends. It was time to dinghy home. We thanked the bartender, wished him well and turned to go.

"*Señores!*" shouted the bartender, "but who will pay for the beers?"

I stopped and turned to Cazador. Then we both laughed. It looked like the Cubans were ready for American tourists after all.

In contrast, when we returned to the *Varadero* Marina, Cazador met a fellow (let us call him *Señor Amable*), who invited us to his home for dinner. Though private *paladars* (home restaurants) were legal in some areas, they were not in the tourist area where *Señor Amable* lived. But he was a cooking impresario, who grew his own vegetables and spices right outside his home, in the middle of the oil fields. The six of us sat at his table inside a ten-foot square room, while his wife bustled about washing dishes just off my elbow. The pigs grunted happily outside in their pen, and the oil derricks clicked, whirred and bowed their heads for as far as we could see out the front door.

Señor Amable did what he could with what he had and created a culinary miracle: a large, steaming platter of seafood *paella* with lobster and fish in seasoned yellow rice, a fresh garden salad with bright red tomatoes, the local Cuban tuber *boniata* sautéed with butter and onions, delicious *Mayabe Cerveza* (Cuba's finest beer), and tiny *café cubanas* with creamy flan for dessert.

Then, another miracle: We had such a good time with *Señor Amable*, his wife, his kids, the neighbors who wandered by and the happy pigs who eventually broke from their pen to get in on the action, that the smiling and energetic *Señor Amable,* who lived so simply and needed every penny he could save, would not accept our payment. Go figure. The Cubans might need dollars, but never at the expense of their expansive Cuban *corazones* (hearts).

A few days later, we took a ride up the peninsula to find a mansion we had sailed past and wondered about. We were struck by its bold and elegant prominence on the cliff overlooking the ocean - like the bridge deck of a great cruise ship, the mansion even had port (red) and starboard (green) lights. We wanted to find out just what the incredible building was about.

We motored along the highway past commercial buildings and storage yards that backed the European resorts along the beach. We came to a gate, and through it we could see the rolling green hills and pruned trees of a golf course. The guard at the gate hardly looked at us as he waved us on, and we proceeded up a narrow road bordering the green grass of the fairways and ended in a circular drive in front of the mansion.

The mansion was, until the revolution, the home of E.I. Dupont. It had a three-story, stone exterior, and a marble and mahogany interior. Over the wood paneled and satin draped walls hung oil paintings depicting Robert Louis Stevenson's *Treasure Island*. A plaque framed the words to Coleridge's poem *Xanadu* and proclaimed the vast estate and the entire peninsula the property of the Royal family of Delaware: the DuPonts. *In Xanadu did E.I. DuPont a mighty pleasure dome decree...*

We were visiting a monument built by a mineral and chemical magnate and commemorating United States capitalism. As we stood on the tiled porch atop the seaside cliff, we stared north over the blue ocean toward the States. I could imagine the DuPonts and their guests taking in the same view after a day at the links on their private golf course and thinking, "Ah, yes, because of what we have accomplished there, in the land of industry, we own and enjoy what we have here, in the land of leisure. Life is good."

The mansion spoke of sensual delights. The dining room still held the last echo of gentle laughter from forgotten banquets. The wine cellar spoke of expensive and refined tastes. The billiards room conjured up visions of after dinner cordials and cigars. The whole place spoke of the rewards of financial success, the American dream. And the contrast, it presented to today's Cuba was insane.

As we led the kids from room to room, we felt a peculiar attraction to the place. We had been in the third world Caribbean for a long time, and Cuba was an extreme example of the Caribbean's third world economy. In contrast the decadence of *Xanadu* was intoxicating.

"What is it about this place? " I whispered to Diane, as if we were in church. "I love it."

"I know," she said. I guess, at heart, we're capitalist pigs."

We climbed a circular staircase to the third floor of the mansion and found a bar surrounded with broad columns and fronted with floor to ceiling windows. The decor was Egyptian, and the view, as from the patio, was a panorama straight north over the blue ocean toward the United States. We were the only people in the bar, and we felt like royalty. We woke a bartender wearing a starched white shirt and tie. He smiled. He was thrilled to have customers, and he bustled over to our table. After some pleasantries and questions about my family, he asked me my name. And I could not resist.

"My name," I said, "is DuPont."

The poor man choked, and his face went pale.

I was immediately sorry for my prank, and I quickly jumped up from my seat, patted the man on his back and reassured him that I was only kidding. But there was something about the place, my *Norte Americano* sense of property and the idea of E.I. Dupont losing *Xanadu* (but probably writing it off) that had made me joke with the man. I was, I guess, uncomfortable with the way my *Norté Americano* sense of property, wealth and security could turn so suddenly on the whim of a people. I bought the man a beer to help anesthetize my hurt.

White Oxen and Red Coffee

I t turned out that Carlotta was right. Land touring through Cuba was the best way to see the eastern mountains, the endless green sugarcane fields, the southern rainforests and the crazy, mounded limestone hills of *Pinar del Rio*. We saw (and ate) crocodile in *Boca de Guama*, and we visited (and prayed) in the santería (voodoo) church in *Trinidad*. In the voodoo church, Christianity met the Congo, and as our guide explained with a sly smile, *everyone*, no matter what religion, eventually slipped in to make a food, tobacco or rum offering. We sniffed some of the 300 orchids grown in the *Soroa Orchideria*, and we watched Cuba's national bird the Tocaroro sing, as it swelled its red, white and blue waistcoat. Cuba had caves we boated through, waterfalls we swam under and rainforests and fields of red ripening coffee and green tobacco we hiked through. In Old World plazas and cathedrals, the colonial citizenry was already saying mass and riding about in leather carriages, while the colonists in North American were just beginning to hack away at the wilderness.

We could have toured by bus or train, but driving was a bigger adventure. In poor Cuba there were not many cars to contend with; but the horses, donkeys, sugarcane carts, jaunty carriages and thousands of bicyclists and pedestrians made up for any excitement lost to motor traffic. On every main highway we saw hundreds of Cubans waiting along the roadside for a ride: businessmen in shirts and ties, farmers with turned up cowboy hats and mothers with wrapped infants pressed against their shoulders. In Cuba the classic hitchhiking pose was palm down and waving, as if to say, "Stop right here. Stop beside me. Take me with you so I don't have to spend another hour, perhaps the whole day and even tomorrow waiting, waiting to get where I'm going."

And we did stop. We met musicians playing *guitaros*, young blushing couples, a lady, hair plaited in corn rows and held back with a white comb the size of Gibraltar, and an old man who smiled and shouted through his toothless mouth under the impression that gringo tourists could understand Spanish better if it were blasted at them like a summer squall. Every Cuban we picked up taught us something and added to our adventure.

Near *Pinar del Rio* we gave a handsome young couple a ride. They were shy, polite and grateful. The young man did the little talking there was, and I asked him where he was headed. They were traveling to a small town in the north, their hometown. They were doctors on their way home from the clinic. They put me in mind of a conversation I had had with a Brazilian cruiser at the marina. He had told me that Cuban doctors earned about $20 per month.

"Per month?" I gasped.

"That's right. And if they want to make more money, they can make ten times that bartending at the *Varadero* resorts."

"You're kidding."

"Look," he said, adopting the attitude of a patient professor. "You're looking at all of this through your *Norte Americano* sunglasses. Just because one fellow chooses to be a doctor and another fellow chooses to be a stone mason, should one make more money than the other?"

"Well," I countered, "for one thing, the mason can learn his trade in a month. But the doctor has to study for at least eight years. For another, the doctor heals people and saves lives."

"Doesn't the stone mason build walls for people and build them because he wants to build them?" asked the Brazilian.

"I suppose so ... in an ideal world." I answered warily.

"And doesn't the doctor heal people because he wants to heal people?

"Yes, but..."

"Well, why should the doctor make more money just because he wants to be a doctor?"

The Brazilian's argument had made me think ... about avocation and vocation, about the ranking of human contributions. Our two, young hitchhikers seemed contented enough. We dropped them off by a field, where a donkey wore a straw hat. The young doctors thanked us, waved and smiled, and we drove on.

In Cuba, hitchhikers were indispensable, because driving in Cuba meant getting lost in Cuba, and only Cubans knew where anything was. There were no road signs. Our guess was that this was not an oversight but a clever plan to thwart an invading army, which would only become frustrated and run out of gas before finding anything. Taking on hitchhikers helped. They knew where to turn even when there were no signs. Heck, every Cuban knew that in order to reach *Pinar del Rio*, we had to turn left after the rice field, where the farmer stood knee-deep and his placid white oxen pulled shoulder to shoulder through the red earth.

Near the end of our trip to Cuba, we visited Trinidad, a beautiful colonial city of narrow cobblestone streets, bell tower cathedrals and gurgling courtyard fountains tucked behind wrought iron fences. We were walking back toward our car after our visit to a cigar factory, when we came upon three boys sitting on the stone stoop of a small apartment. Two of the boys held well-used, dry and cracked baseball gloves. The third boy, a lock of black hair dangling over his forehead and across his eyes, was aimlessly whacking at small rocks with a sick. Diane turned and grasped my elbow. She asked if I would wait with the girls for a moment. She would be right back, and I knew where she was headed.

In a few minutes she returned, and she walked straight up to the boy with the stick "bat." He brushed the hair out of his eyes to consider her, and the other boys roused from their bored reveries. In polite Spanish, Diane greeted the boys and held out the present she had been concealing behind her back. All three boys jumped up at once, their eyes shone, and their mouths were open. The boy with the bat hesitated, but then he looked back into Diane's face, and she encouraged him by extending the present. In her palm rested a new, leather baseball – white and perfect inside its clear plastic package. "*Gracias,*" said the boy, *mile gracias.*" And off he darted, the ball held high over his head and his friends charging behind him. Kids suddenly appeared from all corners. They formed a tiny mob with the baseball, white and shining, at its epicenter. Then the mass of children rounded a corner and disappeared behind a cloud of dust.

"I guess there's gonna be a game," I said.

"Play ball," said Diane.

After a fine lunch of broiled snapper, fried plantains and rice, I was alone up in the bell tower of the convent *San Francisco de Asís* and enjoying the view: green hills, red earth and colonial Trinidad laid out in miniature beneath me. To the south the blue-green Caribbean dissolved into a hazy horizon. Lost in the view, I did not notice the little lady who climbed the steep stairs and stood beside me, until she offered a soft and smiling *"Buenos dias."* The blue badge she wore identified her as a tour guide. Her Canadian tour group was still puffing its way up the steep ladder to the bell room, so shyly, but true to her profession, she asked me whether I knew where I was.

"Trinidad?" I offered.

Polite smile. Yes, but did I know where I was standing? We were, she said, over the *Museo Nacional de la Lucha Contra Bandidos* (National Museum of the Struggle Against Outlaws).

Yes, I knew that. I had just toured the museum and had been impressed and somewhat disturbed by the display of the twisted United States Air Force engine cowling from the U2 spy plane shot down over Cuba in 1962. In fact, in my vista reverie I was still pondering the novelty of having visited, for the first time in my life, a war museum in which my home team was featured as the loser.

The polite little woman asked me another question. Did I know who the *Bandidos* were?

Yes, I replied, "me."

Her reaction could not have been more extreme. She started and looked away. And when she looked back, she was blushing, but her eyes were wide and serious, and she came closer to me - her hands out and nearly touching mine. No! She said. That was in the past. The *Bandidos* were a different people in a distinct time. Today we were friends, dear friends, and I should always feel the warmth and grandeur of the Cuban *corizon* (heart). Touched, I reassured her, and said that I understood, but I am not sure I did then or do now. I only know that she meant what she said, and that the urgent and honest look in her eyes was proof of her sincerity.

Behind us in the bell tower hung an ancient clock mechanism. Rusted weights, counterweights and gears were strewn about the dusty floor waiting for someone with the time, money and technology to restore them to life. I could see the maker's mark stamped on the silent bells: "Boston, Mass 1852." Even though we had just met, this lady and I, we had a long relationship going back hundreds of years. Whatever this relationship had been, sometimes mutually beneficial, sometimes parasitic, it had been an intimate relationship. But on that particular day we were friends.

This affinity between the United States and Cuba is more than geographical, and as felt by the Cubans, it may be hard for U.S. citizens to understand. I do not believe Cubans extend this same feeling toward Europeans or Canadians, who visit Cuba freely. Their special relationship with the U.S. might be a bit like the relationship between two brothers – one of them very rich and famous. They grew up together, and the relatively poor brother admires his wealthy brother – he might even want to be something like him. But he does not want his rich brother to tell him what to do, to rule his life. He simply wants him to be his brother.

When we sailed away from Cuba, we left the Jewel of the Caribbean with mixed feelings. Cuba was a beautiful place. It still held the treats that only the most pristine hideaways of the Caribbean could offer. The *Cubanos* had many reasons to dislike us, but they not only treated us with polite interest and respect, they often hugged us with a spontaneous affection my Teutonic mind could not fathom. As Diane and I had promised when we had first sailed past Cuba in 1988, we vowed once again to return. Otherwise, I do not think we could have left.

CUBA

By Sawyer Grey Scantlebury, age 9
Cuba, Cuba, Cuba
Pretty, sweet and clean
Through the *Canal de Buba*
Water clear, serene
Empty white sand beaches
Lobster but no peaches
Shells of red, white and pink
Crabs in the kitchen sink
Water 75 degrees
Lots and lots of palm trees
No more hamburgers, hot dogs or fries
But Cuba is beautiful in my eyes

We were only ninety miles away from our home as we sailed out past the *Canal de Bubba* and back into the wind and waves of the Caribbean. The unknowns of the land I knew, the United States, once again occupied my mind. What would we do now? How would we live there? What shape would our lives take? But I took satisfaction in remembering that had we "abandoned ship" in Cumana or chosen to quit cruising when we first returned to the States, I would have missed the treasures of our last two years of cruising.

Sawyer, quiet but always listening, had overheard Diane's and my earnest discussions about plans after returning to the United States.

En route back to the Keys, she presented us with a penciled list – the proposal she and her sister had drawn up for making a living in the United States. The list included growing herbs, raising goats, making cheese, gathering eggs, making Christmas baskets and giving cross-country skiing tours. The proposal was entitled "Farm Business." It turned out Sawyer and Riley had been discussing the next direction our family should take at some length before committing it to paper. We were to live on a farm, at which time the girls were also to get a puppy.

And oddly enough, that is where we are today: on a farm with a puppy that has grown into a galloping dog. Yet we are still on passage – a landlocked passage, but a passage just the same – just as uncertain and just as beautiful as any voyage we have ever taken. Our tans are now farmer tans - brown arms to the line of our t-shirt sleeves. Our girls think of school, sports, friends and, gulp, boys. But Diane and I sometimes think about living on a boat again. On my bureau is a Father's day card that Riley wrote for me while we were cruising *Manta Raya*. It is a gift token - a promise to "Do Customs" with me. One day I just might hold that girl to her promise.

The Girls at the Helm

Appendix 1 - In Their Own Words

An Interview with the Girls (daughters Sawyer age 10 and Riley age 7)

(1.) What was your favorite part about living on a boat?

Riley: "Swimming - being able to dive off the boat and swim with my sister."

Sawyer: "Nice beaches with no people, finding shells and swimming."

(2.) What was your least favorite part?

Riley: "Passages. They were boring. All I could think to do was look at books."

Sawyer: "Being seasick [on passages]."

(3.) Tell me about one of the scariest things that happened.

Sawyer: "When the anchor came up in St. Martin, and I had to do the gears to the engine.

Riley: "When we were motoring toward a place and something got tangled up. We were in the middle of the ocean, and you had to dive in, and we were afraid you'd get eaten by a shark. We didn't know how we'd get into the island."

(4.) What was one of your happiest times?

Riley: "Starfish Island [in the San Blas Islands] that nobody was on. It was like our own island except for a few fishermen. I liked being able to pick up starfish and get them sucked on my head."

Sawyer: "Lunches with crackers and stuff, when we'd all talk and sit in the cockpit."

(5.) Do you think other families should try living on a boat?

Sawyer: "Uh huh, because it's really nice to swim, to see different places and meet different people."

Riley: Not if they don't want to. If you want to and you know some kids on a boat, you could ask 'em, but [what they tell you] may not be right, because they might not have gone to the places you're thinking about, and they might have a different view, so you just have to go out and try it yourself."

(6.) What advice would you give to kids who do move onto a boat?

Riley: "Don't bring some of your favorite things like electronic stuff, because saltwater ruins it. Bring something you like and could play a lot."

Sawyer: "Bring lots of books. Only bring toys you really like to play with, 'cause there's not much room for junk."

(7.) Any other thoughts about living on a boat?

Sawyer: "Keep your hair short. You don't have to look great for school or work or anything."

Riley: "Your family might say 'hi,' but go on a boat where you can get to know each other. Try to find a great island and go to it."

Appendix 2 – Who's Going?

What is *cruising*? Who are the people living on boats, and why do they sail across the planet's watery world? And in the name of all that is sane and responsible, why would a family abandon the security of home, school and income to sail on the ocean?

I once interviewed an insurance agent I came to respect very much, and to use the word "respect" in the same sentence with "insurance agent" is proof I can surmount a large hurdle of my own prejudice. The man's name was Al Golden, and he sold marine insurance to offshore sailors, mainly cruising sailors who wished to cast off and see the watery world without worrying whether they might lose their life savings. In 1978 Al and his wife had sailed from Bermuda to Portugal and on to Israel and the Caribbean. I asked Al whether he had insured his own voyage, and he laughed. "There was no offshore insurance for cruisers back then. You just went."

Being an enterprising lad, when Al got back to the States, he started talking to insurance underwriters and trying to convince them to take on the cruising sailor as part of their risk. During one of these discussions, an underwriter derailed his spiel with a telling question: "Wait a minute," said the underwriter, "You mean these people actually *live* on their boats?"

When Al cruised in the seventies, he was part of a small company of sailors who followed the example of a previous and even more select group of cruisers. In 1898 Joshua Slocum was the first solo-sailor to circumnavigate the globe. In the mid 1900s, cruising pioneers like Eric and Susan Hiscock and Miles and Beryl Smeeton wrote about their adventures. After them came sailors like Tristan Jones and Don Street. These folks sailed off on boats that were, to the commercial marine community, *very* small. They motored the canals of France, sailed through the Mediterranean, crossed the Atlantic, explored the Caribbean, and sometimes, fantasy of fantasies, cruised through the exotic South Pacific. The stories they told were inspirational: friendly island natives, exotic foods and pristine, palm fringed, uninhabited islands. These cruisers were pioneers, real high seas adventurers. They were Captain Cooks in miniature - without the crew, the royal charter, the pay or the scurvy.

In the early cruising days, these globetrotting cruisers were a select club charting blue water passage routes and sounding out new anchorages. In the unlikely event that they met one another along the way, they were thrilled to share otherwise empty anchorages. They were a tiny band of world travelers sailing in small boats, and they were bound by their love of voyaging, or, if you are not so inclined, their particular insanity.

Cruising World magazine was launched in 1974 just when the sailaway cruising revolution took off. By the early eighties there were 85,000 loyal subscribers to the magazine - mostly hopeful, armchair sailors, but some actually casting off and sailing over the horizon. One reason for the cruising revolution was the groundbreaking or, if you will, the wave parting of the original cruisers, who wrote about their adventures in "how-to" tomes like the Hiscock's <u>Voyaging Under Sail</u> or Don Street's <u>Cruising Guide to the Lesser Antilles.</u> A more subtle reason for the growth of cruising in the seventies may have been the seventies themselves, when kids in their teens and twenties "dropped out" looking for new adventures and new lifestyles. Robin Lee Graham on *Dove* was my hero. Heck, the boy took off alone, was, at the time, the youngest kid to sail alone around the world AND he brought back a girl. Perfect.

My friend St. Frank cruised during the seventies. He grew up on the Chesapeake, and he has always loved boats. As a licensed captain, he continues to live on boats. He has waypoints on many of the charts of the world, and when he steps onto a dock wearing his baggy shorts and scuffed topsiders, other sailors seem to sense his experience and flock to him like dolphins to a bow wave. They ask him for sailing directions, passage advice, safe anchorages and other nautical tidbits that might fill the sails of their seafaring hopes. And with humility and heartfelt encouragement, St. Frank always obliges.

St. Frank has always owned a boat, starting with a sailing dinghy and working up to a 38 foot sloop he built from scratch - from its hand poured lead keel to its mirror finish mahogany trunk. During brief intervals when St. Frank was between boats, he tended to grow quite anxious, so anxious that he often kept an eye on "surrogate" boats he might "borrow" from the marina, should the need arise. Until securely on his own deck again, his surrogate boats were his aces in the hole - just in case the world's problems were to escalate and he would need to flee back into the welcoming arms of Mother Ocean.

Hoping to avoid dangerous duty during the Vietnam War, St. Frank joined the Merchant Marine. But he found himself anchored off Hanoi one deck above a hull filled with grenades. On the return voyage to the States, St. Frank was trying to think of a new angle when his captain announced that the crew's term of duty would be extended for another year, whether they liked it or not. St. Frank had been shanghaied. So when the captain anchored off the Bahamas with the crew confined to the ship, he stowed away in the life vest locker on the officers' launch and, once ashore, disappeared into the palm-thatched recesses of the island. For two months he lived in a shack with an old Bahamian fisherman and helped him with his nets. Then another merchant ship came along and St. Frank hopped aboard bound for New York. Before long he was back in the Bahamas aboard his own boat, a confiscated drug runner.

St. Frank's early-seventies cruising crowd was a small, can-do bunch, and they managed their cruising any way they could. Don Street was sailing *Iolaire* and charting the waters between St. Thomas and the Grenadines. In St. Barts, Jimmy Buffet was entertaining the fleet with his laid back, rum punch ballads. The Nicholsons, who had sailed into dilapidated English Harbour, Antigua in the late forties, found themselves hosting a growing Caribbean charter business. Entertaining Jolyon Byerley sailed up and down the Windwards and Leewards writing raucous tales for *Yachting* magazine, while Peter Spronk on Dutch Sint Maarten began dreaming up designs for big, fast world cruising catamarans. Other cruisers worked at the island resorts, shuttled mahogany and Mayan cloth up from Central America or imported goods of more questionable legality. But in those days, smuggling was a Robin Hood adventure, not the cutthroat crime it is today. Some of the seventies cruisers built their cruising kitties at night, in the dark, up tiny inlets along the coastal United States. For them, earning a questionable living was a natural extension of leading what most folks considered a questionable life.

Word of the grand sport of cruising kept spreading. While original mentors like the Hiscocks, Tristan Jones and Don Street continued to write and publish sailing directions, new liveaboard writers like Katy Burke, Nigel Calder and Lin and Larry Pardey started telling their stories, giving advice and charting the courses for yet more cruisers to follow. A tough new composite plastic called fiberglass allowed boat builders to mold and assemble boats in a production line. And the world voyager, an offshore cruising boat, once the luxury toy for rich yachties, came within the reach of more sailors. The sport grew.

Despite a few financial dips in the eighties and nineties, first world opulence outshone third world poverty to such an extent that travel to the Caribbean, Latin America, Turkey, Egypt, Thailand and any other foreign shore specked with huts and dugout canoes was a cheap and enticing proposition. Loran C, a radio beacon navigation tool, allowed the first fixes (finding one's place on a chart) without plotting a line of position with an intimidating sextant. And in the early eighties, satellite navigation, weatherfax machines and self-steering autopilots made ocean passages even easier.

World weather forecasting, radio transmitted weather maps and broadcasted passage advice provided, whether real or not, a sense of security. And satellite navigation, a tool that has nearly turned the world's blank oceans into mile-marked, exit-signed interstate highways, made every anchorage a pinpointable destination. Cruisers were no longer forced to learn the dark secrets of the sextant or perform its dizzying calculations. A push of a button (and these days, the button of a palm held, $50 gizmo) told every John, Dick and Cruising Wannabe exactly where they were and which way they needed to turn for their next anchorage - all accurate to within a few feet. These techno gizmos made cruising more palatable.

So how many sailors are out there plowing through the world's oceans now? When asked this question, Tim Murphy, the executive editor of Cruising World magazine, said: "You're on to the question that I don't think anyone knows the answer to, on account of the fact that sailing is such a blissfully unregulated sport." According to Jimmy

Cornell, the guru of world cruising and world cruising routes, between 1974 and 1984, the number of cruising boats calling at international ports doubled. Mr. Cornell believes about 150 to 200 boats circumnavigate each year, and though this number has held steady through the past few decades, the cruising boats coming through major ports has grown, because the number of cruisers voyaging to desirable sailing grounds has grown.

The Panama Canal saw roughly 500 cruise boats in the mid-eighties. In the mid-nineties, 1000 voyagers passed through the Canal. Cabo San Lucas, the destination port for many West Coast cruisers heading down Mexico's Baja Peninsula, saw 100 boats in 1985, while 600 boats cleared into Cabo in 1993. In the mid seventies, cruising boats carried U.S., U.K. and French ensigns. Now South Africans, Australians, Italians and Germans have joined the fleet, with German boats alone completing more Atlantic crossings than U.S. and Canadian boats combined. At least 1,000 European cruisers come to the Caribbean each year. World cruising numbers are up, and Mr. Cornell thinks the popularity of "local" cruising in, for example, the Med and the Caribbean may be increasing even faster. He figures 6,000 boats are spread throughout the eastern Caribbean, and that Trinidad alone saw 4,500 boats in 2000. Combining these cruising boats with the charter fleets, there are at least 10,000 boats bobbing about in the Caribbean each year.

But why? Why would we want to go cruising, and why has the sport grown so popular? Certainly technology has made the sport *feel* safer. But something more fundamental has gotten folks out of their homes, into little boats and out upon the intimidating sea. Is it their love of travel? Maybe. But there are lots of ways to see the world, and most do not require staring wide-eyed at towering walls of water while you clutch your stomach and wish you were back on *terra firma* with your mommy. Is it cheaper to see the world by boat? It is certainly cheaper to live in a floating home than a hotel, but boats cost a lot in the first place, are expensive to keep up and, like rusting mobile homes, depreciate to nothing in no time.

When *Cruising World* magazine was first published, the magazine's founder and editor Murray Davis wrote: "For many people the world is moving too fast. They want to get off for a bit to look around and take a breath. Cruising offers just that opportunity."

Writer Jonathan Raban says boaters love cruising because by living on the water they gain a particularly sublime slant on the world: *No house, and certainly no other vehicle, grants you such privacy and good solitude as a small boat a mile of or more out from the land. It is pitched at a slight angle to the rest of the world. Life aboard a small boat is often anxious and troublesome, and sometimes seriously nasty, but even at its worst it manages to borrow something from the deep and various nature of the sea on which you are afloat. The most timid of amateur sailosr is prone to the besetting mariner's conceit, that he can see and think things that are closed to the people on the beach. A mile out, with one sail up on a sunny afternoon, and he's Captain Ahab, he's Marlow, he's Slocum. He has the whole sublunar world in his spyglass, and it looks strangely small to him.*

Then there are those who appear to be cruising just to make their mark on the world. Marvin Creamer circumnavigated without instruments from 1982-84 - no compass, no sextant, not even a wristwatch. In 1965 Robert Manry, a Cleveland newspaper editor, took a thirteen and a half foot daysailer from Massachusetts to England. And in 1998 Papa Neutrino sailed with three crew from Newfoundland to Ireland aboard *Son of Town Hall*, a floating recycling statement cobbled together from scavenged West Side Manhattan building materials and touted as the first "scrap vessel" to cross the Atlantic.

And there may be other explanations for the lunacy of cruising. Marjorie Kinnan Rawlings, who at one point in her life lived in central Florida in the midst of swamps and beneath Live Oaks dripping with Spanish Moss, wrote that everyone should have a home surrounded with some sense of enchantment. And Mother Ocean, her islands, reefs and glorious sunsets, possess their share of enchantment. Whenever cruising sailors choose, they can pull up their anchors, sail out onto the ocean and arrive safely at the Shangri-la of their choosing - all according to their own wit and wherewithal.

Talkin' 'Bout My Generation

And I have a theory about why a particular subset of us feels the urge to go cruising. If you were born in the fifties, and in particular the mid to late fifties, you may have felt, at one point or another during your business career, a bit odd. For the sake of exploring this feeling, let us call it the "little lost, a bit confused, and trying to hang on to the happiness" feeling. If my theory is correct (and few are), I would propose that the "L.L.B.C.T.H.H." feeling is particularly relevant to the Sputnik generation; not because of the satellite or the space race that followed it, but because the Sputnik generation occurred between two diametrically opposed generations. My generation was sandwiched, as it were, between folks so different and contradictory that one wonders how we all come out of the same country in the span of two decades.

Perhaps, if you are a member of my generation, you read Tom Robbin's <u>Another Roadside Attraction</u> or Ken Kesey's <u>Sometimes a Great Notion.</u> Perhaps, if you had older siblings, you watched them first wear saddle shoes, then penny loafers, and finally sandals along with their beads, beards and ponytails. Maybe, as a youth staring out the car window, you saw flowery, tie-dyed hippies and thought them a bit odd but interesting. Perhaps you became thoughtful reading biographies like Tom Wolfe's <u>The Electric Acid Kool-Aid</u> Test or back to Nature guides like the <u>Foxfire Book</u> or the <u>Whole Earth Catalog.</u> Maybe my generation was a bit young to digest Kent State, but we knew something significant was happening as we watched television and read *Life* magazine. When we reached young adulthood, we were at the tail end of a generation that had gotten quite riled, a generation in protest, but a generation that preached peace, love and back to Nature.

In 1979, one week before I graduated from college, my roommate walked up and plopped a magazine down on top of the book I was reading at the time: Rachel Carson's <u>Silent Spring.</u> "Take a look at that," he said. "It's what's on the way."

I looked down and read the name of the magazine on its glossy cover: "SELF." But at the time I thought nothing of the first edition of the magazine, except perhaps that it was odd, a joke of some sort.

Five years later when I was working at a medical products company, I was asked to speak to a bioengineering class at the University of Arizona. My presentation was simple. I described a series of experiments I had been conducting. I took the students through a real world problem: the mechanical testing of a vascular graft (a vein replacement). I showed them the experimental design, the testing methods, the results, the math needed to interpret the results, and finally, the real world presentation of conclusions that had to be made to Federal regulatory scientists and cardiovascular surgeons. No theoretical lecture, this; I was presenting the real world life of a biomedical engineer.

I had samples of the grafts and slides of the testing apparatus. The students could see, feel and ask questions about everything I presented. And to make sure the students stayed interested, I showed gory, blood and guts pictures of surgeries - always an attention getter. Throughout the presentation I hoped to deliver one message: "Here is the real world.

You are studying for a profession in which you will get to use your brain and help mankind, and that's cool." It was the lecture I wish I had received when I was in school.

When I finished my presentation, I turned to the class, smiled and asked for questions. Three hands shot up immediately, and I called on a lady in the front row.

"How much do you get paid?" she asked.

I was floored. Still, I felt a new level of attention in the room. I felt just how rapt and focused the students had suddenly become.

I stumbled through a response that came nowhere near naming my salary, and I got the feeling that this somehow annoyed the class. Still, I dismissed the girl and her question as outliers and quickly turned to another student who continued to hold up his hand.

"What courses," asked the young man, "would help me get the best paying Bioengineering jobs."

So much for the outlier. Again, I was stunned, and again I flailed through a nonsensical response.

Long after the students had left the room, I remained standing, rooted to the spot where I had fumbled their questions. I blinked rapidly as I looked over the empty desks and chairs before me. From the back of the room, the professor who had invited me walked forward. He was balding, and his remaining grey hair was tied in a ponytail. As he approached, I saw that he was chuckling.

"Surprised?" he said.

I shook my head.

"Times have changed since you went to college, eh?"

"Changed?" I said. "It feels like I'm on a different planet." I threw myself down in a chair and sat silently for a moment before feeling something close to outrage. "What," I asked, "happened to the enjoyment, the love of the science? What happened to studying something because you might be able to do some good with it?"

"Oh," said the professor, still smiling, "it's still around, but it's playing second fiddle to a more important motivation: income. These days the kids come into the university with their minds made up about what they are going to study and just how much money it will make them."

I thought about my own meandering in college: first toward environmental science, then toward engineering. For a short time I thought I might like to be a lumberjack, but in the end I studied medicine and engineering. I went where my interests took me…everywhere, but they steered me right in the end. Now, if the professor were right, the kids were aiming at only one thing from the very beginning: their paycheck.

My roommate had been right. At the end of the seventies, my generation passed the baton to the "Me Generation." And no matter what we might have thought about those self-serving folks, they brought us some interesting headlines: junk bond scams, generic drug hoaxes and the savings and loan debacles. With the Me Generation's push to get rich quick, the stock market soared. The computer industry, and Silicone Valley in particular, fueled the rocket. Even in my little sector of the financial world, the medical products industry, I watched young professionals do *whatever* they had to do to make their company's stock soar. After all, they had stock options, and they could, if Wall Street turned its headlights on them, become millionaires overnight. We are, I believe, still paying for their shenanigans and the shenanigans of those who have followed in their sneaky footsteps.

So why might my generation feel a little startled, a bit confused and somewhat lost? Perhaps we are looking for a middle ground between the two generations, something besides a cabin in the woods, where we make our own soap from lard, and a five-bedroom house, where we stew in our Jacuzzis on a redwood deck just above the Hummer in our three-car garage. Then again, maybe my theory is only that: a theory. Maybe the reason the brothers and sisters of my generation feel the urge to go cruising is that they simply want a break…. with a good tan in the bargain.

Overall cruising does appeal to folks hoping to cut back and simplify. In a world of fast food, phone menus, cell phones, and manic, multi-media marketing, our families sometimes appear to be under siege. And we just might be approaching the limits of our ability to digest and consume. Though the United States and Western Europe hold about 11% of the world's population, we do almost two-thirds of the world's spending. In 2002 we spent $446 billion on global advertising, an almost nine-fold increase over 1950, and half of this advertising was in the United States. In 2000 we threw $20 trillion at goods and services, up from $4.8 trillion in 1960. How we spend our money is one thing; but how we spend our time may also be driving us crazy. On average we spend over an hour behind the wheel every day. Worldwide in 2002 our cars rolled off the assembly line at a rate of 4,700 per hour - five times faster than in 1950. And our demand for more cars and other consumables might be driving us wacky. It took our 18th century ancestors four years to produce the "necessities" we now make in a week. One would think this efficiency would leave us more time for invention and leisure, but we still want more "things." And working to pay for all these "things" might just be killing us. U.S. citizens are among the most overworked peoples of the industrial world. We put in nine more workweeks than our European counterparts. It is no wonder we are looking for a break.

In the October 1984 edition of *Cruising World* magazine, John Vigor wrote: *There comes a tide in the affairs of men that, taken at the flood, sucks them swiftly away from the sea and boats and stands them for the best part of two decades on the reefs of Marriage, Career, and Bringing Up Children. By the time they and their partners are ready to fulfill their dreams, they are 40 or 50 and fainthearted. They no longer have that youthful zeal so many imagine to be the prerequisite for cruising. You see such people sitting disconsolately in RV parks all over the country...And they sit there quite unnecessarily, because it is possible to start cruising in middle age. More and more couples are doing it. I've done it myself. So if you've been tempted in the past, if you've dreamed of trade winds and desert islands, remember that it's not too late. All it takes is a bit of guts.*

And what sorts of gutsy folks go cruising? The early cruising accounts were written by salty dog, single-handed sailors - usually men. Though women cruisers like Susan Hiscock, Blondie Hasler, Beryl Smeeton and Lin Pardey were sometimes one half of the cruising couple. Solo sailors like Clare Francis, who was the first woman to skipper the world Whitbread race, were rare. But all of these women's stories, like the stories of early male sailors, must have made an impression on other women. (Did women begin to think, "Heck, this sailing stuff might not be so hard. I can pull it off without the barking sarcasm of Captain Bligh."). By 1989, *Cruising World* magazine was being run by its first female executive editor, Bernadette Brennan. And one of Ms. Brennan's first accomplishments was to encourage and co-author a book by teenager Tania Aebi called *Maiden Voyage* – the story of the youngest woman in the world to circumnavigate the planet.

And what about voyaging families? When did they start sailing the Great Blue? If we review the early cruising accounts, few families appear to have sailed off into the sunset. But then again, the folks sailing as a family may not have had time to take notes and write a book.

With exceptions like Beryl and Miles Smeeton, who sailed with their daughter, there is little evidence in the literature of families heading off to sea. Cruising stories are told either by young and childless sailors or older and retired sailing couples - their kids perhaps off somewhere and shaking their heads at mom and dad's tomfoolery.

Granted, the idea of taking diaper clad toddlers on a slippery deck over a great and bucking sea is not the sort of adventure new parents generally seek for their children. A guided stumble across the living room carpet, little fists wrapped around mommy's fingers, is adventure enough. Safe homes, schools and neighborhood friends are hard to find in the middle of the ocean. Still, some folks have started out by rearing their children afloat, and some have even sailed far a field. Murray and Barbara Davis, Australian founders of Cruising World Magazine, sailed to the U.S. with their children Kate and Paul, aged 6 and 5, in 1967. "It was more with the idea of enjoying our family in an experience together, before schooling demanded a more settled experience ..." Wrote Murray Davis. And Wayne Carpenter wrote about sailing with his wife, his two daughters and his mother-in-law... bless that man for his courage. One has to admit that the image of an entire family in the cockpit of a cruising boat, kids yanking on the sails, steering, fishing and laughing together, not only as crew but as family, is damned romantic.

But I will tell you a secret from when Diane and I first cruised in 1987 B.K. (before kids). We leapt into the sea before we had our girls, and we were impressed with the rare but interesting families we met afloat. But we were not quite ready for children. We were enjoying one another and the freedom of our cruise. Not once did we consider the extra ballast of children, until one evening, anchored off *Isla Mujeres* in Mexico, we watched a boat arrive at sunset. It was making landfall after a two-day passage from Houston, Texas. The father was at the wheel. The mother was on the foredeck. Two handsome young boys, toe-headed brothers about six to eight years old, were seated behind their mother. Sails were hurled on deck, proof of a rough passage, but now the boat was gliding safely into calm water. The sun cast a warm light on the mother and her two children, and both Diane and I were captivated by the moment, struck by the heart-stirring image of a loving family back-lit by the red sky. Just as the boat passed by us, I remember slipping my hand into Diane's palm, and we heard the mother speak to her children. She said, "So help me God, if you poke me one more time, I will throw both of you into the ocean!" In the fading light, we could just make out the boys giggling, as they jabbed their fingers into her back one more time, and then scrambled to the safety of the cockpit.

Despite the obvious challenges of family cruising, more families are taking to the water. Cruising destinations like Georgetown, Exuma in the Bahamas, have become not only adult race and party destinations but rendezvous points for cruising kids. The annual spring party schedule includes races and games just for kids. By the year 2000, Georgetown, which was once the Holy Grail rendezvous for a hundred or so cruisers, had become the site of a mega-anchorage festival. In the mid nineteen nineties so many cruisers gathered on the porch of the popular Peace and Plenty bar that it collapsed and dumped them into the sea.

But whether sailing solo, as a couple or with kids, are cruising sailors *special*? Do you have to be some sort of hard-core Antarctic explorer, manic athlete or America's Cup winner to cruise? Joshua Slocum was an accomplished sailor and captain, but just as you and I might get to feeling at the end of a lifelong career, he really went cruising because he looked around and realized he was not ready to settle down. He saw the mechanized steamships coming, he mourned the passing of the great windblown merchant ships he loved and he decided to set sail. He simply had to go. He was an accomplished sailor, but he dealt with the same hurdles any of us face when we coil our lines and watch the dock disappear. At times he was lonely to the point of illness; and though his manly writing does not often reveal it, he was sometimes very scared. Chased by pirates off Africa or clinging to the top of his mast as the waves covered his boat off Cape Horn, he had to be petrified. But globetrotting cruisers have gotten their start without the sort of lifetime sailing experience Joshua had. Some did not even know the difference between a jib sheet and a bed sheet, and they did just fine.

Eric and Susan Hiscock, though they became accomplished sailors, had to start from the same place all sailors start: from the shore staring out to sea. Sensing this, their simple instructions for setting two anchors in tidal flows or storing eggs by coating them with Vaseline help novice sailors see they are getting advice from regular folks – folks like their grandparents. It's just that, unlike our grandparents, Eric and Susan ended up smoking a pipe and knitting cardigans at anchor off Mozambique.

If we do our research, we find that the revered cruising guide writers and open ocean demi-gods were just people. They got lost; they made silly mistakes; and, well, in the telling they sometimes *expanded* upon the salty dog reality of their adventures. Did Tristan Jones really walk out to the end of a dock in a near hurricane holding an open jar with a lit candle inside to gauge whether the winds were suitable for sailing? Jolyon Byerley, the sailing sage of the Leewards and Windwards, was honest enough to admit when he fell on his sailing prat. Jolyon was a ferocious Francophobe, and while charter skippering his 70-ton schooner *Lord Jim* off the Tobago Cays in the Grenadines, he came upon a group of Frenchmen "banging away" with a "fusillade of gunfire" at the seabirds around Jamesby Island. "Full of righteous fury" he threw down *Lord Jim's* helm and steered straight at them:

> "…what I really intended escapes me now but, with a few feet to go, we ran up the gently sloping sand and stopped dead. Why that long-suffering rig didn't carry on going beats me. Anyway, with gunmen and crew all frozen to the spot in stupefied amazement, I stood up and with imbecilic pomposity shouted, "*Vous êtes une vache, alors!*" (You are a cow.) With that brilliant rapier thrust, *Lord Jim* jibed all-standing, heeled over and trundled off into deep water, and I sat down feeling more stupid than usual. One of the charter party, new to the game, commented seriously, "Hey, how 'bout that? I never thought a sailboat had brakes."

Yes, all of the globetrotting and wunderkind cruisers were human. They went aground. They forgot to close thru-hulls and flooded their boats. And they took careful sextant sightings only to find themselves on the wrong side of the planet. One sailor I know found his way to Jamaica entirely by the strength of the radio signal on his AM radio. When the music grew faint, he retraced his path and turned this way and that until the reggae was once again loud and clear. All cruisers reach foreign shores through a combination of luck and skills learned at the School of Hard Knocks. Their accomplishments and their frailties are their legacy. And the legacy they left us, like a lighthouse, guides us on our way. We too can go cruising.

Appendix 3 – How to Get Started

When Diane I first considered traveling on a boat in the eighties, we looked for someone who had lived aboard a boat and could tell us what life afloat was like. We had a lot of questions. We wondered what we would need to learn, what sort of boat we ought to have, what equipment should go on her and how much it would cost to cruise. We had a thousand questions. As young as we were, our yahoo enthusiasm was tempered by the suspicion that, though we were immortal and capable of anything, we just might not know everything we needed to know about going to sea.

We looked for a mentor, someone who had been to sea, or better yet, lived on a boat. But trying to find a liveaboard sailor in Arizona was like trying to find a Navajo hogan in New Jersey. Then a friend told us she knew of a liveaboard sailor in Seattle, a wonderful gentleman who might be able to help us with our questions. His name was Chris, and he would become, through the many letters we sent back and forth, our cruising guide, guardian angel and waterborne pen pal.

Our first letter to Chris included only a hundred or so of our thousand questions. I did not want to scare him with the first epistle. What Chris sent back was a long letter that addressed none of our questions; but in a lyrical way answered every question we would ever have about living on a boat. He wrote of the beauty of Seattle and the islands he had sailed there. He described the peace of returning to the water each evening after a long day of work in the city. He praised the character of the people he had met living on boats, and he was grateful for these interesting and caring friends. Then he posed his own question. He asked us whether we owned a boat, and if so, how much time we had spent aboard her together.

If there are "factoids," there must also be "questionoids." It seems that for most of my life the essential questions I should have asked myself were buried beneath a pile of inconsequential interrogatives. We did not own a boat. We had sailed nowhere together. Chris, in his next letter, suggested we rent or buy a lake sailor, a little boat on which we could learn to sail. When we felt comfortable, he suggested, we might want to go sailing for a few days at a time and work up to a week or more together. "Then," he wrote, "have a chat about how it feels."

Iced Tea in the Face

Life afloat and the great cruising escape, as romantic as they might sound, are not for everyone. Take for example the F.B.I agent and his wife who came to visit us after we had been living aboard *Manta Raya* as a family for nearly three years. At the time we were tied to a dock in northeast Florida. We had one foot on our boat and one foot on land, since we were docked in a canal directly behind a house owned by some understanding and kind friends. There was a long umbilical chord, an electrical line, stretching from their home down through their yard and out to our boat. We were using their showers and bathrooms. Life was good.

The F.B. I. agent called because he was about to retire and wanted to cruise the Caribbean with his new wife. He was considering buying a catamaran and wanted to bring his new wife to see our boat. He planned to sail with her into the tropical sunset.Over the phone in Florida, the F.B.I. agent sounded quite confident about sailing and living on a boating. He owned a powerboat and had chartered sailboats in the islands. And his wife? Well, she was just going to love it.

The F.B.I. agent arrived in a yellow Corvette. He had slicked back, pompadour hair and his new wife, certainly much newer in terms of her time on this planet, wore a pleated red skirt and starched white blouse. Her lipstick, hair and brooch pin were in perfect order, which made me feel a bit underdressed in my sandals, baggy shorts and ripped t-shirt. But the newlyweds had not come to see me, they had come to see our boat - our home.

At the sight of *Manta Raya* (and she looked quite large with her 23 foot beam wedged into the forty foot wide canal) the F.B.I. agent whistled and nodded appreciatively. But his wife simply blinked and smiled. In retrospect she looked a bit like a Texas cheerleader confronted with the Space Shuttle.

I introduced Diane, and the four of us sat down on the porch and exchanged pleasantries. The F.B.I. man was actually a nice fellow, funny and interesting. He had led a full life. But as he told engaging stories about crime scenes and Florida money laundering, his new wife was silent. She simply continued smiling. She did, however, stare rather intently past me toward our boat, and then she would glance over her own shoulder to the patio door of our friends' home. I figured she was becoming a bit uncomfortable with the morning's climbing heat and was a bit wistful about the more comfortable environment promised by the hum of the house's big air conditioner.

"Well," I suggested, sensing the passing of the morning and a bit of the new wife's anxiety, "shall we take a look at the boat?" The F.B.I. man clapped his hands and rose, and his wife, her smile suddenly gone, spoke her first words since our greeting.

"How do we get on?" she asked.

Considering her question and glancing down at her footwear, I now understood the anxious stares she had been giving our boat. We had a narrow gangplank, a board actually, leading from the dock to our boat, and the lady was wearing shoes with stiletto heels. I assured her that the gangplank was sturdy and that she could simply remove her shoes or borrow some of the sandals we had lined up at the dock, but she just laughed, shook her head and said, "No way."

"Water," she said pointing down at the canal, "I get nervous standing over water."

There was a long silence as we all turned and stared at the canal. The F.B.I. agent ran his fingers through his pompadour, and I considered calling off the visit. But Diane came up with a plan.

"I'll come around with the dinghy and pick you up. We'll just walk right onboard using the stairs at the transom."

While the ladies took their ten second dinghy ride, the F.B.I. agent and I walked aboard and began talking rigging, engines and fiberglass. Diane led the new wife up the transom steps. The new wife was in her stocking feet and still smiling, but I could see that the smile was starting to crack.

The F.B.I agent and I quit talking about manly winches and chains, and we all went below to look at *Manta Raya's* interior. The new wife saw the little "kitchen," the miniature propane stove and the tiny sinks. Her comment: "Oh, it's so..., er, cute." I noticed she had started gripping her fingers with alternating hands, as if she were milking a cow.

When the new wife tried to step down into the starboard float to see the "bedrooms," she banged her head before I could warn her to duck and back down the stairs.

"Backwards?" she asked.

"Yes," I said.

From below, I tried to help her, but because she came at me rump first, the procedure was more than I could handle gallantly, so I turned away. She slipped, there was a bang, and when I turned around, I saw she had fallen into the hanging locker. I pulled her out, and her nervous laughter went falsetto, heavy on the false. This manic laugh, which I did not think could rise much higher, went up another octave when I showed her how to pump the "toilets" in the head.

Safely in the cockpit, Diane served iced tea, and we tried to restore some calm. I made a point of steering the conversation away from all things nautical, until Riley showed up and became an object of attention for the new wife, who decided to engage Riley in wide-eyed exclamations about living aboard a boat.

"What a life you must live, honey!" said the new wife to Riley, "I mean, how *do* you manage? It's all so primi...eh, rustic... then again, you have everything you need, don't you. You even have showers downstairs. I saw them."

"Oh," said honest Abe Riley, "we don't use those."

"You don't?"

"No, we've got solar showers."

"Goodness, dear, what is a solar shower?"

"Here," said Riley reaching into a locker. "See? It's a bag, and you put the water in here and the sun heats it up. Then you hang it over your head like this and open up the hose."

The new wife stared back and forth between Riley and the bag she had suspended over her head. "You mean you take showers here... out in the open, where everyone can see you?"

Riley started to explain how there usually was not anyone around, and if there were, how she could shower in her bathing suit or sit so no one could see her; but she stopped in mid explanation when she heard the lady's titter grew into a chuckle, expand into a manic laugh and then burst into a sort of hysteria that sounded a bit like a scream.

Riley was fascinated. We were all fascinated. But the scene was a bit too much, and I looked down nervously into my iced tea, wondering whether I should throw it in the woman's face. Probably, I thought, I should take the ice out first.

But the lady eventually calmed down. We managed to get her off the boat and dinghy her back to the dock. The F.B.I agent appeared unfazed. He praised our boat, thanked us for our hospitality and then retreated up the hill with his silent wife under his arm. They climbed into their air-conditioned car. And we waved as they drove away toward the suburbs. But as much as we tried not to, when Diane and I turned to face one another, we burst into laughter. We could not help it.

Learning to Sail on Lake Powell

My brother Mark (not his real name) and I were in the cockpit of our O'Day 22 "Lucile," our little lake sailor on Lake Powell named after my smiling, indefatigable grandmother. It was 1986, and my wife Diane and my sister-in-law were below. Jamie, Mark's golden retriever, was sitting with Mark and me in the cockpit. We were learning to sail on a famous and yet impossible body of water, Lake Powell, where over 1,200 miles of red and tan Grand Canyon cliffs meet the blue water of the Colorado River. I was to learn later that a lake sailor and world cruiser would declare two bodies of the world's waters most troubling and treacherous: the Sea of Cortez to our south and Lake Powell, where we were about to learn our first valuable sailing lesson.

We were becalmed off a famous point on Lake Powell called Dinosaur Rock. At this particular section of the lake, three canyons met in an open bay. Though we did not know it yet, big summer winds swept off the hot desert plateaus above us and were channeled and focused by the canyons so that they converged like train cars on colliding tracks.

But Mark and I were oblivious to such geologic and meteorological phenomena. In fact, after a long morning of fishing in the sun with ample beers to quench our thirst, we were oblivious to just about everything. Our mainsail hung limply, and the only movement in the sweltering afternoon heat was our tillers' lazy swing as the boat danced over the wake of passing powerboats.

At the time Mark and I were exploring an invention we called the "sponge-o-snort." We were wetting a big sponge, wringing it out and holding it over our noses as we breathed in cool, humidified air. If you have never been in the southwest, it is a land so arid that water vanishes almost immediately. Sweat disappears without a trace, and a wet rag or sponge, particularly if air is drawn through it, gets downright chilly as the water in it quickly evaporates. We had been taking turns cooling off by diving into the clear blue lake, but our noses ached in the dry desert air, so the "sponge-o-snort" seemed like quite the invention, at the time. I was, as I sat at the tiller holding the sponge over my face, expounding on the delicious feel of the novelty. Mark was reaching into the cooler for another beer, and I was lying on the cockpit seat with my head resting on the transom combing. Had we been looking up the canyon, we would have seen warning signs of trouble - ruffled waves with white caps sweeping before a freight train of wind.

The first blast hit us and sent us straight over, mast into the water and sails submerged. Mark fell into the ice chest. Diane and my sister-in-law rolled off the lazerette onto the cabin sole. I climbed up the high side of the cockpit like a terrified monkey. And Jamie the dog, her claws scrabbling over the fiberglass deck, managed to hang onto the deck coamings. To this day my sister-in-law recalls staring out the porthole, which had moments before presented a broad view of redrock cliffs but now, like a glass bottomed boat, looked straight down into the deep blue toward the Colorado River bed eight hundred feet below us.

I became very sober, very quickly. I reached back and released the mainsail sheet, and despite the shrieking wind and spray which blew across her, the boat took care of herself. Released from the wind and water trapped in her mainsail, she pulled herself out of the water and rounded up to face the wind. I grabbed the tiller and pulled in just enough sail to get us moving, and Mark went forward and threw himself on the thrashing jib. Everyone went into action. My sister-in-law helped Mark pass the jib thought the bow deck hatch. Diane untangled and sorted lines from the overturned cooler and jumbled fishing equipment. And I began to sense "the dance." I could see each blast of wind coming as the whitecaps raced before it, and we fell off for each gusty punch. "Float like a bee. Sting like a butterfly."

We limped across the bay toward a point where we hoped to duck out of the wind. But before we could get there and as suddenly as the wind had come upon us, it left us. The bay went flat. The sun shone and the sky remained an unperturbed blue. That is when I thought to check on Jamie the dog. She was still up on deck. But her back was arched, and she had the nails of her front paws wrapped around the toerail.

With her tail between her legs, she was staring into the water. Then with one look back at me as if to say, "I've had it with you ridiculous humans," she jumped into the water.

We sailed around Jamie, called to him, whistled and pleaded, but he ignored us. We even tried apologizing, but he paddled on toward shore. When we reached shore, we were all exhausted, and we camped for the night. The dog was not happy about getting back on the boat the next morning.

Our Lake Powell adventures taught us the sobering Truth about sailing - a Truth that is important for weekend sailors and downright critical for liveaboards. On a boat, one rarely escapes the variety and verities of Nature. Winds can whistle at any time. Waves can rise up, curl, leap and become as jagged as saw teeth. Tides will rise and fall, sometimes with a rush of current so strong they can foul anchor lines, yank anchors from the seabed and suck small boats and people out to sea. And though Nature can give us breaks, she is an indiscriminant mistress who demands constant attention. All animals know this. Even dogs.

Appendix 4 – Buying a Boat: They Fly through the Air and They Sheet

For many of us, the word "boat broker" just like the word "realtor" might be anathema. To discover I actually admired and would eventually befriend the agents involved in the sale of our family cruise boat *Manta Raya*, a.k.a. Toon's Boat, was a surprise. To date I had lost no love on "boat pimps," but Claude, the broker for the seller, and Lisa, our broker, were to be exceptions.

Lisa and Claude were two very different sailors from two disparate parts of the world, but together they suffered that enigmatic passion that bonds real sailors and defies distasteful financial reckoning. They had peddled their passion into a pastime. Claude was a big man with sandy, tradewind tossed hair, a thick frame and a moustache so big and bushy it looked like its own animal. Lisa was a tiny woman, with a slight frame that belied her strength. She was a tough New Englander with traditional boat values, and she had built and raced Ted Hood boats from Rhode Island. As a mother of three and a sailor, she ended up wanting our cruise to happen as much as we did, maybe more. Had the two brokers ever met in person, Lisa would have been dwarfed by Claude's thick Belgian frame. But his bulk belied his artistic delicacy. He was a craftsman. He had left Europe on a Piver catamaran, and in an African port along the Gold Coast after a deal lubricating bottle of Courvoisier, he had traded his Piver straight across for a Chinese junk, because the boat "captured his heart." But he soon traded the junk ("she sail backward faster than she sail forward") for a romantic, 120 ft

Bogart era motor yacht - brass ports and teak rails curving around elegant wooden side decks. Unfortunately the great yacht's hull was sprung, and its engine was submerged in oily saltwater. But Claude raised the thing, replaced her wood and brought her back to life - until one fateful day when his welding torch burned her to the waterline.

"*Ce va*," he said, with a Frenchman's characteristic shrug and a puff of his mustache. "So now I am selling boats." Claude's latest floating possessions were a fifty foot outrigger sailboat, a dagger-hulled, single outrigger with rudders at both ends, so that she tacked by turning 180 degrees and sailing "backward," and a barge he was converting into a floating home for his wife and two children. The barge had a large patio with hammocks and a lathe filigree of blue and white jumping dolphins about its cabin top. Claude was a dreamer *and* a doer - an inspiration to all men who peer over the flimsy walls of their office cubicles. In the 70's he had bought a palm covered, white sand beach island off Belize. He had never been back to see the place (and he asked us to visit the island for him, which we eventually did).

Like many of life's great decisions, the path to our boat was well thought out, planned and direct. We started by going to Boston to meet with Lisa, and after several false starts and roundabouts from Maine to California, we ended up wandering about the little Dutch and French Island of St. Martin in the West Indies, where we eventually stumbled on *Manta Raya* by accident.

For two years we had been collecting boat information: articles, brochures and spec sheets. I had compiled a lengthy spreadsheet comparing the boats - their dimensions, strengths and weaknesses, costs per model per year, etc. The ponderous analysis may have done little more than confuse us, but it had taught us one thing. We would not be buying a new boat. Our finances dictated that we would have to find a boat that had been previously loved.

I do not remember how it happened, nor do I know how the Fates conspired, but in the anxious process of finding the right boat we also found Lisa. We met her first in Marblehead, Massachusetts and began traveling with her along the northeast coast peering at boats under tarps in storehouses, boats bobbing at the ends of rocky piers and boats buried in backyard weeds. During our travels together, she took us under her wing.

Lisa liked sturdy, heavy and deep-keeled boats. But she was willing to listen, and the more we looked at the traditional Bristol cutters in

Rhode Island or the solid Sabers in Maine, the more trouble I had shaking a nagging desire that had seized me in the eighties. Indeed, it was only a footnote at the bottom of my boat spread sheet wish list, where I had written a few notes about "multihulls."

Multihulls are just that, boats with more than one hull. Though their design concept dates back a millennium to Polynesian outrigger canoes, their more recent incarnations were the trimarans from California and the catamarans that were just beginning to leak their way into the U.S. from France. For American sailors, they were, and perhaps still are, new and odd floating questions. Sailors were skeptical in the States - particularly in the grey, brown and navy blue states of New England. There were, at the time, no New England insurance agents willing to insure them.

When we had first started searching for boats, I had talked my boat-building aficionado and sailing mentor friend St. Frank into a trip to look at a catamaran in the Chesapeake's sailing capitol of Annapolis, Maryland. After an afternoon of walking about one of the things, which looked something like an airplane mated with a trampoline, we gathered in a nearby pub to mull over our findings. St. Frank, who would not say poop if his mouth were full of it, praised the boat's light and modern construction, its speed and the space above and below deck. She would, he said, certainly be an agile and quick vessel.

But I knew I was not getting St. Frank's unguarded opinion, so I set about easing the Truth out of him with the only time saving lubricant I knew: alcohol. After a number of hearty drafts and some diversionary conversations that took St. Frank's mind off the boats and put it on the darkening harbour and the greater world of real ocean sailing, I sprung the question on him again: What had he *really* thought about the multihull?

St. Frank squinted at his beer mug. Then he recalled how at one point in the afternoon he had begun pushing the "space craft" back and forth from the dock. It had moved, he said, as easily as a plate on ice. "Hell," he said, "I never felt a boat skitter across the water like that. I don't know... it just seems that when the *Big One* hits, the ultimate storm, when you have to give up on skippering, because you can't even pretend you have any control, when you've buttoned up the boat, gone below and left your fate in the hands of almighty Neptune... Me? I'd want to be in something more solid, something that could take a 360 degree roll and come up standing."

In Marblehead I brought the multihull idea up with Lisa, and despite her similarly traditional view toward sturdy monohulls, she did not flinch. "Well Todd," she said, "we're not going to find any of those boats up here. We'll have to look south." I did not realize at the time, just how *far* south she meant.

When we found *Toon's Boat*, the catamaran that was to become our *Manta Raya*, Claude helped us through the panic of boat buying. Despite the mechanical and emotional pitfalls of buying any boat, and especially a French boat in the Caribbean, Claude felt all was doable. And to my many anal retentive, North American queries ("How hard is it to convert European fittings to U.S. fittings, how do I take possession of a boat registered in another country, how, how, how...") he responded patiently, knowing all the while, I am sure, that my Yankee hysteria would soon evaporate in the Caribbean tropical sun. On only one point of cruising was he adamant: no pets. "They are a problem," he said, "especially zee moonkey. I once had a moonkey. He sheet everywhere. In zee storm, he jump through zee air and he sheet." Claude closed his eyes and shook his head at the memory. "Never sail with a moonkey."

Appendix 5 - Ten Ways to Get Away

D
o not get me wrong. I am not opposed to society. I do not think we cruisers should disappear like mad hermits, wild-eyed, seaweed in our hair and throwing shells at hapless boaters who wander into our solitude. Peering into the Big Lonesome often gave our family the willies. We needed humanity and companionship. And cruisers do generally make good company. Still, nothing amazed us more than the cruising sailors who gave up their safety, their comfort and sometimes their fortunes to travel obediently with the pack. They sailed an illusory highway defined by a best selling cruising guide and wedged themselves into crowded anchorages as if they had never left the suburbs.

And the anchorages are filling up. Cruising has gotten popular. When Joshua Slocum sailed alone around the world, he was a one-of-a-kind oddity. When the Hiscocks wrote their cruising wisdom in Cruising Under Sail, they were considered pioneers. But today, with production boats suited for blue water within the grasp of more pocket books and with most of the rhumb lines mapped out, crossed and crisscrossed *ad nauseam* to the GPS second, more and more sailors are finding their way to once empty anchorages. Heck, there are more than a quarter million folks reading *Cruising World* magazine who either sail or are considering sailing over the horizon, and that does not include the folks reading the motorboat rags. Those folks can blast by the sailing slowpokes and fill up anchorages before the windblown sailors can get there. These days, with the buzzing generators, outdoor speakers, all night cockpit parties, disco tour boats, jet skies and fuel spills in formerly "lonely" anchorages, sailing cruisers might as well stay home and camp out in their driveways.

For sailors seeking private anchorages and the Holy Grail epiphanies of lonely sunsets, new strategies are required. And so I offer you, dear Reader, ten ways to lose the crowd and strike out on your own to find secluded anchorages. **And, as an added bonus, I have listed idyllic hideaway anchorages never before revealed in cruising guides or other boating periodicals!**

But first, we must discard two getaway tactics that used to work; but, alas, are no longer effective:

(1.) Looking Dangerous; and

(2.) Getting Naked

When anchoring along the East coast in the eighties, Diane and I hailed from the sailing capital of Flagstaff, Arizona. Back then, the bold, homeport lettering on our transom was disquieting to fellow sailors from real ports with real nautical features, like water. Our Arizona state flag conjured visions of prickly cactus and range cattle stampeding plum *loco* through the anchorage. Accordingly, boats kept their distance. But with the growing cruising community hailing anywhere from Laramie to Llahasa, estranged hailing ports are no longer effective crowd deterrents.

Second, and speaking from personal experience only, the few, full length *au naturel* glimpses I allow myself in the mirror these days are not only disquieting but gastronomically challenging. When we were learning to sail on Lake Powell, naked anchoring kept the houseboats away. We could often hear folks as they drew near: "...Oh, my goodness, Harold, I think...yes...eeeeuw!...Those people are naked!" followed by the sound of engines in full reverse and a rapid departure. But now, in the islands and particularly in the French West Indies, the nudity ploy is not only unsuccessful, it is counterproductive. Instead of being a deterrent, appearing on deck without clothes is an invitation. You will soon hear the "plink, plunk" of light ground tackle about you as the crowd moves in, drawn as if by magnet. Suddenly it is Bastille Day. In short order you will have gathered an entourage of frolicking nudists offering you paté and pastiche. *Mon Dieux!*

More ingenious ploys are required:

I. Ignore the Common "Wisdom"

As we re-learned in Gaunaja, the cruising gossip, especially as it was whispered by those who had not really been there, could keep cruisers out of paradise. When considering advice about a possible destination, also consider the source, and act accordingly. One man's dread might be your dream come true.

II. Be a Long, Lazy or Late Bird

The cruising fleet migrates as a flock. The migration starts on the East and West coasts of the United States in October and turns back near Georgetown, Bahamas and *Cabo San Lucas*, Mexico in April. Although it may be scary to leave the flock, those who venture further South can leave the crowd and the windy Northers astern. Then, when the fleet returns home in April, sailors who have traveled further South can make a more leisurely return North by staying just on the warm side of the retreating Northers. Like feasting seagulls following a shrimp boat, they can enjoy the spring weather laid out before them. What used to be a boating freeway in February turns into a quiet country lane in June.

After Northers the next weather phenomenon in the Caribbean is Tropical Waves and their progeny "named storms" or hurricanes. Although the Coastal Pilot tells us these storms can appear as early as June and July (one reason for the early retreat of the cruising fleet), sizable and damaging storms are much more likely in the fall. With an eye to the weather, migrating cruisers who dally into the summer can enjoy empty anchorages left behind by the fleet. Better yet, those cruisers who can afford to make a year of it can hole up further South in Panama, Venezuela or the Dutch A, B, C's and leave named storms to the North. Come winter, these birds will already be enjoying the tropics when the cruising flock has just started flying south.

III. Throw Away Your GPS

The GPS has been the past decade's boon to the cruising sailor. It has also been the bane. Now every Tom, Dick and self-propelled floating conveyance can find it's way to the most remote destinations by shelling out a couple hundred bucks for charts and electronics. But a GPS will not steer you through "uncharted shoals and numerous coral heads" that sprout randomly in skinny water. Thank goodness for charts that carry such warnings, they are like "Private Property, No

Trespassing" signs. But enterprising cruisers can get into these forbidden Shangri-La's. Forget the warnings in the cruising guide, ignore the GPS coordinates, choose your light and use your eyes. Learn how to read depths and coral with guides like Hiscock's Cruising Under Sail. Slow down. Do not let your speed in knots exceed the depth in feet beneath your keel; and, given a soft bottom and rising tide, do not be afraid to use your keel as a depth sounder, gently. It won't hurt you one bit. The angst of the exploration will give way to the joy of accomplishment when you find your way into a beautiful, secluded and secure anchorage that few or none have managed before. Go gunk holing!

IV. Get Skinny

Most cruising guides are written for sailboats with moderate to deep draft (say 6 feet or more). The same guides contain warnings about places like "Wader's Lagoon" or "Keel Breaker Cut," where entry is "accessible only to shallow draft vessels" or where you must "rely on local knowledge to avoid uncharted shoals and depths." Wouldn't you like to explore and anchor far into these shallow treasures and enticing, untouched cruising grounds? An intrepid cruising couple we know took their trimaran through 20 miles of empty, clear waters marked as "Unsurveyed - numerous coral heads and submerged reefs" in *Los Roques* off Venezuela. They did not see one other boat on their adventure, not even the kind with local knowledge. Sorry all you San Francisco Bay deep-water plowers, but you cannot take your boat where no boat has gone before.

Shallow draft has it advantages, and shallow drafted multihulls create their own reserved parking. I know it is bad form to come into a crowded anchorage and squeeze to windward in front of the fleet, but a multihull can fit itself into shallower and calmer water toward shore and leave plenty of room to leeward. Anchored away from the crowd, a bit of magic begins. As if the multihull were exerting some sort of invisible force field, monohulls will rarely come near, even if the multihull is in ten, twenty or even thirty feet of water. Honest. The reason? Traditional monohull sailors think: "Dang, there's one of those damned multihulls with no draft whatsoever pulled up into knee deep water. Whoa. I had better spend the night out here in the chop and swell where it's safe." Not a bad piece of conjuring for a bit of solitude.

V. Rely on Cruising and Charter Guides

Get the popular cruising guides, and if you are near the charter fleets, stop by headquarters and ask about their recommended destinations. Now you know which anchorages to avoid. The charter companies want their boats returned in approximately the same condition they leave, so they feature only the safest, all-weather anchorages (which you may end up needing anyway). Cruising guides only briefly mention or warn against questionable anchorages. The unmentioned and the dicey are what you want. We spent three days off Mustique on an island referenced in an outdated guide as a "lunch stop only." Given that the anchorage was prone to swell and presented a considerable slog to windward, the charter companies did not mention it on their charts. We had to watch the weather, but we had the island to ourselves, hiked a windswept mountain with wild goats and ate lobster donated by a lonely fisherman - all within a day's sail of the civilized splendor of Mick Jagger's island estate and the massed charter fleet.

VI. Camp Out and Wait

Daily, near the tourist Meccas of the Caribbean, tour boats disgorge pasty skinned vacationers by the metric ton on defenseless offshore islands, where a volleyball net and bamboo tiki bar await the onslaught. Two hours after the invasion, when rum punches have had their effect, the sunburned tourists stumble back aboard their tour boats and then clap and sway as a tanned Adonis on the foredeck leads the crowd in a disco samba: "....da room, da room, da room is on fire; and we don't need no water to put it out!...," until the tour boat disappears over the horizon. Since the booming tour boat weighs anchor every day at three o'clock, by five o'clock the cormorants have returned to their mangrove roosts and by six o'clock, where acres of flesh had been sizzling in the unremitting UV, an empty beach is now warmed by the glow of a soft pink sunset. Cruisers who wait can reap the rewards of these times. Get some provisions, stake a claim and camp out. Time can turn your busy campsite into paradise.

VII. Go Far Young Man!

For Caribbean cruisers, anything beyond Georgetown or, really stretching it, perhaps Venezuela, looks extremely far away. But I am told we can, and I have met folks who did, travel further without dropping off the edge of the known cruising world. Brazil sounds nice. Come to think of it, some of the nicest folks I have met were from Brazil. Chile also sounds interesting. A fisherman I know says the place reminds him of the U.S. in the fifties - everything open and unlocked, friendly folks hitchhiking without concern. One California cruising couple spent an entire winter (Chile's Summer) gunk holing the coast. They saw only one other cruising yacht, and it was Chilean.

VIII. Take Your Licks

We sailed the "Cartagena Triangle," where wind and waves conspired to create a permanently dangerous bulls eye on the Pilot Chart off Cartagena. We sailed messy, cresting, fourteen-foot waves in forty knot winds to get to Panama. We took our licks but then reaped the rewards of the pristine San Blas islands. As trite as the "no pain, no gain" maxim may sound, it holds true for cruising. Few are willing to pay the price of admission for some of the best destinations, so by gritting our teeth and spilling a bit of our nervous sweat, we can get to the "out there" places.

IX. Local Knowledge

Liveaboard cruisers are blessed with the opportunity to take a slow, grass roots approach to the places they visit. Nonetheless, they are tourists. They might know who they are, but the locals do not. For all the locals know, they could be Dirt Pimps looking to develop beach condos. In Aruba it took an entire month before the "permanent" cruisers, who wind surfed every day, while exotic ecosystems grew on their hulls, would tell us where they snuck into hotels to get their laundry done. After all, if they told everyone where to find these sudsy resources, their "privileges" might be taken away. The same "local knowledge" advantage holds for protected anchorages, miraculous dive spots and empty stretches of beach. The locals (cruisers or residents) know where they are, but they also know that by telling you, they could lose their treasures.

You might have to hunker down at the bar to lubricate the reticent sage; you might have to overcome shyness and spend some time hanging off someone's transom; or you might have to invite fishermen aboard and share soft drinks along with your recent copies of National Geographic. But remember that whatever effort it takes, the value of the advice you get is inversely proportional to the ease with which it is given. Earning someone's trust can take a few minutes or it can take a month. But whatever it takes, local knowledge is the key to a treasure box of idyllic getaways. Take the time to make a friend.

X. Don't Tell

The discovery of each anchorage, each gift of solitude, comes with a responsibility: you can't tell. Some sailors make their way by writing cruising guides about their travels, but, with few exceptions, even they understand the obligation they have to stay mum on special, empty and pristine anchorages. Sure, they might point generally to some areas, say, certain reefs off Honduras for example, but these gems must be discovered through a cruiser's perseverance, their willingness to test their mettle outside the established cruising grounds.

And so, alas, I must confess to subterfuge. If you skimmed this section of the book hoping to copy down the lat/lon locations of unpublished cruising grounds and idyllic anchorages, I am afraid I have to disappoint you. Even if I did know (and mind you, I am not saying I do), I could not tell you. You will have to make these discoveries on your own. And when you do, when you sit floating on a silent blue sea by a perfect, palm crested isle warmed and colored by an evening sunset, you might not thank me, but you will smile, because you will have made that pristine landfall all by yourself.

Appendix 6 – Coming Home

C oming home after an extended cruise can be tough. Landfall is a bit disorienting, for everyone. Maybe, dear Reader, you are considering cruising for the first time, and for you this section of the book is irrelevant. But if you take the leap one day or if you are a sailor considering returning home, I offer you the following, because the cruising lifestyle ought to come with a warning label:

> WARNING: DUE TO DAILY EXPOSURE TO PERSONAL FREEDOMS AND OPEN HORIZONS, YOU MIGHT DEVELOP A DEPENDENCY ON THE UNFETTERED OUTDOORS, LIMIT YOUR ABILITY TO ACCEPT REGULATION AND LOSE YOUR TOLERANCE FOR SOCIAL DENSITY. SIMPLE ACTS LIKE SHOPPING AT A WALMART SUPERCENTER MAY BECOME INTOLERABLE.

Just after living on our boat in the Caribbean for two years, Diane, the kids and I visited our first Walmart Supercenter. We huddled, held hands and bravely made our way through the pinballing cars across the ten-acre parking lot. Once inside, we pulled up short and gaped at the expanse of the place: endless merchandise, flashing signs and banners beneath miles of pale green fluorescent lights. Glassy-eyed shoppers were lined up ten deep and dutifully waiting for the beep of the bar scanner. Diane was the first to offer an observation: "We've been to islands smaller than this place."

Take It Slowly

Life's big changes are tough. After a few years or even a few months at sea, the sudden return to shopping centers, cell phones, TVs and traffic can feel as pressing as gravity to the returning astronaut. Slowing reentry can help. On our first return from cruising in the 80's, Diane and I lived on our boat in downtown St. Petersburg, Florida. We walked or biked wherever we went and ate grilled Cuban sandwiches before beating the afternoon heat at the museums or the baseball stadium. We let the traffic, the routine, and the pace of the place work back into our lives gradually. On our second return to the US after Cuba, we again eased the transition by living aboard. Even after finding a home, we continued to sleep onboard, waking to the soft lap of waves instead of the din of an alarm clock, until the day our boat was sold.

From "deck to desk" is not an easy transition. After all the time outdoors, jumping into a corporate gig with a windowless cubicle might give you the willies. Your trip might have taught you that former jobs, like mergers and acquisitions (or, as a good friend of mine calls them, "murders and accusations") are not as appealing as they were pre-cruise. Rushing back to old habits or haunts can be tough. Instead, some cruisers work from their boats or around boats for a spell. They take one step at a time and test the "real" world carefully as they wade back in.

Don't Forget What You've Forgotten

Memory is a tricky thing. One of its better tricks is its ability to whitewash the past. Sometimes this whitewashing is good therapy; other times it is a mistake.

Six months into our family cruise through the Caribbean I recall sweating and cursing over my steaming diesel engine. I was sponging up the salt water that had, for the third time in one month, exploded from the exhaust elbow and filled the engine compartment. On each breakdown our only warning had been the engine's strangled "pucka, pucka" before it drowned under the rising water. There was sweat in my eyes, or maybe it was tears, as I bent over the hot engine. I had spent more time hugging, caressing and talking to that damned machine than I had my wife.

I also recall the tail end of the month we anchored out on a remote atoll off Venezuela. We were at the end of our provisions, and my kids were staring suspiciously at their plates, where the last of the canned goods was masquerading as fruits and veggies - a pile of fluorescent orange mandarin bits and some slimy, institutional green beans morphing into pea soup. I also remember the stormy, seasick passages, the maddening weeks of cabin fever without friends or family to ease the strain, and the scary, mid-ocean encounter with a suspicious Honduran boat and her derelict crew. But let us not dwell on the bad, or should we?

Back on land, we remind ourselves that our home does not rely on a diesel engine. There is little danger we will drag our foundations or sink into the yard during the night. Fresh strawberries have just come in at the grocery store, and dear friends are a short drive or phone call away. The cruising life is wonderful, but lest we forget, there are times when shore life is an improvement.

Don't Believe for a Second that You Won't Go Back

In a rare, wistful moment, Riley once remarked, "I'll never clean the 'poop chute' out of a lobster again." You may not think of this as a *fond* memory, but our biologically oriented Riley was thrilled by the pre-dinner dissection. The point is, she liked that part of cruising, the wild part, in Nature; and she misses it.

After our first cruise in the 80's, we settled on land long enough to build a cruising kitty and family. In the 90's, after we had taught the kids how to float, we set sail again. Maybe it's a decade thing. If we manage our resources, we might be catching, cleaning and eating lobster again within the next few years. Or as a young adult, our daughter might revisit the coral gardens on her own. Who knows? Perhaps one day she will teach lobster anatomy to her own inquisitive kids.

Do not Expect Society to Behave Like Nature

One of our first tasks back in the US was insuring and registering our car, which we had put in storage. Did you know, dear Reader, there is an "Exemption from Motor Vehicle Financial Responsibility Requirements - De-Insured Certification" form? There is. Fortunately, we had filled out just such a form. Unfortunately, when we sent it in, it was promptly lost. Our state D.O.T. informed us they would need proof we had been out of the country. This proof, the helpful official explained, would have to be presented in person. I pointed out that a live appearance would require that I drive my unregistered vehicle almost all the way across the continental United States to the D.O.T. office. Never mind. Those were the rules. Besides, even if the D.O.T. could re-register our vehicle by mail, and they could not, they would only send the registration to the address of record, which was - you guessed it - back home 2,000 miles from our boat.

A sailing friend happened to wander by the phone booth just after my chat with the D.O.T. He said he was drawn to the site by the phone book pages and bits of turf he had seen flying in the air. He asked me what the problem was, and after listening to considerable whining on my part, offered the following advice: "You know what your problem is? You've been at sea too long. When a storm comes up, you think you can reef. When the wind dies, you think you can just haul out bigger sails. But people don't work like that, and society is people. Welcome back to the 'real' world."

O.K., maybe managing the daily routine is easier Out There on the ocean. When you run out of water, you wait for rain or go hunting shoreside with your jugs. Dinner is on the end of a hook, not across town, through traffic and wrapped in cellophane. Here, in the real world, bombarded by absurd regulations, advertisements, and hyper deadlines, it is no wonder we're a bit confused. The wonder is that we are not shell shocked. But that's us. It's our society. We built it, and when we cruisers come home to it, we had best be ready to live with it.

Don't Talk About It, Live It

After your own Great Adventure at Sea, you may be tempted to talk about it...to everyone, everywhere and whenever possible. When we first came back and some innocent asked me about my trip, I got an urgent, frenzied feeling, and a scene from the movie *Blade Runner* popped into my head. Rutger Hauer, a spooky sci-fi clone describes his life as a universe traveling warrior: "I have seen things you people wouldn't believe: attack ships on fire off the shoulder of Orion..."

Maybe landlubbers have not reefed sails in rolling storm waves, made the only tracks on an empty, white sand beach or traded fishing tips with Cuna Indians; but for goodness sake, my adventure did not give me the right to preach to folks as if their lives were some bland purgatory from which only my thrilling insights could save them. Judge Not Thy Fellow Landlubber! Besides, no matter how much I wanted to share my adventures, most folks did not want to or could not hear them.

Though we spent a month in a Venezuela boatyard keeping flies off the kids, while a nervous guard toting a sawed off shotgun paced around our boat, our friends like to think we were swaying in the tropical breeze and toasting the sunset each evening, so we let them. No matter how many times I remind one particular friend that we merely sailed around the Caribbean, he insists on introducing my family as "the family who sailed around the world." I have given up. Now, when he introduces us as circumnavigators, I just smile weakly and nod.

Instead of trying to pound the realities of our trip into the uncomprehending ears of hapless landlubbers, we try to share the gifts of our cruise with them. Without the distraction of television, traffic, phones and leaf blowers, we heard Nature's Rhythms, and they sounded something like a waltz. Piddling along at two knots or sitting in a third world custom agent's tepid office, we had to slow down and wait for natural outcomes. Back in civilization, the "convenience" of dotcom mania, phone menus and overnight everything, has tied folks in knots and made them believe they need it all, yesterday.

The same rush affords us little time for one another. Last week I found myself in a long queue at the bank. But I once spent two hours in a Cumana, Venezuela bank line, and not one person got fussy. A few of us even made friends. But back in the U.S. bank, the crowd felt like a lynch mob. When I reached the teller, her head was bent as she worked frantically over a tangle of paperwork. Without looking up, she mumbled, "I'll be with you in a moment," so I reassured her: "No hurry. Take your time." In that moment, the harried teller looked up, and her eyes melted. It turned out she was a wonderful Portuguese lady with stories about Brazil, which she took the time to tell and I took the time to hear, despite the exasperated sighs and anxious shuffling of feet behind me. Time is on our side, and it can be shared one moment and one decent deed at a time.

In the Windward Island section of A Cruising Guide to the Caribbean and the Bahamas, entertaining Jolyon Byerly writes: "Some of the following anchorages will not appeal to everyone. They may be too lonely and exposed for the average taste, but to me solitude is a great luxury, becoming rarer as the world gets smaller."

Solitude is a gift and a burden for the voyaging sailor. Anchoring alone in a coral atoll in the middle of the ocean with an unbroken vista from horizon to horizon, he begins to change. Time slows to the present. Layers of protection built up over years of fast-paced living peel away to expose something much more attentive underneath. When he comes home to the maddening crowd called civilization, the sound of that lonely atoll plays in his head like a melody, a lovely but persistent reminder that he needs that solitude like breath itself. Anything less would not be living.

So be it. If the price we must pay for cruising is a constant yearning for solitude, my checkbook is out. Cruisers may be able to dive off their transoms into enchantment every day, but those of us back in the "real" world will have to find it where we may. Perhaps we will be Out There again one day. In the meantime, we will try to take it slowly and give back part of the gift we were given. Hopefully we will remember that cruising was no *panacea* and that as trying as *terra firma* can be, there is also much to be thankful for in the "Land of Stuff."

Acknowledgments

My thanks: This book grew out of an attempt to write an article about "family cruising" for *Cruising World* magazine. (Contrary to the snide comments of some of my friends, *Cruising World* is not a dating scene review but a thoughtful and inspiring monthly magazine for sailors roaming or wishing to roam the world.) Like the octopus we wrestled off Panama, the article grew so many arms (strange arms - some seemingly detached from the main body) that the scope of the message grew beyond a periodical. The folks at *Cruising World* encouraged my early writings, some of which appear in this book. They are kind and understanding folks, landed sailors who spend a good deal of their time dreaming about their own future voyages. I thank them for cushioning the fallout of our anxious landfall.

I also owe this book to my brother, who said my articles were "O.K." but supposed I would never write an entire book. As with our sibling leg and arm wrestling, he kindled a rivalry that fueled my writing. I also thank my car mechanic Matt, a dad, who when I told him I was a writer, thought immediately of books rather than magazines. With wide-eyed enthusiasm, Matt said "Man! A book about sailing with your family? That's a great idea. When you're finished, I want to read it." And so, Matt, thanks for getting me started.

The Author

    Todd Scantlebury now lives with his family on a small farm and ranch in central Arizona. Over the course of two cruises and four years, he sailed over 7,000 miles through the Atlantic Ocean and Caribbean Sea from Providence, Rhode Island to Providencia, Colombia.